The ABCs of
Human Survival

Global Peace Studies

Series Editor: George Melnyk

GLOBAL PEACE STUDIES is an interdisciplinary series that publishes works dealing with the discourses of war and peace, conflict and post-conflict studies, human rights, international development, human security, and peace building. The series is global in perspective, and includes works on militarism, structural violence, post-war resconstruction, and reconciliation in divided societies. The series encourages contributors from a wide variety of disciplines and professions including health, law, social work, education, and the social sciences and humanities.

SERIES TITLES

"Bomb Canada" and Other Unkind Remarks in the American Media
by Chantal Allan

The ABCs of Human Survival: A Paradigm for Global Citizenship
by Arthur Clark

The ABCs of Human Survival

A Paradigm for Global Citizenship

ARTHUR CLARK

Published by Athabasca University Press in conjunction with the Consortium for Peace Studies at the University of Calgary.

AU PRESS

© 2010 Arthur Clark

Published by AU Press, Athabasca University
1200, 10011 – 109 Street
Edmonton, AB T5J 3S8

LIBRARY AND ARCHIVES CANADA CATALOGUING IN PUBLICATION
Clark, Arthur, 1943–
    The ABCs of human survival : a paradigm for
global citizenship / Arthur Clark.

(Global peace studies, ISSN 1921-4022)
Includes bibliographical references.
Also available in electronic format (978-1-897425-69-5).
ISBN 978-1-897425-68-8

1. World citizenship. 2. Political participation.
3. Civil society. I. Title. II. Series: Global peace studies

JZ1320.4.C53 2010   323.6   C2010-901184-8

Cover design by Rod Michalchuk, General Idea.
Book design by Laura Brady, Brady Typesetting & Design.
Printed and bound in Canada by Marquis Book Printing.

A volume in the Global Peace Studies series:

ISSN 1921-4022 (Print)

ISSN 1921-4030 (Online)

In respect and gratitude for the life and love of
IRENE MARIE PETZINGER
October 1948–July 2008

Into the darkness I will reflect your light.

CONTENTS

ACKNOWLEDGEMENTS

I wish to thank George Melnyk and the Consortium for Peace Studies at the University of Calgary for their support in publication of this book, and Paul William Roberts for reading the manuscript and urging me to move it forward to publication. I am grateful for help from Scott Anderson in editing and from Joyce Hildebrand in copyediting the manuscript. As always, it is the author who is responsible for any failures of the final text. I also thank all those at Athabasca University Press who patiently guided me through the process of getting the manuscript ready for publication.

This book is about practicing citizenship. Practicing citizenship involves working with others toward outcomes you couldn't have achieved without them. The work I describe in this book depended on contributions from so many others that I would not know how to list them by name, but I should express thanks to several individuals whose contributions were particularly important to my own efforts: Julie Hrdlicka, David Swann, Dijla Al-Rekabi, Donn Lovett, and Tareq Ismael for work related to Iraq; Kelly

Dowdell and other program managers of the Parhad programs at the University of Calgary for the achievements of those programs; Marc Boutin, Mike Robinson, Kelly Dowdell, and members of the Board of Directors for the Calgary Centre for Global Community — Mary-Wynne Ashford, Michael and Judie Bopp, Naushad Dada, Gail Davidson, and Yasmin Kanji — for their help in moving the vision of the Centre forward; and Tom Hanrahan for his work in hosting the Parkhill Pulse.

FOREWORD

When I became active in the nuclear disarmament movement in 1984 I thought the only way to bring about change was to protest with placards. I quickly learned that issues of social justice, women's rights, violence prevention, and peace education were all interlinked and that nuclear weapons were a symptom of a dysfunctional global society. Governments and the military-industrial complex had become so enmeshed they were no longer able to fulfill their responsibilities for the well-being of society. I learned that there are many ways to support education, and that most were more fun than carrying placards—although I found peace marches were wonderful in their own way. Musicians, artists, dancers, educators, women, religious groups, and scholars all found their own ways to support changing attitudes toward peace, human rights, and the environment.

Today it is cliché to say that humanity stands at a crossroad, but perhaps this is cliché because everyone recognizes that we face life-threatening decisions. It seems to me that humanity stands not at a junction of a road, but at the edge of a cliff. If we continue business as usual we will crash into the abyss. As the saying goes, we must change direction or we will end up where we are going. No one can ignore the crises we face: modern warfare, threats of nuclear weapons, abuse of human rights, economic collapse, climate change, crop failures, environmental destruction, and loss of species.

Many people respond to the scale of these challenges to our survival with hopelessness and helplessness. It seems clear that governments are unable to respond quickly to the need for fundamental changes in our institutions and our attitudes. In fact, change is most likely to be initiated by civil society, or "people power" as it has been called. This book outlines clear guidelines for the essential paradigm shift from militant nationalism to a healthy, collaborative society integrated with the natural world.

There are three pillars of a healthy society: government, a strong economy, and civil society (Perlas 2000). Civil society brings conscience to bear on the decisions of the other two sectors. Until recently, civil society has been the weak pillar, and the results have been global destruction of nature, war, and grave social injustice. Over the past twenty years, civil society has become a formidable force for change, and governments have been forced to take citizens into account as they make decisions. Instant international communication is a powerful tool for civil society. On the one hand, citizen journalists expose corrupt and secretive governments and businesses; on the other hand, they share successful strategies and new ways of thinking with those working on social change in distant communities.

Things are getting tough for dictators these days. Since 1986 when the Filipino dictator, Ferdinand Marcos, was toppled by massive civil disobedience, some sixty dictators have been thrown out of office, most of them without violence (Mack and Nielsen 2005). We must credit Gandhi for the first overwhelming demonstration of people power, which happened when he led the resistance that forced the British out of India. Civil society has learned to stand up and, unarmed, defeat government by moral suasion. Nonviolent resistance brought down the Berlin Wall and led to the end of the Soviet Union and many other dictatorships. As people connected across borders, they began to reject the notion that other nations were enemies. Instead, they pressed their governments to find diplomatic solutions to conflicts.

We can feel optimistic about the capacity for civil society to bring about change when we consider some of the many successes brought about nonviolently by ordinary people working in their own communities and in international groups.

Several civil society organizations united in a global campaign to ban landmines, and to their amazement caught the attention of sympathetic governments, who moved the process forward. Canadian Foreign Minister, Lloyd Axworthy, worked collaboratively with international nongovernmental organizations to bring like-minded governments to Ottawa, to discuss banning these weapons. Because so many countries were supportive, the process moved ahead quickly and in 1997, only five years later, the treaty to ban antipersonnel landmines was signed. Continued pressure from citizens led to the recent banning of cluster bombs, which had not been included in the original treaty.

In the early 1990s, civil society pressed the United Nations to request the International Court of Justice in The Hague to give an opinion on the legality of nuclear weapons under international law. The Court ruled that not only are nuclear weapons illegal, but also that the nuclear-weapons states have a solemn treaty obligation to eliminate them. This ruling has had far-reaching implications for governments and for international law. It has been successfully cited in court cases against activists using civil disobedience to protest against nuclear weapons bases in Europe and the UK. The protestors argued that they were acting to prevent their countries from breaking international law, and the courts agreed and acquitted them of charges. At last we can begin to be optimistic about progress toward a Nuclear Weapons Convention that will ban these terrible weapons.

For many years, human rights activists were appalled that brutal dictators had immunity from prosecution for genocide, war crimes, and crimes against humanity. People demanded the founding of a court that could try individuals and hold them personally responsible for such crimes. Once again, governments agreed with this civil society initiative. They founded the International Criminal Court, which came into force in 2002.

Other trends offer more cause for optimism. A surprising report in 2005 from the Centre for Human Security, *War and Peace in the 21st Century*, (Mack and Nielsen 2005) shows a strong global trend away from war since the end of the Cold War in 1991. Between 1991 and 2005, major wars (more than one thousand battle deaths per year) and genocides declined by 90 percent, and wars in general dropped by 40 percent. The number of international crises dropped more than 70 percent in the same time period. Some one hundred armed conflicts have quietly ended since 1988. The researchers credit the increasing successes of the United Nations in nation-building, the founding of the International Criminal Court, and the increasing influence of civil society with bringing about this change. Civil society organizations now play a significant role in resolving conflicts and bringing warring factions together.

Women have long argued for a place at the table during negotiations to resolve political conflicts. According to the UN, women make up 70 percent of workers for peace and social justice in the world. Research confirms the importance of women in changing the context of conflict. One author measured the empowerment of women in a society by whether they have the vote, can stand for office, hold paid employment, and control their fertility (Caprioli 2005). In states where women have these rights, the likelihood of their country using military force to resolve internal conflicts is markedly lower than in states where they do not.

Many countries, particularly in the developing world — in places such as India, Nepal, Bangladesh, Pakistan, and Rwanda — have ruled that at least one third of seats on local councils must be reserved for women (Ashford 2006). The requirement for these offices to be filled by women has led to rapid increases in programs teaching literacy and numeracy to women. Balancing the genders in decision-making is leading to improved educational opportunities, especially for female children. The role of education in reducing prejudice and encouraging critical thinking is important in preventing war and environmental destruction. Learning nonviolent means of parenting is a deeply satisfying way for young adults to influence the future of society.

Citizen journalism is a formidable force for change, particularly because of the ease of transmitting video from all corners of the earth. When we hear from those who live in difficult circumstances, we begin to understand that a military response will not solve their problems. In some countries radio programs are being used to build understanding of different groups in order to reduce inter-ethnic hostilities. The programs are plotted like soap operas, placing the characters in situations that require them to rise above their prejudices. They have had a remarkable impact on building understanding in communities at risk.

These are only a few examples of successes of civil society affecting communities, governments, and the United Nations. There are hundreds of such stories — many you know in your own neighborhood — which refute the tired dogma that you cannot change the world. We can change the world, but not without hard work.

This book is based in a keen awareness of the challenges we face, the evidence that we are capable of meeting those challenges successfully, and the ever-present danger that we may fail to activate that capability. The crises we face today cannot be resolved without you and me and everyone else on the planet. This book sets out the steps. Let's take them together.

MARY-WYNNE ASHFORD, MD
February 2010

References

Ashford, Mary-Wynne. 2006. *Enough Blood Shed: 101 Solutions to Violence, Terror, and War.* Gabriola Island, New Society.

Caprioli, Mary. 2005. Primed for violence: The role of gender inequality in predicting internal conflict. *International Studies Quarterly* 49 (2): 161–178.

Mack, Andrew, and Zoe Nielsen, eds. 2005. *Human Security Report: War and Peace in the 21st Century.* Vancouver BC: Oxford University Press.

Perlas, Nicanor. 2000. *Shaping Globalization: Civil Society, Cultural Power and Threefolding.* Quezon City, Philippines: Centre for Alternative Development Initiatives.

Introduction and Overview

Martin Luther King Jr.'s concise and memorable statement describes the choice we face as human beings: "We must learn to live together as brothers, or perish together as fools."

A great deal of twentieth-century history, and early evidence from this century, suggests that as a species we are choosing the second option. And we seem to be making this choice unconsciously, almost completely unaware that we are even involved in a process of choosing. We see the consequences of our choice but fail to recognize them as such, and fail to understand where they are taking us.

Personally I prefer the first option as described by King, which I will refer to throughout this book as "Option A" — learning to live together as human beings. When the term "Option A" appears in the text, you can remember it as the advantageous option. I will refer to King's second option as "Option B." You can remember it as the bad option.

Option A and Option B will be expressed in various ways in the pages that follow. In this book, "perishing" is taken to mean not only the extinction of human beings as a species (which might not happen for a long time to come), but also (and more importantly for my purposes) the extinction of human options that would give us a much healthier global community than we now have. In that sense, we have been perishing as fools for centuries.

This book is about a way of thinking — a paradigm — to enable progress toward Option A. I propose here *a way of thinking about world affairs, personal well-being, and the interdependence of the two*. The paradigm is new in the sense that it is not the currently dominant way of thinking about world affairs or about personal well-being. In the conventional view, these two domains are largely disconnected. We tend to think of our personal well-being (self-interest and the pursuit of happiness) as isolated from world affairs, unless we happen to be living in some part of the world where this conventional paradigm is challenged by local realities.

Our thinking about personal well-being is often characterized by cynicism (self-interest in a narrow sense of that term). A cynic can be defined as "a person who believes that only selfishness motivates human actions and who disbelieves in or minimizes selfless acts or disinterested points of view" (Random House Dictionary of the English Language). In contrast to cynicism is the view that a very large measure of self-reliance is essential to healthy psychology at the individual level, and self-reliant individuals are best able to contribute to their communities. Human society depends upon interactive support systems involving all its members. Enlightened self-interest recognizes the importance of a healthy society, and therefore the responsibility of each member to contribute to the common good. Narrow self-interest (selfishness) is likely to overlook such aspects of reality. When a culture becomes too tolerant of narrow self-interest, it makes the community weaker than it otherwise would be.

In our culture, fraught with consumerism, we are inclined toward narrow self-interest, particularly when it comes to world affairs. Lack of attention to civic responsibility is a critical failure in our society. We pursue our careers, provide for our families, plan our futures, insure our houses, and perhaps contribute to some activities in the local community. We may vote and we probably pay taxes, but world affairs are left to our "leaders" and the "experts" who advise them. Our political leaders and the experts who advise them serve in political and cultural institutions rooted in the paradigm of nationalism.

The pathology of nationalism

Pathology is malfunction, caused by the inadequacy or loss of normal control mechanisms. For example, cell division (controlled proliferation) is essential for a healthy organism, but when the controls of cell division are inadequate to keep cell proliferation in check, the result is cancer, which can kill the organism.

The term *nationalism* is used in various contexts, including *civic nationalism*, in which the nation is thought of as an inclusive political entity with equal rights for all its citizens. This contrasts with *ethnic nationalism*, in which rights are chiefly recognized for a particular ethnic group.

Civic nationalism can be the cultural and political basis of a healthy society. However, when any form of nationalism breaks out of the constraints of law, it becomes malignant. The tendency for nation-states to break out of the constraints of law remains characteristic of nationalism today, particularly in militarily powerful states. Throughout this book, I refer to this kind of nationalism as militant nationalism or as malignant nationalism, or simply as nationalism, since, because it characterizes the behavior of the most powerful states, it is the dominant form of nationalism today.

As such, nationalism is the dominant paradigm for thinking about world affairs. It is the paradigm that led to World Wars I and II, and the box within which foreign policy analysts and political leaders do their thinking. Nationalism is also the box within which large parts of the general public think about world affairs.

Nationalism is an us-versus-them ideology in which it is acceptable for one state to invade another state and overthrow its government, killing tens of thousands of people in the process — provided, of course, that it is "us" or one of our allies who are carrying out the invasion against an adversary and not the other way around. Nationalism is pervasive in our culture: "We support our troops" is a currently popular assertion of nationalist sentiment.

> Nationalism creates a morality.... It lays down that loyalty to the nation — and in established States, the State — ought to take priority over all other loyalties, including that to the family, and that the crime of disloyalty is treason, the punishment for which is frequently death.... National interest also allows a member to disregard moral principles in defence of the nation — it is permissible to lie, to steal and to murder. (Harris 1990, 16)

Prominent intellectuals (many of them political "realists") often tell us that there is no other choice. It is a mark of sophistication to be able to expound on the necessities, if not the virtues, of nationalist competition for power and of its (particularly malignant) outcome, warfare. In other words, the choice posed by Martin Luther King Jr. is a delusion: Option B is the only option.

Choosing the future

The notion that we have no choice but to continue toward Option B is factually incorrect. For example, although the history of nationalist conflict between France and Germany is indeed long, and its costs incalculable, the fact that France and Germany have since World War II moved away from their militant nationalism, and from Option B, is clear enough. In *The Unconquerable World: Power, Nonviolence, and the Will of the People*, Jonathan Schell provides a detailed refutation of the idea that we have no choice. Schell's book is one of many resources on the topic, a few of which will be mentioned in this book or listed in the section on Further Reading.

Whether we can move toward Option A at any given time or place is an empirical question. Like the question, "Can we find a cure for cancer?" the question "Can we find a cure for nationalism?" can only be answered through serious, sustained, and constantly renewed efforts to find the cure. And a thousand failures do not answer the question. The question can be answered definitively only when the cure is found, and then the answer is yes. As it happens, there is abundant and growing evidence that prevention and cure are achievable.

In the old way of thinking, any discovery of prevention or cure would have to come from our political leaders and experts. Ordinary citizens are not experts in world affairs and foreign policy, so they should mind their own business, go shopping, pursue their careers, advance their knowledge and expertise in their professional fields, and otherwise follow their own "self-interest." This is old-paradigm thinking, and it dominates the thoughts, the discourse, and the patterns of behavior in our culture.

It has been said that life is like a mirror, reflecting back at us what our thoughts project into it. And so it is with history. If we are unable to think of paths toward Option A, if we are unable to even imagine what Option A might be like, then history will reflect this void in our imagination.

If we wish to move toward Option A, then we will have to abandon the cynicism and nationalism that currently dominate our culture. The reason is simple and familiar: we cannot solve the major problems we face by using the same patterns of thinking that created the problems in the first place.

Because we are making definitive choices about our future within the confines of cynicism and the nationalist paradigm, we are in effect choosing Option B. We are perishing as fools, and in this century or the next, the perishing may drive us to extinction as a species.

The direction in which our choices are leading us is extinguishing hope for the future as well as options for the here and now. The nationalist paradigm does not permit us to envision anything better than the darkness and pessimism of perpetual violent conflict, and the squandering of public resources to sustain it. This pessimism exerts a pervasive negative effect on our society. In military families, it is associated with suicide, domestic violence, and depression. More widely, it creates a cancerous social malaise related to the idea that human life is cheap and of very limited significance. It is postponing, perhaps forever, the pursuit of options that are much more life-affirming. Pessimism obscures even the awareness that a healthier global community and greater self-fulfillment are possible.

This book calls for a paradigm shift. I refer to nationalism and the ideology of us-versus-them as the "old paradigm" because it is the established way of thinking about world affairs, the one in which we have been indoctrinated. It is characteristic of the old paradigm in its present-day form to insist that state power, not international law, is the necessary basis for advances in human rights. Proponents of the old paradigm may become quite strident about this, especially as they carry out their violations of international law.

Today, this way of thinking faces a challenge from a different one that recognizes the necessity of international law for reliable progress in human rights. In this book I refer to this way of thinking, which prioritizes human well-being, as "the new paradigm." In various forms, however, this "new paradigm" has challenged the old paradigm again and again throughout history, as I explain in the section below entitled "The Personal is Political."

The new paradigm abandons the nationalist delusion that we are first of all Americans or Canadians or Germans or Japanese, Jews or Christians or Muslims, or members of some other subgroup.

It abandons the cynical delusion that we are first of all consumers or professionals or some other socio-economic entity. The new paradigm recognizes a more basic aspect of reality: we are first of all human beings and members of a global community.

The new paradigm is a conceptual guideline toward Option A. Human well-being is the priority. The old paradigm is a conceptual guideline toward Option B. Political power is the priority.

In the conceptual framework of the new paradigm, patterns of human thinking and behavior can be evaluated in terms of their effects on human well-being and on the chances of human survival. Such considerations are viewed as alien or marginalized in the conceptual framework of the old paradigm.

Whatever the challenges to human survival, we will meet them more effectively using evidence-based thinking directed toward Option A. Our choice of paradigms has historically had consequences of life-and-death importance. It has defined the limits of what we can learn from history as well as the limits of our current options.

The necessity of democracy and law

Just as the market can provide, from countless sources, information essential for economic decisions, an effective democracy can provide information essential for wise political decisions. Political power isolated from democratic constraints inevitably succumbs to the pathology of power.

Power must also be constrained by law. Democracy and law are in fact interdependent. Increasingly, as the fact of global community becomes a part of common sense and universal awareness, law means international law.

International law encodes these new-paradigm concepts, making them a universally accessible and assessable set of standards. International human rights law articulates the basis for a healthy global community: the civil, political, social, economic, and cultural standards essential to human well-being. International humanitarian law specifies the responsibilities of belligerent and neutral states, as well as individual combatants, in time of warfare. Their actions and the consequences of those actions, as they involve each other as well as involve non-combatants and protected persons — chiefly the civilian population — are subject to international humanitarian law. Together, these standards of international law provide a framework for measuring the human security performance of governments. This body of law includes the law of non-aggression and the UN Charter. Warfare is the most basic of all human rights violations, for in war the necessary conditions of all human rights are undermined.

Nationalism has a well-documented contempt for law:

> The illegal we do immediately; the unconstitutional takes a little longer. (Henry Kissinger, quoted in Kraft 1973)

The choice between international law and nationalism is the choice between Option A and Option B.

The personal is political

The new paradigm aligns with healthy human and social psychology. It is more basic and more realistic than the old paradigm. Human endeavor — even warfare — depends on the health of community to support it. It depends on trust and human well-being. The old paradigm and the warfare system it sustains undermine the health of communities, trust, and human well-being. For this reason, the old paradigm is self-contradictory and unrealistic. Even in the most powerful state, old-paradigm thinking gradually erodes personal well-being, social cohesion, human security, public resources, and confidence in the future. New-paradigm thinking enables sustainable development in all those domains.

New-paradigm awareness emerges in the work of social psychologists and writers such as Erich Fromm, in a wide range of work by contemporary authors, in the visionary work of countless individuals and non-governmental and non-profit organizations (civil society), and in the principles and purposes of modern international human rights and humanitarian law.

New-paradigm thinking is also at the core of the world's major spiritual traditions. In those traditions we find profound insights into sound human and social psychology. A fresh and irresistible way of seeing that human and social well-being are connected, and depend on something much more basic than any political authority, constitutes a potential threat to the existing political power structure.

Thus each of the major spiritual traditions conveys a new paradigm, a fresh way of seeing the world and experiencing life. As such, these spiritual traditions have threatened established, old orders and the old paradigm that served the political power structure of the times. Predictably, the new paradigm has been attacked again and again, and later subverted and corrupted by old-paradigm thinking.

Christianity, for example, was initially a threat to the existing authorities, whose attacks and efforts at suppression failed to destroy it. Step by step it was simply subverted and corrupted, and that process has had a very long-lasting success. At its origin, we see the Sermon on the Mount (new paradigm, Option A). Centuries later, we see the Crusades and the Spanish Inquisition (old paradigm, Option B). Today many of the people who call themselves "Christians" are locked into the same destructive old-paradigm, Option B patterns of thought and behavior.

For centuries there have been Option A Christians, Option A Jews, and Option A Muslims. For centuries there have been Option B Christians, Option B Jews, and Option B Muslims. That distinction between affirmation of life and subservience to power, between Option A and Option B, is far more important than the label of Christian or Jew or Muslim. But only those who have eyes can see the difference.

This book is not about something so grandiose and remote as a clash of civilizations, but about another kind of conflict, more subtle, pervasive, and personal: a clash of convictions about the value of human life. Like a person uncertain of her own worth and considering suicide, the global human community is wrestling with the possibility of extinction. Within each of us, that conflict between self-doubt and self-affirmation is playing itself out, day by day.

Ignorance of the value of a human life and lack of empathy for other human beings leads to violence in world affairs. It is closely associated with ignorance of and lack of reverence for our own worth as individuals.

War is a disease: The case of Vietnam

War is a disease in the same sense that HIV/AIDS and cancer are diseases. Warfare kills people, devastates lives, and blots out the gift that each person afflicted with the disease might have brought to the world. The cause of warfare is to be found in patterns of human thinking and behavior. If we can change the patterns, we can eliminate the disease.

The case of Vietnam was the wake-up call for a generation of North Americans. Something was rotten in the state, and many of us began to look for some way of thinking that could account for the pathology. Governments and cultural institutions rooted in the old paradigm were not going to help much with that process. Instead, they would obstruct the paths of discovery. Predictably, the old-paradigm institutions have made a sustained, well-funded effort to use Vietnam in restoring the pathology of the warfare system. "This will not be another Vietnam!" became one of the catchphrases used in recruiting support for the next invasion, the next war, and the next, and the next.

> The evil that is in the world always comes of ignorance, and good intentions may do as much harm as malevolence, if they lack understanding. On the whole, men are more good than bad; that, however, isn't the point. Men are more or less ignorant, and it is this that we call vice or virtue; the most incorrigible vice being that of an ignorance that fancies it knows everything and therefore claims for itself the right to kill. (Camus 1947, 131)

Occasionally this insight expressed by Albert Camus in *The Plague* dawns on someone who has suffered from that kind of ignorance and who makes the effort to understand what went so disastrously wrong. The following excerpts are from Robert McNamara's book *Argument Without End: In Search of Answers to the Vietnam Tragedy* (McNamara et al. 1999).

McNamara, who had been Secretary of Defense during the Vietnam War era, went through personal agonies over that catastrophe and the part he had played in it. His book is based on a project he led involving scholars and former government officials from the United States and their counterparts from Vietnam in a series of dialogues held in Hanoi between November 1995 and February 1998. Although the book does not completely escape from the old paradigm or envision the new, it expresses a passionate awareness of the problem. The honesty and introspection of the author can be used to intelligent advantage for our future, if readers pay close attention.

> In fact, the dialogues themselves reveal what seems to have been one of the central failures — perhaps *the* central failure — in both the United States and North Vietnam: a failure of *empathy*. Each side fundamentally misread the mindset of its enemy. The fact that they became and remained bitter enemies for a quarter-century is testament to the depth of the misreading, the

utter inability of leaders in Washington and Hanoi to penetrate the thoughts, perspectives, and emotions of those on the other side....

... In every way, American ignorance of the history, language, and culture of Vietnam was immense. The chapters in this book are filled with illustrations of that ignorance. (McNamara et al. 1999, 376–77, 397)

Ignorance and lack of empathy are major causal factors in the disease of warfare, and they can be overcome.

The practice of medicine and the practice of citizenship

In many parts of this book, I will use concepts or analogies drawn from the field of medicine. Analogies are not very useful as proofs, but they can clarify intended meaning, accentuate important issues, and serve as a source of ideas for solving problems.

For example, in considering the qualities important for responsible, effective citizenship, I can ask myself what qualities I would expect in a highly effective physician. These qualities would certainly include personal well-being: a physician preoccupied with personal problems or hobbled by pessimism or depression will tend to be less effective than a physician who does not have these impediments. A highly effective physician would also have empathy and respect for others, not only patients but also the people she interacts with in everyday life. She would have a sound basis in the principles of medicine and experience in applying those principles in case after case of challenging problems. Identifying problems and seeking solutions would have become second nature to an effective physician, and optimism would be a pragmatic necessity.

Such an inquiry can be used to identify analogous qualities of responsible, effective citizenship. Responsible, effective global citizens are at work in every society; the range and genius of their work are astounding. Civil society worldwide has in effect assumed the role of physician to the global community. Because civil society is much less hobbled by the old paradigm than established institutions, it can move with much greater speed and adaptive intelligence in identifying and solving major problems.

This book has a bias, essentially identical to the bias of medicine: human well-being and the conditions of global community necessary to foster that well-being take priority over support for any particular government in its contests for power. I am a human being before I am a citizen of this or that state, and I have a responsibility to other human beings that is more basic than my responsibility to any government. The pathology that threatens human well-being can be identified in the violations of international law by governments, particularly by militarily powerful governments and their allies.

When my government or one of its allies violates international law by committing an act of aggression or by threatening another government, it is thereby placing the global community at risk. Since I am part of the global community, those violations of law are threatening me. As a citizen, I am expected to obey the law; as a citizen, I expect that same standard of behavior from my government. That is my bias. The ideas I present here as fundamentals of responsible global citizenship serve that bias.

A personal journey

I am a citizen of the United States. I served for two years as a captain in the U.S. Army Medical Corps. The Vietnam War was ravaging lives in Southeast Asia, but I was stationed with the Second Infantry Division just south of the "demilitarized zone" in Korea. It was remarkably quiet. I had time to read and think about causes and consequences of current events. By the time I was discharged from the army, I had pieced together my own way of understanding the war. Soldiers often figure out the most important things for themselves, although usually much too late. Their governments will not help them with that kind of enlightenment, for reasons I have already mentioned.

I am a physician, currently a professor in the Faculty of Medicine at the University of Calgary in western Canada. I am a citizen of Canada, and the widower of a woman from Iraq, Irma Parhad, with whom I shared my life and work. She was born in Mosul and attended high school in Baghdad and college and medical school in Chicago. We met during our neurology residency years in Albany, New York, served on the faculty at Johns Hopkins in Baltimore, Maryland, and moved to Canada in 1984 to establish a neuroscience research program. She made countless contributions to the lives of people in southern Alberta. When she died of cancer in 1994, the part of the world that she had illuminated went dark forever. That is what happens when a human life is extinguished.

Since Iraq's invasion of Kuwait in August 1990, I have been on a long search for answers to questions. The questions presented themselves to me as they did because I was the person I was. The same events must have had very different effects on others, and for some, perhaps they raised no questions at all. As the months and years went by, leading to the 2003 invasion of Iraq, my questions and answers became a journey, and it was the road as much as the destination that commanded my attention. Each question and what it revealed, each point along the journey, led to other questions, the next part of the road.

I was looking for a basic and comprehensive way of thinking about the case of Iraq and similar catastrophes that were extinguishing human lives and wasting resources. I wanted something pragmatic to help guide my own decisions and actions as a citizen. I read countless books and articles by intelligent and articulate observers, with some emphasis on works by "neoconservatives" and "neo-liberals," with whom (I assumed) I would disagree. I found a great deal that was important and informative. I also found much that was astonishingly shallow, incoherent, even dishonest. Among the sources I read, I did not find the pragmatic conceptual framework I was seeking. What I learned on the road provided it.

About this book

I needed something like a text on principles of medicine. Principles of medicine facilitate the physician's interpretation of data for a specific purpose: to contribute as effectively as possible to the health of the patient. I needed a basic and comprehensive text that would facilitate interpretation of world events for a similar purpose: to contribute as effectively as possible to human well-being. Because I did not find a text of this kind, I have had to write it myself.

The approach I use has evolved over more than a decade and a half. Its conceptual basis is somewhat different from that of the peace movement although I find important synergies with that movement. The world in which human beings are inflicting pathology on other human beings presents to me a challenge somewhat like what a physician would face in the midst of a plague. It calls for an active process of questioning complacent assumptions, identifying and defining problems, and testing potential solutions. And so I have chosen the analogy of medicine to clarify the concept of global citizenship presented in this book. The process, which is ongoing, also involves healing myself, which is sometimes the most difficult part of the work. In this process I have experienced personal growth in a way I had never known before I began it.

This is not intended as a scholarly tome. It is intended as a conceptual framework for a life of action and transformation — or at least for understanding why we human beings keep driving ourselves toward catastrophe. Historical details are sometimes mentioned, particularly in the case study of Iraq in chapter 5. However, most such details are beyond the scope of this text. The book is intended to be easy for the general reader to follow. The practice of responsible global citizenship does not require academic credentials, which may even be an obstacle. The investment that some scholars have made in their many years of old-paradigm scholarship may undermine their ability even to consider the concepts put forward here. Nonetheless, the book carries a message intended for scholars as well as the general reader.

The reader may notice my repetition of concepts. A concept that appears in the introduction and in chapter 1 may reappear in one or more of the subsequent chapters in a different context. The introduction and overview is designed to give the reader an extended synopsis of the text; chapter 1 sets the background for subsequent chapters, particularly for the thirty principles that appear in chapters 4 and 6; and chapter 5 provides a more detailed case study illustrating the Principles of Global Community. Hence some redundancy is inherent in the design of the book.

The reader will notice in some parts of the text my impatience, even irritation, with "the establishment" — old-paradigm intellectuals, elected and appointed officials, and others. If that edge makes the text more persuasive, then I am satisfied that it remain. If it has the opposite effect, consider it due to my own shortcomings and move on. Don't let it deter you from optimal use of other parts of this book.

The manuscript for the book was initially submitted in October 2008, and I have been urged to provide updates, particularly with regard to developments since Barack Obama took office as president of the United States. I will do that here briefly, and at occasional points in other parts of the book.

Barack Obama seems to me wiser and more emotionally mature than most of his predecessors in that office, and certainly I have great respect for him as a human being. Many of his statements and initiatives since taking office are commendable and important. From the perspective of this book, he may well be providing openings for democratic renewal that are unprecedented, and if we neglect those openings the fault is ours, not his.

However, Obama faces largely the same constraints in the office of president that you or I would face if we held that office. He cannot escape the gravitational field of the old paradigm, and his actions since taking office give abundant evidence of that constraint. The bottom line: his genius and wisdom will be wasted if we fail to live up to our responsibilities as citizens. This book is not so much about criticizing the failures of elected officials as about how to take up our own responsibilities and fulfill our own potential in contributing to a healthier global community.

The foreign military presence in Afghanistan and the extension of its violence into Pakistan are contrary to the principles and purposes expressed in this book. The U.S. attack on Afghanistan has been from its inception a violation of international law. Article 51 of the UN Charter gives states the right to self-defence. The UN Charter, including Article 51, is intended to control cycles of violence; responses to an attack must be proportionate and limited. It does not permit the destruction of a state that supports terrorism; if it did, it would be a license to destroy (for example) each of the states that hold a permanent seat on the UN Security Council. Agents of terrorism have long been supported by Russia, the United States, and other militant nationalist states. There is nothing in international law that permits the destruction of such states.

Under international law, the lives of human beings matter, and not just the lives of citizens of powerful states. Governments must comply with law in their responses to political violence; otherwise they will perpetuate the cycles of violence against human beings, as they have done in Afghanistan. That's Option B.

This book is a contribution to and not a substitute for the excellent work of others. Some of the many books from which I have benefited are included in the section on Further Reading. Lists of websites are provided in some of those books. Search engines and the Internet have changed the way books are written. For this reason, I mention the names of authors and books in various parts of the text to enable the reader to search for more from that source. The resources available for the practice of responsible, effective global citizenship are endless; those who engage in this practice will continue to find their own resources as their lives and experiences unfold.

Those who have the most to contribute to the community are often the busiest and may not find the time to read a book from cover to cover. If you read and understand this introduction and overview, you will have a general idea of the concepts in the book.

Chapter 1 ("Choosing the Future") draws attention to the process of choice whereby we determine the course of human history and develops related themes such as pragmatic realism and the relationships between personal well-being and a healthy global community.

Axioms are basic concepts, self-evident and requiring no proof, on which a larger conceptual system can be built. An example from plane geometry is: "The shortest distance between two points is a straight line." Chapter 2 ("Axioms") specifies five axioms that I consider important for the discussion of world affairs. These are concepts so basic that they could be used to test a person's contact with reality.

This introduction has given a glimpse of an old and a new paradigm, and has called for a paradigm shift. Chapter 3 ("Paradigm Shift") explores the tenacity of the old paradigm and the power of the new paradigm, develops new-paradigm themes, and suggests some ways to make the shift.

A synoptic list of thirty principles is included in this Introduction and Overview. The first twenty of these are designated "Principles of Global Community" and are developed in chapter 4. Chapter 5 ("The Case of Iraq") illustrates some of the principles of global community using the example of Iraq. Chapter 6 ("Principles of Global Citizenship") develops principles 21 to 30, which are intended to facilitate effective, responsible engagement in public life.

Chapter 7 ("Practicing Citizenship") deals with the experience of practicing citizenship as I know it, including the importance of the imagination in opening paths for exploration. It describes the background and evolution of two related projects with which I have been involved here in Calgary: one aiming to revitalize local communities and the other to connect communities globally while enabling individuals and local communities to realize a little more of their full potential.

This book is not much concerned with predictions of doom but with the pragmatics of hope. Chapter 8 ("Prognosis") emphasizes the difference.

What I present here is not intended as some sort of edict or "final word." As with a text on principles of medicine, it is intended as an articulation of some basic concepts to be examined critically, used appropriately, and modified as indicated by experience.

Above all, it is intended to prompt readers to use their creative and responsible imaginations and to engage in redirecting the course of world events. The familiar concept that "imagination is more important than knowledge" should at least emphasize the importance of the imagination in determining the course of history. Our ability to co-operatively imagine optimal conditions for the global community and to implement what we imagine can be used to enormous advantage at both personal and global levels.

PRINCIPLES OF GLOBAL COMMUNITY
AND GLOBAL CITIZENSHIP
A synopsis

1. *We are in the process of choosing between a healthy global community under a rule of international law (Option A) or ongoing violent contests for power driven by militant nationalism (Option B).* The choices resulting from this process have largely determined both the course of world events in the past and the current conditions of human security. The process of choosing diminishes or expands our ability to envision possibilities and to explore the farther reaches of the human spirit. It creates opportunities or challenges for the generations who will follow us. The choices we make will continue to determine the course of world events, the conditions of human existence, and the chances of human survival in the future. Outcomes are likely to be better if we become more conscious of the choices available to us and better informed about alternatives for the future than we have been in the past.

2. *We cannot be part of the solution until we understand that we are part of the problem.* Responsible global citizenship requires not only understanding that we are contributing to the problem but also an ongoing inquiry into *how* we are contributing to the problem. As we pursue this understanding and inquiry, we progressively enhance our ability to help solve the problem.

3. *Warfare is pathological.* Warfare ravages human beings physically and psychologically. The causes of this pathology include multiple interrelated factors: environmental, political, economic, cultural/ideological, social/psychological, and others.

4. *Militant nationalism drives the global community toward Option B.* The Option A priority is human well-being. The

Option B priority is political power, and in organized states, state power. Militant nationalist culture denies, obscures, rationalizes, or ignores the conflict between these two priorities.

5. *Power must be constrained by law.* Reliable progress in human security can be made only within a framework of international law protecting human rights, counteracting the pathology of power, and constraining violent contests for power. This is a basic requirement for progress toward Option A.

6. *A rule of law depends on respect for the inherent justice of the law and on justice in its implementation.* No police or army can long enforce a law that is self-negating. There can be no rule of law if the most powerful can violate the law with impunity or if the law is applied in ways that violate its most fundamental principles and purposes.

7. *Democracy and law are interdependent.* An effective democracy is the only reliable enforcer for international law. International law is the guarantor and guideline of effective democracy.

8. *Democracy and law are evolving.* This dynamic can be measured in terms of Option A and Option B: whether the evolution of democracy and law is moving us toward a healthier global community and improved conditions of human existence, or whether democracy and law are degenerating into false forms, carrying the names "democracy" and "law" but not their Option A reality, and so leading us toward the pathology of warfare, militant nationalism, and diminishing human security.

9. *Nationalism has both creative and destructive effects on the state itself.* An *inclusive nationalism* can mitigate conflicts among ethnic communities and promote cooperative effort for the public good. This potential accounts for much of the historical success of nationalism. But nationalism has a strong tendency to become malignant: to make political power (and state power) an end unto itself. This *militant nationalism,*

the dominant form of nationalism today, is pervasive in the culture of militarily powerful states, and it influences the culture of their allies.

10. *Every powerful state has both conveyed significant benefits and committed major atrocities.* Without exception, every powerful militant nationalist state in history has facilitated major achievements that benefited the citizens of that state. Without exception, every powerful militant nationalist state in history has been responsible for murderous atrocities.

11. *Nationalism is legitimate only when it serves human well-being within the constraints of international law.* Its limits of legitimacy are defined, for example, by international human rights law, by the law of non-aggression, and by concepts in social psychology such as those in the work of Erich Fromm and Abraham Maslow.

12. *Violence begets violence. Militant nationalism sustains that dynamic in the global community.* Warfare is *intentionally* sustained by a warfare system; militant nationalism is its ideology.

13. *Militant nationalism begets militant nationalism.* Militant nationalism in one state or ethnic group tends to trigger militant nationalist responses in other states and ethnic groups.

14. *The warfare system sustains and is sustained by a culture of cynicism.* In our militant nationalist culture we are taught that it's a dog-eat-dog world. By choosing to think this way, we make it "normal" to have extremes of wealth and poverty, conspicuous consumption, cutthroat competition, and endless warfare.

15. *Militant nationalism is associated with contempt for law, democracy, and human rights. It is associated with the pathology of power.* The tendency of power to corrupt is well known. We have seen murderous examples of that tendency in our own time and in the behavior of our own governments and their

allies. This self-destructive tendency of militant nationalism is associated not just with a failure of governments to *represent* responsible citizens and the best interests of human beings but also with a failure even to *respond* to the efforts of citizens to initiate responsible behavior in governments. The contempt that powerful governments have for law is expressed in their behavior and is often even made explicit by the intellectuals who advise them.

16. *Militant nationalism has destructive effects on individuals, families, and communities.* Militant nationalism is a deeply pessimistic ideology based on the false premise that we have no choice but to continue destroying each other. This pessimism has destructive effects physically, psychologically, and socially. It leads to permanent physical and psychological disability, depression, suicide, domestic violence and dysfunction, and pervasive social malaise.

17. *A militant nationalist government is a threat to its own citizens.* Any government that violates international law by its threats against other governments thereby constitutes a threat to the global community. Since citizens of the militant nationalist state are part of the global community, every militant nationalist government is a threat to the citizens of its own state.

18. *Militant nationalism is particularly toxic to the global community when it dominates the culture and politics of a powerful state. Powerful states are the major violators of international law and the major threats to global community and human survival.* Weak or fractured states such as Colombia or the former Yugoslavia or Rwanda or Sudan have committed murderous atrocities and violations of international law, but the criminality of such states does not have the global reach of a superpower and cannot corrupt and obstruct the UN Security Council and other institutions designed to advance the purposes of international law. Only powerful states are capable

of that kind of obstruction and perversion of international law and its institutions.

19. *International power politics provoke internal repression, dictatorships, and civil wars.* Internal repression tends to increase as external threats increase. Even very powerful states with comparatively democratic traditions will sharply curtail civil liberties in times of major wars. Civil wars may arise because of unequivocal violations of basic human rights by a politically dominant group, because of militant nationalism within an ethnic group striving to establish autonomy or its own independent state, or (as is usual) because of a combination of such factors.

20. *Militant nationalism is an ideology whose time has passed.* The corruption, waste, and hypocrisy necessary to sustain militant nationalism have critically undermined its credibility. Enormous resources are currently being squandered to maintain this ideology. The sooner the resources being squandered on Option B are redirected toward Option A, the sooner we will see the light of dawn.

21. *Elected and appointed officials are limited by the paradigm of the political institutions they serve.* Those who serve in a militant nationalist government are limited by the militant nationalist way of thinking. There will be intense pressures on them to carry on "business as usual," severely limiting their ability to move events toward Option A.

22. *Civil society has emerged as the Option A leader in world affairs.* Civil society is the non-governmental, non-corporate sector of society that is dedicated to the public interest and the common good. Civil society organizations are variously concerned with environmental or social justice issues or other challenges. Organizations and individuals in civil society have moved with an adaptive intelligence and speed, which governments cannot match, to identify problems and potential solutions of life-and-death importance to our future.

23. *The Option A responsibilities of any national government include compliance with and promotion of international humanitarian and human rights law and the law of non-aggression, as well as the promotion of mechanisms, structures, and competencies for effective democracy.* The claim of any state to be a leader in promoting human rights can be reliably assessed by that state's record of compliance or non-compliance with international law and by its record of responsiveness or non-responsiveness to the Option A initiatives of civil society.

24. *Power is essential to fostering a healthy global community under a rule of law.* Power has interrelated political, economic, and cultural domains. The success of Option A initiatives depends on power in each of these domains. Volunteerism and a shoestring budget can accomplish a lot but cannot compete with a six hundred billion dollar-a-year military budget, or with the massive funding going into cultural and political institutions rooted in old-paradigm thinking.

25. *The pathology of powerlessness sustains the pathology of power.* The tendency of power to degenerate into pathological forms can only be averted by effective democracy and a rule of law. Uncritical deference to authority sustains dictatorships and the major violations of international law perpetrated by powerful states.

26. *Problems are there to be solved. Identifying and solving problems is essential to personal growth.* Pragmatic realism involves the ability to recognize a specific obstacle or problem, to define it in terms that evoke possible solutions, and to test the solutions. Pragmatic realism in the service of human well-being is a mark of wisdom and healthy psychology.

27. *The conditions of human existence and the chances of human survival depend largely on respect for self and others. Emotional intelligence is essential at both personal and global levels.* Responsible citizenship includes the capacity of each person to advance his or her personal well-being and to be constructively

involved in the life of local and global community. Effectively implemented, these two processes (personal growth and public engagement) are reciprocally reinforcing. Personal growth is limited in the person isolated from public life through cynicism, consumerism, or careerism. Pursuit of one's career oblivious to personal and social relationships and to the common good makes life — even professional life — less rewarding. There is no natural barrier between the common good and the good life.

28. *Citizenship is a field for innovation, achievement, and creative public life.* The practice of medicine can be taken as a model for the practice of citizenship.

29. *Awareness, support, and active engagement are three stages of responsible citizenship.* Lack of time, interest, energy, and other resources for involvement in public life are real or perceived problems obstructing progress toward Option A. These problems have solutions, beginning with the simple under-standing that awareness of the issues can itself be a powerful catalyst for change.

30. *Optimism is essential; complacency is dangerous; pessimism is a waste of time.*

Choosing the Future

People do the darnedest things. They discover preventions and cures for disease; commit mass murder and rape; create masterpieces of literature; perform levitating acts of kindness and devastating acts of blindness; and invent weapons that can bring their own species to an end.

Because of this astonishing range of human options and abilities, we constantly change the world. The world of 1800 was very different from the world of 1900. No one in 1900 could have imagined what the world would be like today, and no one today can predict what the world will be like in a hundred years. The changes take place incrementally or suddenly. Absolutely essential advances may go completely unheralded; catastrophic changes are usually unforeseen. The work of years can be destroyed in minutes; the work of an afternoon can exert a powerful influence for decades. We cannot predict what the world will be like even ten years from now, yet we influence what that world will be like each day of our lives.

It was not quite a century ago that World War I was called

"the war to end all wars." That cataclysm did hideous things to countless human beings, yet even former peace activists were recruited into it, perhaps thinking this would be the last time. It was followed by an attempt to outlaw war, yet by 1940 we were at it again, descending into World War II. During that particular chapter of our history, we invented nuclear weapons, which are widely recognized as a threat to our very existence as a species.

Sobered by the consequences of our behavior, we humans then conceived the United Nations. The UN Charter, signed on June 26, 1945, opens with these words:

> We, the people of the United Nations, determined to save succeeding generations from the scourge of war, which twice in our lifetime has brought untold sorrow to mankind, and to regain faith in fundamental human rights, in the dignity and worth of the human person, in the equal rights of men and women and of nations large and small ... and for these ends ... to ensure, by the acceptance of principles and the institution of methods, that armed force shall not be used, save in the common interest, and to employ international machinery for the promotion of the economic and social advancement of all peoples, have resolved to combine our efforts to accomplish these aims.

Where are we going?

Recurrent cycles of self-destructive behavior, followed by repeated resolutions to bring the behavior under control, characterize alcoholics as individuals and human beings as a species. There have been signs of progress toward breaking our addiction but also emerging challenges that can undermine the progress. There is the ever-present danger that such challenges might even lead to human extinction.

For the first time in history, it is possible to contemplate a non-biblical "end of the world" scenario — not an act of God but a deliberate unleashing of a manmade, global, cataclysmic chain reaction. (Brzezinski 2004, 12)

As every well-educated person knows, the dangers are not only from warfare and nuclear weapons but also from environmental conditions. Jared Diamond emphasizes a series of environmental challenges that include climate change:

Our world society is presently on a non-sustainable course, and any of our 12 problems of non-sustainability that we have just summarized would suffice to limit our lifestyle within the next several decades. They are like time bombs with fuses of less than 50 years. (2005, 498)

The major challenges we face do not occur in isolation. On the page preceding the statement quoted above, Jared Diamond provides two maps. One illustrates "political trouble spots of the modern world"; the other, "environmental trouble spots of the modern world." The two maps are identical except for the titles.

A person weakened by hopelessness or malnutrition or an immune deficiency is more likely to succumb to an infectious disease than a person who has the same disease but is otherwise in good health. Environmental problems are made worse by militarism. Warfare undermines the basis for all human rights. Public health systems and infrastructure deteriorate when public resources are diverted into weapons acquisition and development.

Our patterns of behavior in North America indicate that we are grossly irresponsible with respect to conditions essential for human survival. This irresponsibility is apparent in our conspicuous waste and consumption, and in our disregard for the lives of people in Iraq and other parts of the world. Such irresponsibility makes all of us more vulnerable, and undermines human options for future generations. The challenges we face do not occur in isolation, nor do the consequences of our irresponsibility. Our own patterns of thinking and behavior are responsible for the self-destructive direction in which we are heading, yet we make daily choices largely unaware of this fact. It is not so much the danger of human extinction but the ongoing loss of human creative potential that chiefly concerns me in this book. We can improve human options and the conditions of human existence, but it will require a basic understanding of why we have been so self-destructive, and active use of that understanding to change ourselves and our culture. Many of our institutions are rooted in self-destructive patterns of thinking and behavior, and serve to perpetuate our self-destruction. We will have to change those institutions. The most essential part of the work, however, must be at the personal level. We cannot be part of the solution until we understand that we are part of the problem.

Where do we want to go?

"Would you tell me, please, which way I ought to go from here?"

"That depends a good deal on where you want to get to," said the Cat.

— LEWIS CARROLL, *Alice's Adventures in Wonderland*

The Cheshire Cat's response to Alice is good advice for us as citizens. We had better think carefully about where we want to go. Leaving the choice to political leaders and the "experts" who advise them is a prescription for recurrent disaster. That's not because political leaders and experts are evil but because their thinking and their options are largely confined to the box of the old ways of thinking and because they serve in political and cultural institutions based on those ways of thinking.

We need effective public discussion about options for our future. The discussion should be ongoing, vigorous, visionary, well informed, well organized, and well documented. It should move freely outside the box of the old ways of thinking. Erich Fromm was a careful observer of human psychology and its effects on twentieth-century society. Noting the much greater attention that had been devoted to ideas of "the good man" and "the good society" in previous centuries, he writes:

> The twentieth century is conspicuous for the absence of such visions.... The absence of visions projecting a "better" man and a "better" society has had the effect of paralyzing man's faith in himself and his future (and is at the same time the result of such a paralysis). (1947, 82–83)

If we cannot make a cooperative effort to focus human imagination on our options, then our choices will be unconscious and poorly informed, and our influence will be haphazard. Something better than that is certainly possible, and it might make the difference between survival and extinction. The question is whether we want to try.

In studying the history of societies that made catastrophic choices, Jared Diamond suggested that the failure could be thought of as having several stages:

> First of all, a group may fail to anticipate a problem before the problem actually arrives. Second, when the problem does arrive, the group may fail to perceive it. Then, after they perceive it, they may fail even to try to solve it. Finally, they may try to solve it but may not succeed. (2005, 421)

The problems are all around us; they have economic, environmental, political, cultural, social, and psychological dimensions. Responsible global citizenship involves an evidence-based, goal-directed engagement in the work of solving these problems. If, as citizens of the global community, we were to take these things seriously and set to work on them, we would need some conceptual frame of reference as a pragmatic guide. I refer to such a frame of reference here as Option A, which I prefer, contrasting it with Option B, which is the self-destructive direction we have been traveling. Each of these options can be expressed in various ways; the sections and chapters that follow will develop this conceptual framework. A concise and effective way of expressing Option A and Option B was provided several decades ago by Martin Luther King Jr. It is worth repeating and memorizing:

> We must learn to live together as brothers, or perish together as fools.

We can greatly improve our orientation in time and space by using this system of navigation. We can evaluate our own culture, history, and process of decision-making at each step in terms of whether they lead toward Option A or toward Option B.

I will refer to the patterns of thinking that tend to move us toward Option B as an "old paradigm" and ways of thinking that tend to move us toward Option A as a "new paradigm." Old-paradigm thinking is characteristic of entrenched power structures, which historically have been challenged repeatedly by the new paradigm. Because they cultivate the old paradigm, empires drive themselves toward Option B (perishing as fools).

Many people are able to break free of old-paradigm thinking, but it would be a rare person who has not been influenced by it. In old-paradigm thinking, which is characterized by cynicism, Option A is "idealistic" or "unrealistic." If you think in this way, you will probably read this book critically. Good.

The practice of medicine and the
practice of global citizenship

The bias in this book is similar to the bias in medicine, a profession in which the first principle is "Do no harm." As in medicine, this book has a specific ethical basis (new-paradigm thinking directed toward Option A: human well-being) and a goal-oriented, evidence-based approach to understanding the conditions that influence human well-being. The same bias was articulated by Albert Camus in his novel *The Plague*:

> All I maintain is that on this earth there are pestilences and there are victims, and it's up to us, so far as possible, not to join forces with the pestilences. (1947, 253)

In the practice of medicine, the purpose of identifying and examining disease-producing factors and mechanisms is to find ways to cure and prevent the disease. *Pathogenesis* is the medical term for factors and mechanisms that produce a disease. The study of human self-destruction is essentially the study of a form of pathology. The question addressed in the next section — "Why are we so self-destructive?" — has an obvious similarity to the question "How does cancer get started and grow and metastasize?" This book presents a way of understanding the pathology that we human beings inflict on ourselves. The self-destructive patterns of human thinking and behavior, which have undermined the conditions of human existence (and are threatening human survival), are here recognized as *pathological*.

In writing this book, I am interested not just in the solution to a puzzle but also in actively solving the problem. If we define the problem in narrow terms as one of political leadership, we cannot solve it. Only when we begin to see that we are part of the pathogenesis, that our own patterns of thinking in fact support the self-destructive patterns of human behavior — only then can

[33]

we begin to achieve optimal effectiveness in the practice of global citizenship.

Taking the practice of medicine as analogue for the practice of citizenship has a number of advantages. It helps to clarify the new paradigm, to define problems and obstacles in practice, and to identify potential solutions to the problems and ways to move past the obstacles.

Notice the emphasis on learning in the statement by Martin Luther King Jr.: learn or perish. An active process of learning is necessary, or we will perish as fools. But what is it that needs to be learned in order to move us toward Option A? After all, there is plenty to learn in moving in the other direction, toward Option B. There's learning how to plant land mines, how to fire air-to-surface missiles, how to salute, how to display the flag, and how to sing the national anthem. There's always a new book or article out by an Option B intellectual with plenty of new things to learn, lots of details from historical research, all placed in a conceptual framework that reinforces our tendency to move toward Option B. This book (the one you are reading) presents a way of thinking (a new paradigm) designed to facilitate progress toward Option A. Many books, websites, and other sources provide rich additional material that enhances our awareness of Option A. The culture in which we are immersed constantly floods us with information that reinforces either Option A (new paradigm) thinking or Option B (old paradigm) thinking.

The term *pragmatic realism* as used in this book refers to a mindset similar to that of a good physician in the midst of a crisis that threatens human health and well-being. Very much aware of the dangers, the physician is also aware that timely and intelligent action can reduce the dangers and lead to optimal outcomes.

Pragmatic realism recognizes our own part in human self-destruction, but also our capacity for better, more life-affirming human options. It seeks an evidence-based way to promote human well-being and enable optimal development of human possibilities. Pragmatic realism has the patience and concern for the well-being of others, as well as the respect for their value, that characterize a good physician.

Pragmatic realism is essential to the practice of responsible, effective local and global citizenship. Pragmatic realism can drive a positive feed-forward loop whereby the practice of responsible citizenship revitalizes democratic process, and that revitalized democracy steadily reinforces international law. The resulting increase in human security worldwide enables the conditions that foster human creative potential (education, public health measures, community interaction). By amplifying this process locally and globally, and by creating structures and resources for that purpose, this part of the feed-forward loop can foster a sustained application of human intelligence in the service of human well-being, similar to that seen in the best health care systems. That would mean a constant reinforcement of the practice of responsible citizenship, with its feed-forward effects on democracy, international law, and human security.

Pathogenesis: Why are we so self-destructive?

In the 1980s, the Cold War was drawing to a close. Nuclear weapons might have been eliminated, along with a wide range of other costly and destructive Cold War-era policies and practices. Enormous resources could have been freed up and redirected toward more constructive alternatives. The benefits from that line of decision-making would have been beyond our ability to calculate.

Instead, governments chose to perpetuate the warfare system. In the 1990s, violence was escalated again and again when other options were available. We will be paying the costs of this choice — also incalculable — for decades to come. One example of the consequences will be examined in detail in chapter 5, "The Case of Iraq."

Why are political leaders and their advisors so incompetent at breaking this self-destructive pattern of human behavior? It's a puzzle, potentially much more interesting than a murder mystery or a crossword. And the solution will be incomparably more rewarding.

There have been many approaches to solving the puzzle, including Marxist perspectives, comparisons with the territorial behavior of other species, and historicist analyses that emphasize the decision-making processes of political leaders. A critical analysis of institutions that promote the self-destructive patterns of thinking and behavior is also essential. These are a few examples of analytic paradigms for understanding the origins of war.

Even more basic to solving not only the puzzle but also the problem are approaches that help us understand how *we* (you and I) are contributing to human self-destruction. In a book that has become a modern classic (*The Denial of Death*, 1973), Ernest Becker proposes that our self-destructive behavior and much of our culture can be explained by the very human fear of death. Each of us is going to die, and we know it. Culture can be understood as a strategy for coping with the anxiety produced by that awareness. We create "immortality systems," ways of denying our mortality by identifying with something we believe to be eternal. Being a citizen of the Roman Empire, a Roman Catholic, a Christian, a Muslim, a Jew, a patriot, a Communist, or simply being "saved" can serve as a sort of security blanket. I am an American (or a Christian or whatever), and America (or the Kingdom of God or whatever) is eternal and I am part of it and so I am immortal. This "immortality system" makes the very idea of death more bearable.

Referring to Sigmund Freud's book *Group Psychology and the Analysis of the Ego* and developments that followed it, Becker sketches an understanding of why a political leader can so easily induce complicity in acts of aggression and destruction. If "the leader" orders the killing of tens of thousands of people, it becomes "holy aggression." Thus members of the armed forces can kill with equanimity, and a society can remain silent while its government deprives human beings of basic human rights. It is allegiance to what has been declared right and noble and good.

Our awareness of death could remind us of our shared humanity and become part of the basis for creating a healthy global community. Instead, it has become one of the forces producing the dysfunctional global community we inhabit today.

Becker's way of thinking is useful because it draws the connection between something that is deeply compelling at the personal level and something that is profoundly destructive at the level of world events. To understand why we are so self-destructive will take more than this, but *The Denial of Death* can serve as one very helpful reference point.

The countless versions, combinations, and permutations of immortality systems include the one promulgated by imperialist Cecil John Rhodes (1853–1902):

> Only one race approached God's ideal type, his own Anglo-Saxon race: God's purpose then was to make the Anglo-Saxon race predominant, and the best way to help on God's work and fulfill His purpose in the world was to contribute to the predominance of the Anglo-Saxon race and so bring nearer the reign of justice, liberty and peace. (Rhodes, quoted in Alexander 1996, 25)

Mr. Rhodes instructs us that white supremacist policies are "in accord with God's will," and violence in the service of such policies advances God's purpose. Much more recently, we heard such arguments in support of the invasion of Iraq, including the idea that U.S. military action is bringing democracy to the Middle East. Killing tens or hundreds of thousands of people in the service of state power is not an easy sell to normal healthy individuals. If you want to recruit support for the violence you are planning, you have to find some way of disguising its primary purpose (supporting political power). Your publicity for the project must obscure the fact that you will be killing fellow human beings and ruining lives of survivors, and must emphasize some benefit (making the world safe for democracy, advancing God's purpose in the world, whatever) that will appeal to the public and the executioners — the soldiers and others who carry out the orders. As Aleksandr Solzhenitsyn put it,

> To do evil a human being must first of all believe that what he's doing is good. (1974, 173)

One of the reasons we are so self-destructive is because we think we are not responsible. The violence is originating somewhere else, not with me. It was Hitler, it was the Germans, it was the communists, it was the terrorists, it was the Muslims. In the case of Iraq, examined in some detail in chapter 5, it was Saddam Hussein who was responsible for our imposing sanctions on Iraq and the invasion of Iraq. Even if our own government did something wrong by imposing sanctions and invading Iraq, we are not personally responsible for that. It was our leaders and the experts who advised them who are at fault. If someone were to ask us, "Why did you allow this to happen?" we might respond: "I didn't know these things," or "I am not a foreign policy expert," or "It was the President's responsibility," or "We had to stop the evil that was over there," or "Am I my brother's keeper?"

We think of Hitler as a prime example of evil, but support for Hitler came from "good citizens" and "good soldiers" doing their duty for their country. Just like us.

> By far the greater part of violence that humans have inflicted on each other is not the work of criminals or the mentally deranged, but of normal, respectable citizens in the service of the collective ego. One can go so far as to say that on this planet "normal" equals insane. (Tolle 2005, 73)

Democracy by definition is a form of governance in which the citizens are ultimately responsible for the behavior of their government. And "the citizens" means you and me.

Policies of our governments have been responsible for the extinction or devastation of millions of lives over the past quarter century. Most recently, under the banner of a "war against terrorism," we have blatantly violated international human rights law, humanitarian law, and the law of non-aggression. Governments in many parts of the world have been responsible for murderous atrocities. So have ours, in Canada and the United States. The question is whether we are going to apply the same standards to our murderous atrocities as we apply to those of others.

Old-paradigm thinking makes us blind to our atrocities. New-paradigm thinking makes us aware of them:

> First take the log out of your own eye, and then you will
> see clearly to take the speck out of your brother's eye.
> (Matthew 7:5)

That's new-paradigm thinking, as expressed at the origin of one of the world's major spiritual traditions.

Because of our ignorance, because of old-paradigm thinking, irreparable physical and psychological damage has been visited upon countless children, women, and men. Social and economic support systems have been ravaged. Plans for careers, for love, for marriage, for children and grandchildren, for a better future have been incinerated as a result of policies supported by taxpayers. We have almost no idea of the human creative potential we have helped to extinguish, of the chances for love we have helped to destroy, or the seeds of hatred we have helped to sow. To preserve our sanity, we shield ourselves from such knowledge. We return to our immortality systems. We pursue our careers to win the approval of our peers. We read books and articles that make us comfortable by reassuring us about our basic goodness or our inability to do anything about all this — or by distracting us from thinking about it. We can't change the world. We are helpless. It's the best we can do. We didn't know. We didn't know any better. We didn't know anything better was possible.

> The evil that is in the world always comes of ignorance.
> (Camus 1947, 131)

Pathogenesis: Nationalism and warfare

Standard definitions of nationalism include this one:

> The policy or doctrine of asserting the interests of one's own nation, viewed as separate from the interests of other nations or the common interests of all nations. (Random House 1987)

Definitions are important for clarity of communication, but there is much more to be said about nationalism than can be expressed in dictionary definitions. The ideology of nationalism makes it acceptable to fabricate evidence, to torture, and to murder in defense of the nation, or in "the national interest." Nationalism easily becomes an ideological framework for the psychology of the herd, as Sigmund Freud, Ernest Becker, and others have understood it.

Despite the negative attributes of nationalism (or related to them), nationalist *resistance* can be a legitimate and indeed essential response to oppression. Both Gandhi and Hitler appear in lists of prominent nationalists of the twentieth century. Readers who are somewhat acquainted with that history, however, will recognize important differences between the nationalism of Gandhi and that of Hitler.

Erich Fromm alludes to this distinction:

Nationalism is our form of incest, is our idolatry, is our insanity. "Patriotism" is its cult. It should hardly be necessary to say, that by "patriotism" I mean that attitude which puts the own nation above humanity, above the principles of truth and justice; not the loving interest in one's own nation, which is the concern with the nation's spiritual as much as with its material welfare — never with its power over other nations. Just as love for one individual which excludes the love for others is not love, love for one's country which is not part of one's love for humanity is not love, but idolatrous worship. (1955, 58–59)

The boundary between the nationalism of Gandhi and the nationalism of Hitler is the very boundary to which Fromm refers. It is the divide that separates legitimate from illegitimate nationalism. Fromm and many other observers have recognized the destructiveness of nationalism. In this book I use the terms *nationalism* and *militant* (or *malignant* or *illegitimate*) *nationalism* almost interchangeably to refer to the dominant form of nationalism, which exerts such a catastrophic influence in the global community today. When I deviate from that usage (using *nationalism* without the connotation of malignancy), the context should make the meaning of the word reasonably clear. I will specifically use the term *positive nationalism* to refer to a healthy "love of country" that is part of a love of and respect for humanity. Positive nationalism can be thought of as an extended form of civic nationalism. Every human being is thereby recognized as a member of the global community, to whom the provisions of international human rights law and humanitarian law are applicable. International law provides a necessary formal framework for distinguishing between positive nationalism and militant nationalism.

Both Gandhi and Hitler were responding to militant nationalist conditions that preceded them. Gandhi was rejecting British nationalist domination of India (British imperialism). Hitler was rejecting the humiliation of Germany and Germans that followed World War I, of which Versailles 1919 was the cornerstone and emblem. From 1919 to 1933, the humiliation included a series of economic shocks in Germany and ethnic upheavals in Europe.

Gandhi's nationalism carried the therapeutic ingredients that could solve the problem of militant nationalism. It was life-affirming and recognized the shared humanity of everyone involved in the conflict. It was deeply realistic and was calculated to recruit universal support.

Hitler's nationalism carried the pathogens that exacerbated the problem. It was life-negating. It glorified ignorance of the shared humanity of Germans, Jews, and other members of the global community. World War II was the relapse that Hitler's nationalism provoked. Imagining itself to be the salvation of Germany and Germans, Hitler's nationalism was profoundly unrealistic. Within twelve years of its ascendancy, Germany was reduced to ashes.

Gandhi's life and work can be used as a case study in the legitimate uses of nationalism. Gandhi emphasized non-violent resistance, communication, and respect for the other as essential actions and attitudes in the process of rejecting oppression.

International law and the origins of the world's spiritual traditions are on the side of Gandhi's nationalism, not Hitler's. Article 2 of the UN Charter affirms the principle of non-aggression. International human rights law and humanitarian law affirm the priority of human well-being over state power and violent contests for power. Article 51 of the UN Charter affirms the right to self-defense, strictly defined in authoritative interpretations of the Charter.

Christianity and other major spiritual traditions *at their origins* affirmed and actualized a profound respect for human well-being and made allegiance to power dependent upon and subordinate to that priority. International law and the origins of the world's spiritual traditions represent healthy responses to the pathology of power. Because they are prescriptions for the treatment of human self-destruction, they challenge established power structures.

The pathology reasserts itself. States refuse to take the medicine that would cure the pathology. Again and again they have rejected the principles and purposes of international law. The most powerful states subvert the institutions intended to implement international law. Christianity and other major spiritual traditions have been subverted to serve state power. This is evident in the speed and comfort with which the church in Germany accommodated the policies of the Nazi regime and in the support for militant nationalism that comes from evangelical Christianity in the United States today.

At the apex of all this very human pathology is warfare, and the warfare system that sustains it. *Warfare is a disease in the same sense that cancer or HIV/AIDS is a disease: it destroys human life and health.* Militant nationalism rejects this self-evident interpretation, substituting very different interpretations designed to sustain the warfare system.

Nationalism becomes increasingly pathological as it is increasingly associated with domination, armed violence, and contempt for human rights and humanitarian law. *Power unconstrained by law is the major pathogenetic factor in warfare, and it is a defining feature of illegitimate nationalism.*

There was widespread satisfaction at the outcome of World War II. Germany and Japan had been defeated in their efforts at ascendancy. Everyone on "our" side had been instructed in how evil Germany and Japan were: they had done hideous things to millions of people and were trying to dominate the world. Militarism had played a prominent role in their ideology. Germany and Japan were militant nationalist states. Had they not been stopped, they probably would have developed weapons of mass destruction and would eventually have threatened human existence itself. Fortunately, they lost the war and turned their attention to making Volkswagens and Toyotas. What a relief!

[43]

The problem is that the victors were also militant nationalist states and they have not been stopped. It is impossible to solve the problem of militant nationalism by defeating two of the lower-ranking militant nationalist states while militant nationalism itself continues, triumphant and unchecked, in the global community.

Again the question, why are we so self-destructive? Why would anyone choose a way of thinking that is so obviously suicidal for the global community? Nationalism had a powerful influence on twentieth-century history, and it is important to emphasize some of the reasons for its historical success. It is true, and important, that nationalism is potentially a constructive paradigm for the conduct of human affairs. A positive nationalism can foster healthy community and promote the public good. In a multicultural state, inclusive nationalism can ameliorate interethnic conflict (conflicting nationalisms) within the state.

Nationalism can be used as part of a rallying strategy when a society or an ethnic group is ravaged by economic crisis or other challenges, as in Germany during the Great Depression of the 1930s or in Argentina during an economic crisis in the late 1990s and early 2000s. In response to a mortal threat, nationalism can be a powerful unifying and revitalizing force even though it is part of a larger pathological process. The Zionist response to German nationalist oppression and the British response to German nationalist aggression are examples from the era of 1930 to 1945. Conversely, loss of national cohesion often coincides with the violent disintegration of a state (civil war) into competing nationalist entities.

From my own experience growing up in the United States, I know the enthusiasm that militant nationalism can evoke. Singing the national anthem before football games, watching those inspiring war and action-adventure movies, pledging allegiance to the flag in grade school, or reading advertisements for military enlistment — those of us who came of age in the United States are deeply programmed in militant nationalism. There are veterans who look back on their military experience as among the best times of their lives: they felt the *esprit de corps*, being part of a highly disciplined, effective, and closely knit unit serving their country.

Reasons for the emotional success of militant nationalism are easy to find. In part it is rooted in healthy human psychology, the devotion to something larger than the little self and the positive effects of self-discipline in service to others. In militant nationalism, these positive human tendencies are placed in the service of a profoundly destructive pattern of human behavior. Yet they retain their power. There is little wonder that young men can be persuaded to go out and "do their duty for God and country," even if that means killing people or being killed or permanently disabled themselves. Perhaps some aspire to escape from the emotional vulnerability of being human by simply obeying orders — to disappear, as expressed by a writer whose work influenced many Germans in the era of National Socialism:

> War is elevating, because the individual disappears before the great conception of the state…. What a perversion of morality to wish to abolish heroism among men! (Treitschke 1916, 74)

These are ways of dealing with anxiety about death and separation. Becker's concept of the immortality system helps to clarify the pathology that humans inflict on one another. It is better to die for something you believe in than just to die.

But immortality systems don't bring home the groceries. Even when militant nationalism can be evoked, it tends to be transient. To sustain it, an ongoing rewards system must be put in place to ensure that the pathogenetic work will continue. There have to be paying jobs — and plenty of them — to sustain the pathology of nationalism.

Those jobs are available in established cultural, political, military, and economic institutions rooted in old-paradigm thinking and

Option B behavior. Eisenhower referred to a military-industrial complex, but the system is much more pervasive than that. It is a military-industrial-cultural-economic-political complex that provides jobs and an identity. The institutions maintain the pathological value system and the basis for decisions that to a rational observer often appear psychotic.

A paying job, an immortality system, positive feedback from the universities and society — what more could a man ask? It's a very masculine form of pathology, but women are not immune to recruitment. With all that good stuff, little wonder that individuals in a militant nationalist state can have trouble understanding that militant nationalism is pathological.

The road to hell is paved with immortality systems and lucrative job opportunities. Despite all those apparent benefits — and the comforting thought that it's other people's children, not yours, who are going to be hit with the air-to-surface missiles and the economic devastation and the water-borne diseases — militant nationalism exerts a pervasive destructive effect on the militant nationalist state itself. This is true no matter how powerful the state relative to other states in the global community. The United States is considered the world's last superpower. Militant nationalism in the United States leads to post-traumatic stress disorder, suicide, spousal and child abuse, and depression in military families, and to a profound, pervasive social malaise in society at large. Those who think it's alright to ravage the lives of other human beings in "the national interest" are not healthy human beings, and societies made up of such people are not healthy societies.

Particularly since the mid-twentieth century in the United States, militant nationalism has come into tension with consumerist and careerist tendencies in our culture. Harvard graduates and rich folks don't flock to service in the invasion and occupation of Iraq. It's those headed toward poverty who are enticed into the conflagration. While World Wars I and II actually had the effect of increasing social cohesion, with individuals from all walks of life sharing a common purpose, the ongoing preparation and promotion of war has no such effect in our society today. The polarization of wealth is accompanied by the polarization of mortal risk (largely assigned to the poor) and of primary responsibility for directing and rationalizing the carnage (largely a purview of the rich and their close associates). For many, "Support our troops" is a heartfelt expression of sympathy for those who, because of limited financial means, are putting their lives in the line of fire.

Militant nationalism is a chronic societal disease. Public resources are funneled into military purposes instead of into health care, education, and other priorities for a sane society. Joseph Stiglitz and Linda Bilmes, in *The Three Trillion Dollar War* (2008), have estimated that the invasion of Iraq will cost the United States three trillion dollars.

> The Bush administration said the war would cost $50 billion. The U.S. now spends that amount in Iraq every three months.
>
> To put that number in context: For one-sixth of the cost of the war, the U.S. could put its social security system on a sound footing for more than a half-century, without cutting benefits or raising contributions. (Stiglitz 2008)

Political leaders unable to break free of the old paradigm become deaf to the voices of concerned citizens and continue shoveling public resources into the flames. Militant nationalism is an ongoing and perhaps terminal danger to our security. With time and the sustained level of risk inherent in the militant nationalist paradigm, disasters such as the destruction of Iraq and the incineration of the World Trade Center will recur in various forms.

Democracy and international law

In the months preceding the 2003 U.S. invasion of Iraq, I made a series of phone calls to the offices of my two senators in Maryland. With each phone call, politely but firmly, I asked a basic question. Each phone call and letter emphasized a different question, but each in the series of questions was related to the first question I asked: In the senator's opinion, should U.S. foreign policy comply with international law?

Each phone call was followed up with a letter that put the question in writing. The series of phone calls and letters had, of course, an achievable objective: to test the democratic emergency response system. If the senators responded intelligently and openly, it would be a good sign, potentially enabling an exchange on realistic options for U.S.-Iraq relations. If they gave a form response, a brush-off, it would be a bad sign. Either way, it would provide important information about how U.S. democracy works in the months leading up to a crisis in the global community.

The senators' offices failed to answer a single question. Signally, their offices refused — despite repeated requests — to answer the question: Should U.S. foreign policy comply with international law?

That particular failure of the senators' offices is related to a failure inherent in nationalism. As nationalism becomes militant (and it has long been militant in the United States), it becomes increasingly unresponsive to the wisdom of concerned citizens. It blocks effective democracy.

Arguments for the legitimacy of the nation-state are based on its capacity to foster human well-being. Such arguments derive from many writers, including Thomas Hobbes, John Locke, and Jean-Jacques Rousseau. The concept of "divine right" long ago gave way to the concept that even a monarchical rule is subject to this test of legitimacy.

Experience has shown that the best wisdom for governance

comes from an open exchange of ideas rather than from decisions made behind closed doors. Militant nationalism undermines democracy and tends to increase the secrecy of decision-making among those in power.

Democracy draws on the strength of the "marketplace of ideas." Democracy can be thought of not merely as majority rule, but as governance based on the best of the collective wisdom of the people. The majority will not reliably provide the best wisdom, and — as this book emphasizes — the old paradigm that dominates established political institutions leads to recurrent catastrophe. For these reasons, democracy must be guided by sound principles of law. Law must be just; it must protect the minority against the tyranny of the majority. As David Held puts it, "The *demos* must rule, but within the framework of a legal order which is both empowering and limiting" (1995, 222).

Law must also ensure that neither the majority nor the government becomes a tyrant in the international arena. In the twentieth century, international law evolved in response to catastrophic violence in the international system. Rivalries among states for military power, and the idea in international law (under the Westphalian system, dating from 1648) that states were at liberty to pursue their "national interest," had produced apocalyptic violence, particularly in World Wars I and II. This violence threatened democracy itself. The threat that warfare poses to freedom had been recognized much earlier, of course.

> Although the threats to freedom derive, in [Immanuel] Kant's view, from many forms of violence, they stem above all from war and the preparations for war. "The greatest evils which affect civilized nations are," he wrote, "brought about by war, and not so much by actual wars in the past or the present as by never ending and indeed continually increasing preparations for war." (Held 1995, 226)

[49]

Demagogues like Hitler and Stalin, almost by definition, win widespread public support. If democracy is nothing more than government by elected agents, democracy has the capacity to self-destruct. Majority rule will self-destruct unless it is guided by sound principles. For a detailed treatment of this, as well as the interdependence of law and democracy, David Held's book *Democracy and the Global Order* (quoted above) is a useful resource.

Militant nationalism undermines democracy, and with it, our ability to meet a wide range of challenges that will face us in this century and the next. International law — particularly human rights law, humanitarian law, and the law of non-aggression — is an essential part of the curriculum for learning to live together as human beings. We will continue down the road toward Option B unless our governments bring their policies and practices into compliance with international law. Our governments, however, are extremely unlikely to do that unless citizens insist on that compliance. As citizens, we are expected, for good reason, to comply with the law. If we fail to insist on the same standard from our government, we fail an equally important test of citizenship.

Obviously international law will not solve all the world's problems. It is necessary but not sufficient for the global community to move toward Option A. It recognizes as legitimate the measures necessary for human security. International law does not forbid self-defense. It recognizes state sovereignty, including the right of each state to defend itself against armed attack, and the right of other states to come to the assistance of the state that has been attacked. International law does not recognize any right to "pre-emptive self-defense," for obvious reasons.

International law has evolved, and continues to evolve, in full awareness of racism, dictatorships, and the danger to basic human rights from many sources. It provides the necessary framework for any legitimate international threat or use of force. Clearly, further evolution of international law is essential, but that must take place openly and with the full participation of the international community, not as a *de facto* acceptance of murderous violations of law by powerful states. Down that road lies extinction.

A standard objection to international law is that, unlike domestic ("municipal") law, there is no agent for enforcement. No doubt a formal framework for enforcement is needed (and states must take that step), but the basic source for enforcement is quite clear from the standard definition of democracy. Since governments are the agents that must comply with the law, and since democracy by definition places the responsibility for governance with the people, *it is ultimately the citizens of a state who are responsible for their government's compliance or non-compliance with law.*

Ultimately responsible but feeling powerless, citizens are in a precarious situation. It is as if we are being driven everywhere by a chauffeur who pays no attention to our instructions and repeatedly does things that place us in great danger. The question is this: when will we get our chauffeur to drive more safely, follow our instructions, and comply with the rules of the road? That is essentially the challenge we face as citizens: getting our governments to comply with the law and act in our interest.

The rabbi's son from Krakow

In his booklet *The Way of Man According to the Teachings of Hasidism*, Martin Buber tells the story of a rabbi's son from Krakow who, through a series of dreams and a journey, discovers that there is a treasure buried beneath the stove in his own home. He unearths the incredible fortune and uses it to build a prayer house serving the community.

This story appears in other versions in various spiritual traditions. It has received diverse interpretations, and even a parody by Woody Allen. For my purposes, the following interpretation is useful.

Each of us holds creative potential, the capacity to bring to the world a unique gift that may remain undiscovered for years, perhaps forever. To discover that potentially epoch-making gift, we must be aware of the possibility. We have to take ourselves seriously. And of course there is work to be done in finding and developing and bringing to the world our unique contribution.

In our society, this insight is too often obscured. Depression and low self-esteem are rampant. The associated waste of human potential is an incalculable loss — both to the afflicted individuals and to their society.

Yet even in our society, many wise observers remind us of such things and heighten our awareness of ourselves. In doing so, they can also enhance our capacity as citizens. Nathaniel Branden's work focuses on the enabling effect of self-esteem in every part of the life experience, including the contributions we make to those around us. Daniel Goleman, in his book *Emotional Intelligence*, provides a list of seven key ingredients in a "crucial capacity" — how to learn. Each ingredient could be taken as an essential skill in the practice of responsible and effective global citizenship: confidence, curiosity, intentionality, self-control, relatedness, capacity to communicate, and cooperativeness. These abilities emerged as important competencies among children who did well in school, but their value extends far beyond the school years.

"Life is difficult," writes Scott Peck in the opening line of his book *The Road Less Travelled*. Like other experienced observers, he thinks of love as a conscious decision, leading to the difficult and life-long work of developing your potential for the purpose of enhancing your own life and the lives of others.

In the landscape of literature essential for global citizenship, Erich Fromm's work is monumental. He calls our attention to the anxiety that human freedom carries with it and to what he saw as just two alternatives for coping with that anxiety: to accept our freedom by developing our unique capacities through loving relationships with other human beings or to escape from our freedom, losing our true identity in some ideology and deference to some authority. These alternatives faced Germans of the Nazi era, but they also confront North Americans in our time. Fromm said that society itself is insane if it promotes among its members a life-negating escape from freedom rather than a life-affirming acceptance of it.

There is a resonance among the paradigms put forward by many writers concerned with healthy human psychology. Abraham Maslow emphasized the process of discovering and developing one's potential, which he called self-actualization. Self-actualization involves creative effort on behalf of others:

> Self-actualizing people are, without one single exception, involved in a cause outside their own skin, in something outside of themselves. (1971, 42)

Maslow also emphasized the necessity of such individuals to the health of a society, as well as the decisive effect they have on both the conditions of human existence worldwide and on their own happiness.

Responsible and effective global citizenship: what's in it for you? It could be freedom, discovery and exploration, self-actualization. You would have to pursue it to find out.

Choosing the future: Summary

If we have no concept of where we are, the challenges ahead, or where we want to go, then our future will be much darker compared to what it will be if we heighten our awareness of these things. This chapter presents some observations intended to help with a process of heightening awareness. The first of these observations is that as a global community and as a species, we humans are divided against ourselves. Violent contests for power are undermining the conditions of our existence, the possibilities for growth of the human spirit, and the chances of human survival. Resources that are urgently needed for life-enhancing work are being used instead to promote self-destructive behavior.

The second is that we do not have to continue this process of self-destruction. We have a choice. Our self-destruction (the pathology) is based in identifiable patterns of thinking. A shorthand way of describing these ways of thinking is "us versus them." In this book I refer to these ways of thinking as the old paradigm. With practice, we can identify these patterns of thinking in ourselves. They are a necessary (though not sufficient) factor in the pathogenesis of our self-destruction. Old-paradigm thinking leads all of us toward Option B.

In a very important sense, then, the pathogenesis of this disease that threatens our future is different from that of diseases such as cancer and HIV/AIDS. It is volitional (we are making the choices essential to produce the disease) and visible (we can directly experience the choices being made as they happen).

This may make it easier to find a cure and prevention for our self-destruction than for cancer and HIV/AIDS, or it may make it more difficult. Either way, it does make it more directly our responsibility to work toward the cure for this disease than to work toward a cure for cancer or HIV/AIDS. It also becomes obvious that we can only be effective as citizens by being aware of our own part in the pathogenesis.

The old paradigm (the disease-producing pattern of thinking) takes the form of various ideologies. Nationalism in its currently dominant form, militant nationalism, is one such ideology, and it is especially pervasive. Many of our established political, cultural, and economic institutions are rooted in militant nationalism. Militant nationalism is driving the global community toward Option B.

The ideology could not produce the disease without the institutions needed to sustain it. Cultural institutions provide the basic indoctrination in the ideology and shape the "news" and "history" in a way that fits the old-paradigm way of thinking. Economic institutions maintain the daily input of financial and human resources to reinforce and implement the progress toward Option B. Political institutions shuffle the cards in the deck of old-paradigm thinking and deal the hands that lead again and again toward Option B.

In a population of normal, healthy individuals, a minority are able on their own to see through the old paradigm, understand its consequences, and reject it. Others can accomplish this if someone else leads the way. Many individuals, however, will persist in old-paradigm thinking, no matter what the evidence for its self-destructive effects and no matter how clearly that evidence is presented — especially if their incomes and their identities depend on it.

Finding a cure for the plague that threatens our extinction depends on sound personal and social psychology, and on healthy interactions at every level, from the personal to the global. Militant nationalism is a deeply pessimistic ideology that assumes we have no choice but to continue violent contests for power among nation-states. On the contrary: healthy interactions internationally, regionally, locally, and interpersonally are an achievable norm. Militant nationalism tends to make these interactions pathological and to induce depression and psychological dysfunction in individuals, families, and local communities.

At every level from the personal to the global, the process of choosing between affirmation and negation of life is dynamic and interdependent. The society and culture into which an individual is born and comes of age affects the values of that individual, and the values that person develops as he or she matures will affect the culture and the society in which he or she lives.

Competent and responsible citizenship requires more than a healthy personality. A knowledge base and a set of skills, and experience in applying them, are as essential to the competent practice of citizenship as they are to the competent practice of medicine.

The basic principles, purposes, and prescriptions of international law are an essential framework for the practice of responsible citizenship. Viable democracy depends on the active practice of responsible citizenship. International law defines the boundary between positive nationalism and malignant nationalism. International law and democracy are interdependent. We cannot achieve a rule of law for the global community until and unless citizens become aware of the requirements of international law, and of their responsibility to ensure compliance by their governments. Otherwise old-paradigm thinking will continue to drive all of us down the road toward Option B.

As citizens of the global community, we are in a similar situation to that of the main character in Camus's novel *The Plague*. The protagonist is a physician who must do what he can, day after day, as the plague destroys human life and health in the city to which everyone is quarantined. The outlook is too dark for pessimism. Optimism is essential; pessimism, a waste of time.

Each human life is an index of what the human spirit can achieve. What you decide to do with your life will be one part of that record.

CHAPTER TWO

Axioms

On March 19, 2005, I picked up my laundry at a local cleaner. The young woman at the cash register, perhaps in her early twenties, was listening to the radio as she gave me my change. She laughed at something she heard. Explaining her laughter, she said, "If you're rich and famous, you can get away with anything."

"Like the president of the United States," I said.

"Exactly," she said, and laughed again. "Mass murder."

If the young woman had pursued an advanced degree in political science at a major university, she might have learned that mass murder is okay. The fact that she has so far avoided that form of "sophistication" is auspicious for our future. We need to amplify voices like hers, to remind us that the emperor is naked; mass murder is not okay.

Axioms have that kind of simplicity. Axioms are fundamental statements, requiring no proof, that can be used as a foundation in developing a larger conceptual framework. Axioms are often self-evident, yet very powerful. A good axiom, in the hands of a check-out clerk who knows how to use it, could probably hold a Harvard professor at bay.

One of the reasons that intellectual commentary on world affairs is often so shallow and confused is that it is so often based on dubious premises. The axioms are never examined. In *On Equilibrium*, John Ralston Saul illustrates this problem using reference to Solon, a wise political leader of ancient Athens, who resolved an economic crisis by taking action that was intuitively necessary but strongly opposed by some wealthy and powerful people. Saul suggests that today's "experts" would explain to a contemporary Solon in great technical detail why the action (which would solve the problem) would not work. These experts might have university degrees and a long list of scholastic achievements but have lost touch with the kind of wisdom expressed by the young woman at my local cleaner. Saul points out that such intellectuals can easily arrive at a "false sophistication" in which "the complexity of [the] methodology obscures the naiveté of [the] assumptions."

So it is important to keep our basic premises, our axioms, in mind and to re-examine them from time to time. One such axiom was well expressed by Alfred Korzybski in *Science and Sanity*, published more than 75 years ago. He reminded us of something basic about how we think, so basic that it is extended here as the first axiom essential for thinking about the world and how we influence it. Korzybski used the word *map* in much the same sense that I have used the word *paradigm* — a way of thinking about something.

FIRST AXIOM
The map is not the territory.

It is worth remembering (and it is true whether we remember it or not) that our concepts of the world are not the world itself. Any way of understanding reality is a set of abstractions and not the reality those abstractions represent. Our concepts of some aspect of reality have the same relationship to that reality as a map of the Rocky Mountains has to the Rocky Mountains. The map is not the territory.

Accuracy in the factual details of the map is essential, but the map represents only selected aspects of reality, no matter how accurate its details.

What the map represents and what it omits depend on the purposes the map is designed to serve. Some maps will depict the hiking trails in an area; others, the location of mineral deposits. Some maps will emphasize the great benefits a government has conveyed; others, the atrocities the same government has committed. If I want you to support a particular government, I will probably emphasize its virtues. If I want you to help replace or destroy that government, I will probably emphasize its failures or atrocities.

The stated purpose of the map may be quite different from the real purpose the map is designed to serve. If the stated or implied purpose of the map is contrary to its real purpose, it is a false map. A map purporting to show hiking trails or mineral deposits might omit all representation of those features from one specific area if the mapmaker does not want them to be known. Propaganda for war does not come labeled as such.

Words such as *peace* and *democracy* generally evoke a positive response from the public, but they can be false maps if the peace and democracy referred to are in a framework of illegitimate power and oppression rather than of international law.

Another way of expressing the first axiom is "We think in generalities but life happens in detail." Take for example the concept of free will. For a given situation, I might think that I have a choice about what to do. This book is based on the assumption that readers have a choice about what to do with their lives.

The concept of free will is a very useful map, yet with some effort we can discover things about the real world that don't seem to fit the map. Current concepts in neuroscience view our consciousness and thinking as dependent upon the release of chemicals (neurotransmitters) at synapses (connections between nerve cells) in our brains. Obviously we are not consciously making the arrangements to release the neurotransmitters or to carry out the other physiologic events on which our conscious decisions depend. What we experience as consciousness and free will is dependent on something that scientists have only fairly recently described in physiologic and molecular terms — phenomena that remain invisible and largely unknown to us as we experience our exercise of "free will."

Thus neuroscience brings us a map that is remarkably similar to the one expressed in Matthew 6:27–29: Like the "lilies of the field," we are part of something infinitely larger and more detailed than we imagine, and we are dependent upon that reality. We are part of the flow of the universe. That's a different way of thinking about free will and about ourselves, a different map, and that map also serves a purpose: it can give us an appropriate humility. By learning to use the two maps alternately and with facility and for human purposes, we might acquire a dimensionality and depth to our lives and our actions, and enrich our appreciation of the world. Like Socrates, we can learn not to assume that we know something we do not. And even as we acquire that modesty of spirit, we can begin to know ourselves a little better.

SECOND AXIOM
The map changes the territory.

Although the map is not the territory, it does change the territory. "Ideas rule the world" is another way of expressing it. The way we think about the world and about ourselves profoundly influences our behavior, and our behavior influences the world around us. By choosing to think of ourselves as powerless, we set the stage for a life of wasted potential.

In the Vietnam War era, public relations experts for the U.S. government presented a neat map to the American public. To the growing skepticism about the Vietnam War among many Americans, the experts responded: "If you knew what we know but cannot tell you, then you would rally in support of this war." It was called the Big Picture: "If you had the Big Picture, you would understand why we must pursue this war to a successful conclusion."

Of course, the government in Hanoi also had its own Big Picture. Robert McNamara, then Secretary of Defense for the U.S. government, later (with the wisdom of hindsight) had this to say about the Big Pictures:

> The incomprehension seems to have been total and absolutely consistent. Washington and Hanoi, in other words, ... were thus wrong nearly 100 percent of the time.... The fundamental enemy — the root cause of the agony over the Vietnam War — was mutual ignorance. (McNamara et al. 1999, 381)

Yet there were many citizens of the United States who were wiser *at the time*. They were skeptical of the Big Picture. They didn't get their skepticism from having done a doctorate degree at a prestigious university. Their skepticism was born of immediate necessity — the possibility that they or a friend or a member of their family might soon die in Vietnam — and for many of them, from a sense of responsibility to fellow human beings, not only those in the United States but also those in Vietnam. Their resistance to the ignorance, arrogance, and violence of their government, the U.S. government, also changed the territory. They established what are sometimes called "facts on the ground." It became increasingly difficult for those in positions of power to manipulate public opinion.

What a person thinks about herself or himself has a profound influence on the course of history: not only on that person's own history but on the history of the human spirit. When one person, or a few people, demonstrate that something can be accomplished which previously had never been imagined or had been assumed to be impossible, that achievement establishes a historical fact.

There was a time when women were thought to be unfit to vote or to participate in public life. Various "compelling" arguments supported this point of view. Today it seems merely quaint. History was changed because of people who were able to think outside the box of an old paradigm, and then act on what their imagination told them was possible. Their maps changed the territory.

What you think about power, and your relationship to power, also influences the course of history. Uncritical subservience to power produces a pathology of powerlessness, which supports the pathology of power and accounts for a great deal of violence in the world. One of the mantras for the pathology of powerlessness is "You can't change the world." And by accepting that doctrine of impotence, the person making that choice gives *de facto* support to the pathology of power. They do in fact change the world, moving it toward Option B. Your way of thinking about power will profoundly affect your life and work.

Far too many citizens voluntarily surrender their role and their responsibility in a democracy, abandoning the course of world affairs to "leaders" and "experts." The doctrine of impotence can be found both in impoverished and in wealthy societies. Distracted by the demands of a career, consumerism, or the daily struggle for survival, or driven by an ideological deference to power, citizens become marginalized. Relinquishing their own power and intelligence to leaders and experts who are thinking inside the old box, these citizens become part of the pathology.

You have your own maps about who you are. If you choose to think of yourself as powerless to do something important that is in fact well within your power, you will influence the course of your life and the course of history by making that decision. You change the territory of who you are by your way of thinking about who you are.

THIRD AXIOM
We choose our maps.

No one can force you to accept the doctrine of impotence. Consciously or unconsciously, we choose our ways of thinking about ourselves and about the world. And that makes all the difference. We use maps to find our way from one town to another; we also use maps to find our way from dawn to dusk. By choosing a map that includes a defined goal and the necessary daily priorities that enable us to reach that goal, we can accomplish things we otherwise could not achieve. We have become who we are largely because of the ways of thinking we have chosen. If you are highly skilled at choosing and designing mental maps to serve your purposes and your needs, you will be better off than if you lack this facility.

FOURTH AXIOM
Good, bad, evil, important, and unimportant are in the eye of the beholder.

Which team won a particular sports event will be a question to which the fans of both teams will give the same answer, though their feelings associated with the answer may differ. Which team won is an empirical question; rational observers will agree on the fact. Their maps will be identical on the answer to the question. Whether the outcome of the event is good or bad cannot be answered conclusively because the essence of good and bad is emotional, not factual. The maps of different observers will differ on the issue. Whether the fact is good or bad is in the eye of the beholder.

In the natural sciences, empirical questions usually cannot be answered with the certainty of the outcome in sports events. It is standard practice to accept as fact a conclusion that has a probability exceeding 95 percent of being correct. If the evidence indicates that the probability of an association between cigarette smoking and lung cancer is greater than 95 percent (the contrary possibility has less than 5 percent chance of being true), then for working purposes scientists accept the association of cigarette smoking and cancer as a fact.

Cigarette company executives may dislike the fact. They may try to ignore, obscure, or rationalize it. They may make a sustained and strenuous effort to gather evidence to the contrary, because of how they *feel* about the fact. It might even be possible to establish by an opinion survey that most people feel very passionately that the association of cigarette smoking and cancer is a bad thing. They wish that cigarette smoking were not associated with lung cancer. That they have such feelings could then be established as a fact. But is it *really* a bad thing that cigarette smoking and cancer are associated? That is not an empirical question, because the essence of bad is emotional, not factual.

Does this leave us with nothing but moral relativism? Obviously not.

Physicians conduct their professional work based on recognition of the value of human life. The resulting formal, operational set of ethical standards enables outcomes that (we assume) are experienced as good by most of those who are affected by the practice of medicine. A neurosurgeon evaluating a patient who is losing consciousness and considering an operation to control an intracranial hemorrhage to save the patient's life is not distracted by doubts about the value of that life.

It is in human eyes that human life has value. But *those are our eyes.* Major spiritual texts, international human rights law, the medical profession, and human empathy all recognize the fundamental value of human life. That awareness seems to be at the source of the world's major religions. But again and again this recognition is obscured:

> To this day Christianity remains divided between those who embrace Jesus's teachings of love and forgiveness as the foundation of Christian morality and those who invoke

the name of Jesus in the pursuit of righteous vengeance, imperial conquest, and authoritarian rule. (Korten 2006, 122)

Spiritual maps have been falsified to serve the purposes of militant nationalism. It is time to restore the authenticity of those maps.

Those who have written intelligently about evil seem to share this basic concept: evil is what destroys human life and creative potential. This emerges in the work of Albert Camus, Hannah Arendt, Scott Peck, and Roy Baumeister, as well as more theological works grounded in one or another religious tradition. It is implicit in the entire field of books on spirituality, psychology, and self-help.

For purposes of the map presented in this book, good is associated with fostering human well-being and creative potential, and promoting the conditions of global community necessary to sustain them. Even so, those are words, and words that sound very similar can be used to persuade people to destroy human life and creative potential. Instead of using the standards of international law, a persuasive leader can simply use a much more permissive and ambiguous language, such as "fighting for freedom" or "saving the fatherland" or "manifest destiny." Self-righteousness is a deadly affliction. An awareness of destructive tendencies *within ourselves* is an indispensable competency for the future of human survival.

FIFTH AXIOM
Political leaders are not competent to determine the value of a human life.

Much of what we value in life depends on the unique contributions of another person: sometimes a writer or an artist, sometimes a scientist or physician, sometimes a person who advanced the conditions of human well-being we now enjoy. And sometimes it is just someone who has made a very large difference in our personal life. Each human life harbors something unique, potentially a gift that no one else can bring to the world.

Presidents, prime ministers, and other political leaders are not remotely competent to know the value of even one of the millions of lives their policies affect. This is a simple statement of an obvious fact and, in the present context, an axiom. The same concept applies to religious leaders. It is not for popes or presidents to determine the value of a child's life. The same incompetence can be found in the experts who advise them, the intellectuals who attempt to justify their policies, and the soldiers who carry out their orders.

Robert McNamara identified a failure of empathy as one of the major reasons that the Vietnam War was so protracted, so destructive, and such an utter waste of resources. If you lack empathy, you carry within you the fatal flaw that can produce a downward spiral of violence in the future. In medicine, empathy for the patient is formalized in the ethical basis of the medical profession. In power politics, there is no such formal constraint. A physician must bring his emotions under control in order to behave professionally for the benefit of the patient. In politics and in political science, the suppression of empathy and emotion plays a much more questionable role.

Human emotions are immediately relevant to the ethics of daily decisions. Emotions can be inflamed to serve destructive purposes, as in propaganda for war. Emotions can also be suppressed to serve destructive purposes, as in so much of the political, military, and intellectual work leading toward Option B.

Responsible citizens need to be aware of the human costs of their government's violations of law — exactly the awareness a militant nationalist culture tends to suppress. This includes awareness of the human costs to combatants and non-combatants, not just to "our troops." It includes awareness of the costs to future generations of a lawless world. Awareness of the human costs of warfare is essential to responsible global citizenship. Another way of stating this is that responsible citizens are aware of their own limitations: they know that they cannot know the value of a human life.

How effectively we can evaluate commentary from our "leaders" and "experts" during a war depends in part on how immediate our own experience of military violence has been. Many readers will have had no experience of that violence, yet are exposed to military analysts and other old-paradigm commentators in daily broadcasts of news and commentary. Such commentators often seem to be emotionally unaware of the human costs of the events they talk about. Suppressing public awareness of the damage "our troops" are inflicting on fellow human beings is essential to effective war propaganda.

If a failure of empathy is a major cause of warfare, then journalism informed by empathy is a necessary antidote to propaganda for war. That's why such journalism is so valuable to the practice of global citizenship. In the following story, journalist Paul William Roberts describes his visit to a children's ward in a Baghdad hospital shortly after the 2003 invasion of Iraq, and his conversation with the hospital's only surgeon about an Iraqi child.

> Her name was Amina. She was four years old. A bomb had fallen on a house where she lived while she was walking home from the market with her father. Shrapnel and flying glass had smashed and slashed her to pieces. She had not yet been told that her father had died of his own wounds.
>
> "As you see, we have not any bandage here any more.... We must use what we have.... We have no anaesthetic to give her," said [the surgeon]. "And no anti-bio. She is in shock, you see, so is feeling nothing really." He paused and sighed. "She will die today. Yes, I am certain of it..."
>
> The brown pool of that eye in its frame of bloody rags was looking straight at me. Something leapt the space

between us, some form of communication. There was
a little girl in there, a little girl whose body had been
broken and torn. A little girl about to die.

... Could anyone look at this little girl and say that
what had happened to her was justifiable? I would like
to see the manly men of Pentagon and White House take
their photo-opportunity with little Amina, explaining to
her that, painful and cruel as it may seem, the cost — her
cost, not theirs — was worth it. (2004, 199–200)

In what follows that passage, Roberts tries to imagine what
Amina might have accomplished and what she might have enjoyed,
had she lived. His empathy informs his journalism and brings to
his readers one set of "data" essential to making wise decisions.
Roberts considers the possibility that Amina might even have
discovered a cure for cancer that might have saved the life of
George Bush's granddaughter. For the individual case of Amina,
such a possibility seems remote, though there is little doubt she
would have made important contributions to the lives of others.
As the number of lives derailed by political violence increases,
the probability of losses to the field of medicine and other fields
concerned with human well-being also increases.

Millions of stories similar to Amina's remain untold. The waste
and carnage of power politics is beyond the capacity of a human
mind to grasp. The statement "One death is a tragedy, a million
deaths is a statistic" indicates the human inability to grasp the
enormity of decisions involving political violence.

Most of us would not want to board a ship or an aircraft if the
captain and crew had a reputation of violating the rules of the
high seas or airways. We expect not only competence but also
compliance from individuals in positions of such responsibility.
Yet we vote for leaders who, in their policies, threaten human lives.
We do this in part because we think that no other options are
available.

Political leaders are not competent to determine the value of a human life, but they are competent to bring their government's policies into compliance with international law. Political leaders therefore face a *de facto* choice: they can act within their competence or outside it. They can emphasize the necessity of international law for the security of all, or they can ignore, obscure, or rationalize their government's violations of international law. The first choice leads toward Option A, the second toward Option B.

Human emotions underlie all human thought and endeavor. A mathematician experiences the proof of a theorem as "beautiful"; Henry Kissinger describes power as "the great aphrodisiac." It is essential to understand the pervasive emotional forces at work in political events and their potential to undermine or enhance human well-being. Political leaders learn to influence emotions. The mesmerizing effect of Adolf Hitler's public speeches is well known to historians of that era. Contemporary political leaders are selected in part for their charismatic qualities. Public relations experts help with shaping their messages, using phrases that for the intended audience will trigger strong positive emotions. Depending on the audience, the president's or the prime minister's speech is salted with phrases such as "struggle against tyranny and terrorism," "the fight for liberty," and so on. When such phrases are being used to support major violations of international law, they are treacherous, however seductive they may be.

If citizens are ever to live up to their responsibility to humanity, they will have to develop some critical skills, including an ability to see through the rhetoric of "us versus them." They must become aware of their own limitations and those of their political representatives, and the consequent necessity of compliance with international law. Otherwise their lives, their fortunes, and their honor will continue to be sacrificed to illegitimate power. When they learn just how badly they have been fooled, it will always be much too late.

CHAPTER THREE

Paradigm Shift

Asking the right questions and pursuing the answers
energetically can change your life and the course of history. An
example of a very basic question for world affairs is this: What
forms of human behavior are diminishing the chances of human
survival?

Here is one part of an answer. From 1990 to the present, the
government of the United States pursued policies in the Middle
East that extinguished more than a million lives and devastated
millions more. Culminating in the 2003 invasion and occupation
of Iraq, these policies will probably cost the United States more
than three trillion dollars, based on a recent estimate.

In this chapter of human history, we find a technologically
advanced society, which considers itself a "leader" in world affairs,
directing a large part of its public resources into the destruction
of another society at a time when its own public infrastructure is
in a process of decay. Bridges and other physical structures need
renewal in the United States, and social programs such as health
care lag significantly behind those of other countries with far

more limited economic means. Instead of directing public policies and public resources into creating and restoring essential physical infrastructure and services, the U.S. government has directed those policies and resources to the destruction of Iraq's bridges, health care system, and other objects necessary for the well-being of the Iraqi civilian population.

How could the political leadership in any society of *Homo sapiens* behave with such ignorance and incompetence? When will they ever learn? If this form of behavior is characteristic of human beings, we can reasonably assume it is diminishing our chances of survival.

The self-destructive patterns of behavior are rooted in self-destructive patterns of thinking and the institutions that sustain the process. Patterns of thinking can be referred to as *maps* or *paradigms*. I use the terms almost interchangeably in this essay.

Homo so-called *sapiens* has often shown a remarkably limited capacity to change self-destructive patterns of behavior. The observation is a central theme in Jared Diamond's book *Collapse: How Societies Choose to Fail or Succeed* and in Ronald Wright's *A Short History of Progress*. A careful observer can find abundant evidence of the same limitation in our own society.

Thomas Kuhn found it even among scientists. Kuhn's *The Structure of Scientific Revolutions* (1962) gives an account of the process of paradigm shift in the natural sciences. When evidence emerged in a scientific field that simply did not fit the old paradigm, a new paradigm would be proposed that could accommodate all the available evidence. Yet the new paradigm was often accepted only when the old generation of scientists was displaced by a new generation that "faced the facts." Instead of accepting the necessary paradigm shift, the establishment, even in the natural sciences, would sometimes cling to the familiar way of understanding the world.

The resistance to evidence is probably much greater in politics than in the natural sciences. New generations have a choice between facing the evidence or having a lucrative job with an institution that repudiates the evidence. And there are always plenty of young people who will take the jobs. Thus the old paradigm persists, and well-paid human behavior moves all of us toward Option B.

The old paradigm is associated with militant nationalism. It holds that militarism is necessary to protect the citizens of the militarist state. The fallacy in this concept is clear from the historical record. Paul Kennedy's *The Rise and Fall of the Great Powers* (1987) provides an account of how militant nationalist states again and again drove themselves to bankruptcy by playing the fool's game of militant nationalist competition.

Beyond a certain point, investment in what is called "defense" produces insidiously or rapidly diminishing returns, undermining the security of citizens in the militarist state even as it destabilizes the global community. Militarily powerful states have long since passed the point of diminishing returns for investment in defense. Political leaders in these states fail to understand the limits of their maps. The map that emphasizes national defense has critical limits, and if those limits are overlooked, each additional increment of expenditure on military will further undermine the public interest. The old paradigm has long been dangerously obsolete.

There is another way of thinking about these matters, a new paradigm, which recognizes the limits of the old paradigm. *The new paradigm asserts that our security depends on government compliance with international law.* It is based on recognition of the need for a healthy global community under a rule of law. This is absolutely essential to human security in every state.

It is nearly impossible to overstate the power of the paradigm. It limits or expands what we can learn from history and what we understand about ourselves. The conflict between the old paradigm of nationalism and the new paradigm of global community under a rule of international law has been evolving for more than a century. Anyone who is even slightly aware of the history of the twentieth century knows how tenacious the old paradigm has been. Making the paradigm shift is something to which each of us can contribute.

Who are we?

The first person plural is a political minefield. In our discussions of world events, are the words "we," "us," and "our" inclusive or exclusive? Do they refer to us as human beings or to an us-versus-them concept such as "us Americans"? The concept that the destruction of civilian life in Iraq is not affecting "us" is an example of the second (old paradigm, Option B) use of the term. Emotions, including empathy, are integral to political events. Failing to understand this guarantees failure as measured by the standards of responsible global citizenship put forward in this book.

On the morning of September 11, 2001, commercial airliners slammed into the World Trade Center and the Pentagon. A few hours after the attacks, I saw the tape of one of the planes cruising like a missile toward then colliding with the tower, and the instant, irrevocable inferno. People like me were being suffocated, vaporized, crushed, and incinerated in the moments depicted by that tape, and I was utterly powerless to help them.

A telephone call from Kevin Cosgrove to a 911 operator has been posted on the Internet. Kevin was a young man trapped on the 105th floor of one of the World Trade Center towers. At the time of this writing, the text as well as a combined audio/video recording related to this call can be retrieved (search using the young man's name). Read the text or watch and listen to the video, and notice your own emotions and thoughts as you experience this. It affects me first at the level of a very strong emotion (empathy). Once I get past that, as I must, I move to a more analytical level, which recognizes my responsibility to change the conditions that led to the horror. In this analytical mode, I set aside my emotions as well as I can so as to contribute as effectively as possible to an optimal outcome. If you have no empathy in such situations, or if you think it is irrelevant, or if you respond emotionally only when the victims are Americans, or if you see no personal responsibility in connection with these things, then you are different from me in an important way. And that difference will influence how you experience the 911 call, as well as how you react to this book.

It is too late for all those whose lives were lost in the political violence of September 11, 2001 and for those who died in the cycles of political violence that led to those attacks. Rage, ignorance, indifference, and old-paradigm thinking will make it too late for hundreds of millions more.

Political leaders and their experts missed the point. After the attacks of September 11, prestigious sources began to suggest that the attacks were sufficient justification for war. Violence would help solve the problem of violence. If *we* fought *them* over there, we would not have to fight them here. The deaths resulting from subsequent U.S. attacks on Afghanistan soon surpassed the death toll from the attacks of September 11.

Even so, the danger of "terrorism" and other threats to *us* were not extinguished. This was used as part of the rationalization for invading Iraq in March 2003. According to a report in *The Lancet* in October 2004 (Roberts et al.), that invasion led within one year to the deaths of several tens of thousands of Iraqi civilians, most of whom were women and children, and most killed by the invading military forces. Again, that civilian death toll dwarfed the tally from the September 11, 2001 attacks in the United States. But in the minds of old-paradigm thinkers, the civilian deaths in Iraq don't count because *they* are not *us*.

Canadian journalist Paul William Roberts provides an intimate glimpse of a few minutes from that invasion of Iraq:

> The soldier's unit had been told to intercept a vehicle in which high-ranking Iraqi military personnel were thought to be traveling out of Baghdad.
>
> "We lit that fucker up real good," the soldier said.

"Blew the door clean off and the fuckers clean out ...
Asshole had his wife an' kid with him too. L'il girl. She
were standin' there fuckin' screamin', man, an' on fire. She
were fuckin' burnin', man. We was laughin' our fuckin'
heads off, man ... Her face's all black an' she screamin'
... yeah! It were fuckin' tasty, I tell ya!"

I waited for some kind of punch line, but that was
it: blew up the car, set the little girl on fire, stood there
watching her burn and laughing. The soldiers to whom
he was relating this charming little tale of heroism found
it appropriately amusing too. They said things like
right-on and dang, then related anecdotes of their own
experiences that day, all of which involved fuckers who
got whacked or lit up. (Roberts 2004, 145)

If the little girl and her family and other Iraqis are part of *us*,
then *we* are less secure today than we were before September 11,
2001. Obviously, with the more inclusive use of the first person
plural, the invasion of Iraq is a threat to our security. Importantly
and less obviously, the same is true even with the narrower usage.
The patterns of human behavior that led to the invasion of Iraq will
recur, threatening countless human lives in the future, and those
who live in North America will not be immune.

The given reason for the invasion of Iraq was doubly dishonest.
First, the actual purpose of the invasion was not "our" security at
all, but regime change. The purpose was hegemony, not survival.
Second, the invasion actually threatened our security because it was
an assault on the rule of law in the global community, and like it
or not, we are part of that community. The legacy of the invasion
of Iraq, and the thinking that drove it, continues to threaten our
security.

It was almost a century ago that "experts" and "leaders" promoted
World War I as the "war to end all wars." It wasn't, it didn't, and it
won't. Today the promotional tricks have changed; the thing being

promoted is the same. War is not an instrument for ending warfare. For that purpose, a more intelligent use of the first person plural might help.

Pathology of the old paradigm

It is easy to conjecture at least one of the reasons why the American soldier who set the little girl and her family on fire might have had no immediate sense of having done anything wrong. He had been deeply indoctrinated in the paradigm of nationalism, which makes it okay to incinerate human beings. He probably knows that the political leaders of his own country and his commanding officers have no effective compunctions about such things; his actions are likely to go unpunished. For his own good, he should also know that the pronouncements of political leaders on security and defense issues are treacherous.

It is also easy to understand how political leaders and experts for more than a century have been such a miserable failure at providing human security in the global community. They too think within the box of the old paradigm.

There is an enormous gravitational pull keeping soldiers and political leaders, and the experts who serve them, inside the box. Cultural, political, and economic institutions have evolved within the nationalist paradigm. The economic power associated with it ties incomes, careers, and reputations to support for nationalism. This military-industrial-ideological-political complex demands loyalty. There can be dire personal consequences for innovative thinking.

In the old paradigm, security is provided by the nation-state's military power. Sometimes referred to as "defense," this militarism (whatever its defensive functions) becomes a threat to others. Within the nationalist state, "we" are taught to see only the threat that others pose to "us," not the threat we pose to others. The result is predictable: a self-sustaining dynamic of violence.

Einstein had a concise formula for nationalism:

> Nationalism, in my opinion, is none other than an idealistic rationalization for militarism and aggression. (quoted in Nathan and Norden, eds. 1960, 242)

Whether that sounds to you like $E=mc^2$ or more like $2+2=4$, it's a useful concept (depending on your purposes, of course). The national interest is not the public interest. The polarized and exclusive concept of power to be found in militant nationalism is toxic to democracy.

Non-state actors may also use violence, sometimes in response to nationalist state violence or in efforts to establish their own state. This stateless version of violence is selectively referred to as "terrorism" today, but the following standard definition of terrorism makes no such distinction: "The use of violence and threats to intimidate or coerce, esp. for political purposes" (Random House 1987).

Our cultural institutions, driven by the old paradigm, emphasize the terrorism of non-state actors, and do so in a way intended to recruit public support for further violence — state violence operating within the old paradigm. The so-called war on terrorism has perpetuated the cycle of violence. Because the old paradigm is dominant, there are strained and sustained efforts to avoid the standard definition in public references to "terrorism." The term *political violence* can be helpful in restoring the necessary awareness that violence of this kind can come from either state or non-state actors, and that such violence needs to be brought under control, no matter what the source.

In this plague of violence afflicting the global community, we find experts who tell us that there will never be a cure; in fact, that it is not even a disease. In presenting his call for a "robust nationalism," Samuel Huntington writes:

Conservatives know that the end of one conflict creates the basis for another one. They agree with Robin Fox that wars are not a disease to be cured, but part of the normal human condition. They stem from what we are, not from some contingencies of what we do from time to time ("history"). They are, like religion and prostitution, basic responses to basic human fears and hopes. (1999:31–40)

Huntington's statement illustrates the limitations of the old paradigm. The new paradigm expands the boundaries. Murder, rape, warfare, and cancer might all be considered "part of the normal human condition." Whether they can be reduced or eliminated at any given time or place is an empirical question. You have to make a relentless and serious effort to eliminate them if you have any serious interest in answering the question.

After centuries of waste and bloodshed, France and Germany have largely ceased to be a threat to one another and to other parts of Europe. Because of nuclear weapons and other factors that have more recently entered the equation (e.g. diminishing and contaminated natural resources, accelerating climate change, population growth, and economic turbulence), the global community may no longer have the luxury of the time that Europe took to learn the lesson.

Repeatedly, in personal lives and in communities, nationalism has intruded on healthier human responses to change. However difficult it may prove to be, a paradigm shift is essential to the future of human security. Today, our institutions remain locked into the old paradigm: the state will provide for "our" security. The evidence indicates that governments locked into this paradigm are undermining our security — whether the first person plural is used in the narrow or the broader sense. The new paradigm is in accord with that evidence.

Fortunately, there is evidence that the malignant version of nationalism may be drawing to a close. Its recurrent failures, its waste of human lives and resources, its destruction of the environment, and the lies and hypocrisy necessary to sustain it are an open secret. How close to the tipping point we are remains to be seen.

The new paradigm and human options

In the darkest of times human beings are resilient. During my late wife's illness with cancer, I witnessed her courage, tenacity, sense of humor, and relentless creative force. We have great resourcefulness even under harsh conditions, and we can access that capacity now, while time and resources are still in our favor.

Today the global community is afflicted with another form of cancer, the cancer of militant nationalist violence, in which we are both the disease-producing agents and the only hope for a cure. If we drive ourselves into the terminal stages of the disease, no doubt we will find our courage and resilience in those dark times. But why on earth should we not act now and steadily improve our options for the future?

It would be a mistake to underestimate the difficulty of curing this cancer, but a far greater mistake to think it is impossible. We are imposing this malady upon ourselves; therefore, it is within our power to stop it.

> Fifty-eight years after Hiroshima, the world has to decide whether to continue on the path of cataclysmic violence charted in the twentieth century and now resumed in the twenty-first or whether to embark on a new, cooperative political path. It is a decision composed of innumerable smaller decisions guided by a common theme, which is weaning politics off violence. (Schell 2003, 386)

Optimism is a pragmatic necessity. Moreover, history gives good reason for optimism, as it records such achievements as the end of slavery, the mitigation of racism, improvement in the treatment of children, and the acceptance of women's suffrage. History is also

[79]

filled with countless setbacks and the collapse of civilizations. Life is difficult and does not go on forever. There will always be dark times ahead; we cannot have the light without the darkness. That's the deal.

The rhetoric of politicians is a very poor indicator of our chances of finding a cure for the disease of militant nationalism. The best place to take a reading of our chances is within your own spirit and your own sense of responsibility for this task. If there is no hope there, where on earth will hope ever be found?

CHAPTER FOUR

Principles of
Global Community

The paradigm for global citizenship presented in this book is based on the connection between personal and social psychology, between self-actualization and the health of the global community. Like the practice of medicine, it identifies as pathological that which undermines human well-being. It seeks to understand that pathology in terms conducive to effective therapy and prevention.

Effective global citizenship requires familiarity with fundamentals, a set of basic skills, persistent practice in applying the skills toward clearly defined goals, and often intense concentration. Even a familiarity with fundamentals in the practice of global citizenship can itself be a huge step forward, and this book can help with that. Knowing "how things work" that affect your life is an asset as important as your bank account. The ability that some people have to see the relationship between events in their personal lives and events in their society has been called the "sociological imagination." Having this ability can prevent you from being a prisoner of social forces that influence your life (see Shepard 1987, xxxv).

Knowledge of the ways you can affect your society is just as liberating as knowledge of how your society affects you. If you live and work to promote human well-being at the personal, local, and global levels, you can gradually free yourself and others of pessimism. If your experience is like mine, doors will open for you. You will learn to use successes and setbacks in making moment-to-moment changes. Surprising advances, opportunities, and transformations are part of this experience. Again and again, you will transcend what you thought were your limits.

I have used the analogy of medicine in referring to the practice of global citizenship. *The ABCs of Human Survival* is written with the concept of a text on principles of medicine in mind. The important thing, however, is to find the analogy that is most effective for you.

Even the analogy of war can be useful for this purpose. It is often used for sustained effort toward an envisioned goal, as in the phrases "war on poverty" or "war on cancer." Scott Ritter has written a useful book for those who like this analogy: *Waging Peace: The Art of War for the Anti-War Movement* (2007).

The analogy of a game can also be useful because so many people enjoy games of all kinds and because many have been involved in competitive athletics. Skill in playing the game of citizenship can give the satisfaction of skill in a sport.

The principles of global community (in this chapter) and of global citizenship (chapter 6) have evolved over more than a decade from my thinking and experience. This chapter emphasizes how things work in the global community, while chapter 6 emphasizes practice — how individuals change the global community. The separation is somewhat arbitrary: all the principles are relevant both to understanding and to practice.

PRINCIPLE 1

We are in the process of choosing between a healthy global community under a rule of international law (Option A) or ongoing violent contests for power driven by militant nationalism (Option B).

In our society, we consider human sacrifice ceremonies a savage affront to morality, but we consider our own maintenance of the warfare system quite acceptable. As a society, we ignore, obscure, or rationalize the fact that our policies were largely responsible for the deaths of hundreds of thousands of Iraqi civilians well *before* the invasion of Iraq in 2003, as well as the carnage of the invasion itself. Historically, we have always rationalized, obscured, or ignored the atrocities for which we have been responsible.

As individuals, however, we do not have to accept this way of thinking (or not thinking) about our savagery. We have the option of rejecting destructive and self-destructive patterns of thinking and behavior that are officially condoned and promoted. It's a choice. Consciously or unconsciously, we in fact make this choice. Remaining silent or "neutral," and paying taxes, supports the savagery. We not only make these choices, but we are also responsible for the predictable consequences of our choice.

If we choose to believe that Option B is the only option and behave accordingly, then we will continue down the road to Option B. We will be blind to the alternative because our thinking has made us blind.

By rejecting militant nationalism and affirming the necessity of law, we align ourselves with progress toward Option A. We assume responsibility for learning to live together as human beings. The government cannot claim to represent a person or a constituency that explicitly rejects its militarism and its violations of international law. If the person or the constituency is silent, the government can pursue its path unimpeded down the road to Option B.

Rejecting militant nationalism and affirming the necessity of law are essential if we are to learn to live together as human beings, but they are not sufficient. We must also deal with other weaknesses in our society if we want to re-direct the global community toward Option A. One of these weaknesses is social atomization — our isolation from each other, both within our local communities and within the global community.

What are the causes of this social atomization? Certainly one significant factor is the material conditions of our society. The rich and the poor have but limited tendency to dialogue across the chasm created by discrepancies of wealth. But even within neighborhood communities, we often do not take time to talk with our neighbors. This isolation occurs despite, and to some extent because of, the widespread availability of personal computers and email. Electronic communication can be a great asset if used wisely, but it is no substitute for direct, healthy human interaction.

We have imposed this social atomization on ourselves. We do this by our daily choices. We can make different choices. Poorer and less technologically advanced societies have achieved much greater social cohesion than ours, and people in them are generally less isolated from one another than we are in our so-called advanced society. And yet we are quite capable of enhanced social cohesion, as may become apparent during a national crisis. It happened during World War II within the states that were at war; there are those who still remember it.

This social cohesion — the reverse of social atomization — can have measurable and surprising effects on personal well-being. Richard Wilkinson has examined the data on increases in life expectancy that occurred in Great Britain in the twentieth century. For civilians, those increases were greater during the decades of the two world wars (1910–20 and 1940–50) than in any other decade of that century.

> During the First and Second World Wars, British government policy was designed to foster national unity and a sense that the burden of war was shared equally across

[84]

the whole society.... Not only did income differences narrow dramatically among those in employment, but unemployment almost disappeared, and income tax became much more progressive. The policy seemed to have its desired effect: people talked of a strong sense of camaraderie, social cohesion, and common purpose. A remarkable result was that civilian death rates fell two or three times as fast as in other periods during the twentieth century. (Wilkinson 2005, 39–40)

As Richard Wilkinson's extensive work makes clear, however, it is not warfare but human cooperation (social cohesion) that is the essential ingredient in a healthy society. Growing disparities of wealth in a society correlate with reductions in life expectancy and other indices of declining health. Countries with modest economic indices may be healthier and happier than "rich countries" if their level of social capital is high.

Definitions and uses of the term *social capital* vary, but I use it here similarly to how Robert Putnam uses it in *Bowling Alone* (2000): it is value created by social networks and the tendency within such networks for people to do things for each other and for the common good. As such, social capital is an essential asset for effective democracy, and benefits from the participation of individuals with high self-esteem, respect for life, and a creative approach to community.

Wilkinson's finding that indicators of physical and psychological well-being improved as a function of social equality has an important parallel in findings by Amartya Sen and others that famines are not so much the result of food shortages as of a lack of democracy. Frances Moore Lappé has extended this thesis in her books and — along with countless other exemplary individuals in civil society — given it vitality in her life and work.

Social and political atomization makes democracy impossible and places society at risk. Conversely, social cohesion enables a society to address a variety of challenges more effectively. By our choices, we evolve daily toward more cooperative or more atomized communities. By our choices, we accept or reject militarism and its corrosive effects on the local and global communities.

Consciously or unconsciously, each of us is personally involved in this choice-process. It operates at every level from the personal to the global. It involves the influences of individuals on society and the influences of society on individuals. This choice-process has largely determined the course of world events in the past, and it has also determined the current conditions of human security. It diminishes or expands our ability to envision possibilities and to explore the farther reaches of the human spirit. It creates opportunities or challenges for the generations who will follow us. It will continue to determine the course of world events, the conditions of human existence, and the chances of human survival in the future.

PRINCIPLE 2
We cannot be part of the solution until we
understand that we are part of the problem.

Perhaps self-righteousness is the basic driving force in the familiar trajectory of empires: their rise, decline, and ultimate collapse. As a species, we human beings have depended on social cooperation. Yet we have also been catastrophically self-destructive. Careful observers have pointed out that our destructive behavior depends on self-righteousness and a lack of introspection. Hannah Arendt emphasized the "banality of evil," the widespread support given to political leaders who impose savage policies on the global community (1963a). She understood how easily individuals are recruited into support for destruction, and how difficult it can be for them to resist even if they understand what is happening.

We fail the test of introspection when we assume that we are powerless to influence conditions and events in the global community and that we have no responsibility for those events and conditions. Erich Fromm (1941) reminds us that we human beings have a strong tendency to escape from freedom, from responsibility, and from self-knowledge.

Responsible global citizenship requires not only understanding that we are contributing to the problem but also ongoing inquiry into *how* we are contributing. As we pursue this understanding and inquiry, we progressively enhance our ability to help solve the problem. This concept is well expressed in the New Testament: "first take the log out of your own eye, and then you will see clearly to take the speck out of your brother's eye" (Matthew 7:5).

You and I must develop this understanding, but governments must also develop it. Governments cannot become part of the solution until they understand that they are part of the problem. This process involves acknowledging their violations of international law, recognizing that their lawlessness is a major part of the problem, and then bringing their policies and actions into compliance.

PRINCIPLE 3
Warfare is pathological.

Warfare is pathological in the same sense that HIV/AIDS or cancer is pathological. It kills people, including children, and devastates the lives of the people afflicted. Because we are part of the global community affected by warfare, it ravages the resources of our communities.

The diverse causes of war include economic, environmental, and political factors. This book emphasizes a cultural and ideological factor in the cause of warfare — militant nationalism, a pattern of thinking that makes warfare more likely, more frequent, and more deadly.

The causes of warfare might be explored in many venues: the behavior of other species (the "territorial imperative"); human competition for various natural resources (oil, water, food); economic considerations (capitalist competition, the current "profitability" of weapons production); political maneuvering and decision-making in the particular geopolitical context (e.g., historicist or political realist perspectives); or the social and psychological milieu (with deteriorating socio-economic conditions leading to hopelessness and public acceptance of warfare as inevitable).

Most of these ways of understanding the causes of warfare can be applied either in old-paradigm frameworks (which lead toward Option B) or in new-paradigm frameworks (which lead toward Option A). They can be used to serve the purposes of Option A thinkers or Option B thinkers.

Take so-called political realism as an example. Political realists are interested in power relationships among states and coalitions of states. Obviously some understanding of such power relationships is essential to efforts at preventing warfare and promoting a healthy global community. With remarkable frequency, however, political realists have placed themselves at the service of state power in its virulent rivalries (old paradigm, Option B). As a working hypothesis, I suggest that they do so because there are more lucrative jobs available in that line of work. Be that as it may, the fact that the political realist line of thinking has often served militant nationalism (Option B) does not change the fact that political realism, if honestly pursued and applied, can equally well serve a healthier purpose (Option A).

Essentially the same applies to the other ways of understanding the causes of warfare. The old-paradigm thinker can cite the "territorial imperative," or human competition for various natural resources, or economic determinants, or whatever, as the reasons why warfare is inevitable. The new-paradigm thinker takes a very different approach. In new-paradigm thinking, all these causes of warfare are factors that need to be understood and addressed in the process of finding effective therapy and prevention of war.

Whether we can bring warfare under control is an empirical question. If we want to achieve that outcome, we will have to develop a way of thinking that increases the chances of producing it. We will have to make the shift to the new paradigm proposed in this and countless other books, the paradigm that produced major advances of human consciousness through the centuries. The new paradigm recognizes warfare as pathological and aims to do to warfare what we long ago did to smallpox.

PRINCIPLE 4
Militant nationalism drives the global community toward Option B.

Option B extinguishes a largely unexplored world of human options. Every year, and with every payment we make into the warfare system, we relinquish constructive possibilities — in fact, luminous opportunities — for realizing what the human spirit might achieve. The world and our lives might have been incomparably richer and more productive than we have made them. We have failed because we lacked the wisdom, the love, the courage, and the imagination to do better.

We undermine our strength because we permit an ongoing hemorrhage of public resources and human talent into developing, producing, maintaining, and supporting the means of human self-destruction. Of the colossal sums recently approved by the U.S. House of Representatives to support the U.S. military presence in Afghanistan and Iraq, one small part of the bill designated more than seven hundred million dollars for procurement of missiles for the U.S. Army. Missiles are Option B technology.

In militarizing the global community, we have become highly destructive of the natural environment and wasteful of resources. The example we have set as "leaders of the civilized world" gives other states not only a self-destructive model to follow but also plenty of excuses for following it.

"We support our troops" is a popular assertion of militant nationalist sentiment. This phrase seamlessly blends support for human beings with support for militarism: "our troops" are human beings, and "our troops" are carrying out violence against other human beings.

Now is the time for us to support human beings. Support our troops as human beings. Bring them home. Work for a world in which they and others like them have respect and self-respect, and can contribute to the well-being of others. Work for a world in which all of us, including those now in uniform, will end our slavish obedience to militant nationalist authority. Work for a world in which those in uniform and others like them will become responsible citizens rather than obedient and incomplete human beings.

At every level, from the personal to the international, militant nationalism is using our economic, political, social, and cultural capital to drive all of us toward Option B,. The Option A priority is human well-being. The Option B priority is political power and, in organized states, state power. Militant nationalist culture denies, obscures, rationalizes, or ignores the conflict between these two priorities.

PRINCIPLE 5
Power must be constrained by law.

There is an obsolete concept of law in which a "lawmaker" or "lawgiver" (such as an emperor or monarch or dictator) promulgates the law but is himself above the law. That concept is diametrically opposed to modern concepts of law. Modern concepts of law are illustrated by the ideas underlying the U.S. Constitution, which is the source of whatever legitimate authority the U.S. government may have, and by the ideas underlying the UN Charter, which is the source of whatever legitimate authority the UN Security Council may have.

Prime ministers, presidents, government officials, judges, and legislators are all subject to law. To the extent they violate the law, they lose their legitimacy. In their violations of international law, they threaten the global community, which includes the rest of us.

Of the many astute observers of power and its consequences for good or ill, Norman Cousins is one of the most eloquent. A careful reading of history, he suggests, can give us useful insights into the pathology of power:

> The tendency of power to drive intelligence underground;
>
> The tendency of power to become a theology, admitting no other gods before it;
>
> The tendency of power to distort and damage the traditions and institutions it was designed to protect;
>
> The tendency of power to create a language of its own, making other forms of communication incoherent and irrelevant;
>
> The tendency of power to spawn imitators, leading to volatile competition;
>
> The tendency of power to set the stage for its own use. (1987, 23–24)

The exercise of power must be constrained by law. Reliable progress in human security can be made only within a framework of law protecting human rights. In the twentieth century, international law has increasingly emphasized basic human rights. Violent contests for state power were recognized as a central threat to human security.

With the breakdown in order that is inherent in war, all basic requirements of human security are threatened. For that reason, one of the fundamental requirements of international law is that governments must refrain from the international threat or use of force.

Under the UN Charter, the international threat or use of force is permissible only against an armed attack, or under auspices of the United Nations and in accord with the principles and purposes of the UN Charter. Advances in human rights must take place within the framework of this law of non-aggression (Article 2). Louis Henkin, former editor of the *American Journal of International Law* and advisor to the State Department on international law, expresses the relationship as follows:

> Peace was the paramount value. The Charter and the [United Nations] were dedicated to realizing other values as well — self determination, respect for human rights, economic and social development, justice, and a just international order. But those purposes could not justify the use of force between states to achieve them; they would have to be pursued by other means.... The purposes of the United Nations could not in fact be achieved by war. War inflicted the greatest injustice, the most serious violations of human rights, and the most violence to self-determination and to economic and social development. (1991, 38–39)

Far from being an obstacle to control of dictators and tyrants, as has been claimed at times, international law is the only reliable framework within which such tyranny can be controlled and democracy promoted. Dictatorship and tyranny arise precisely under conditions of lawlessness in a dysfunctional global community. Powerful states, driven by militant nationalism, *promote* those conditions. They support dictatorship and tyranny to serve their own purposes, then use dictatorship and tyranny as pretext for war.

The "responsibility to protect" is an emerging concept in international law, with potential for considerable benefit or harm. Under current conditions, this concept can too easily be invoked to cover military intervention with a humanitarian mask. The given reasons for militarism have always been in some sense humanitarian, and there seems little to gain by expanding the wardrobe of disguises for aggression. In conflicts degenerating toward violence and oppression, the international community will usually have abundant signals of the developing crisis and abundant opportunity to assist in resolving it, to intervene, well before the arrival of catastrophe. Instead, powerful states themselves are often promoting policies that exacerbate such crises.

It is these issues that need primary emphasis and attention. They have received inadequate attention in the original document on the responsibility to protect (International Commission on Intervention and State Sovereignty [ICISS] 2001). This is a deficiency that is being redressed in a Canadian initiative, the "responsibility to care," led by Dr. Mary-Wynne Ashford. The use of military intervention as prescribed by the ICISS is fraught with danger until we change the international context, and that change should rapidly obviate the need for military intervention, through international action before the catastrophe has arrived.

This is, of course, a complex issue. *The Hague Agenda for Peace and Justice in the 21ˢᵗ Century* (Agenda 21), which provides an essential conceptual framework for the promotion of peace and justice in the twenty-first century, has endorsed the concept of the responsibility to protect. But without a responsibility to care, and without acceptance by the most powerful states of their responsibility to abide by international law, the responsibility to protect will rapidly become worse than useless.

A rule of law can enhance trust across the global community and reliably diminish the use and threat of force. It can constrain the pathological aspects of power and channel power in more constructive directions. It can free up resources from weapons expenditures and allow those resources to be used for public health, education, and other programs that foster human creative potential. Compliance with international law is in the best interests of all states, including the most powerful.

By contrast, lawlessness encourages criminality and irresponsibility among the most powerful. It diminishes trust, increases the costs of transactions, devastates the global community, and leaves the future to military adventurism and the hazards of chance. Richard Falk, Albert G. Milbank Professor of International Law and

Practice, Princeton, asserts that lawlessness has undermined the best interests of Americans:

> I think that if we re-examine the "lawless" initiatives of the past half-century, we find that few, if any, have benefited the United States or its people. I believe that as an American citizen I would be better served by a government that accepted the constraints of law as surely in international affairs as in domestic. Indeed, I would even contend that the next leap forward in legitimate governance will be giving citizens an enforceable, constitutional right to a "lawful foreign policy." (Falk 1999)

Based on a recent opinion poll, U.S. and world public opinion is in accord with these views. In the United States, 69 percent of respondents concurred with the statement: "Our nation should consistently follow international laws. It is wrong to violate international laws, just as it is wrong to violate laws within a country." The response in most countries surveyed was similar to that in the United States, with well over half of the respondents in agreement. The website www.worldpublicopinion.org carries background and details of this poll.

Law can be used to serve illegitimate power rather than as a constraint on such power, and it is often used for this purpose. Hence the uses of international law today are often contrary to the fifth principle put forward here — and contrary to the purposes of this book. Perhaps schools and universities should have introductory courses in international law in which the Option A and Option B uses of international law are clearly distinguished, so that students can make an informed choice.

PRINCIPLE 6

A rule of law depends on respect for the inherent justice of the law and for justice in its implementation.

International law offers advantages that can make the difference between life and death for our future. To achieve a rule of law, however, certain basic requirements will have to be met. A rule of law must be respected for its inherent justice or it will not endure. Jonathan Schell's *The Unconquerable World* (2003) and Mark Kurlansky's *Nonviolence* (2006) give historical overviews of how non-violent resistance and the rejection of unjust law and illegitimate power played a definitive role in twentieth-century history. No police force or army can long maintain a law that is self-negating.

The law as written must be conducive to healthy community: locally, regionally, and globally. International law recognizes, as it must, the principle of sovereign equality of states, just as municipal or national law recognizes the principle of equality of citizens before the law. Small states such as Guatemala under Jacobo Arbenz, or twentieth-century Costa Rica, or Sweden may provide better role models for the global community of the future than more powerful states such as China or the United States. Protection of smaller states from the bullying of larger states is a *sine qua non* for our future security.

Despite its imperfections, international law, with its increasing emphasis on basic human rights, has evolved in the right direction (toward Option A). Its prescriptions for progress are based on sound principles and long experience. But the most powerful states refuse to take the medicine.

The work of the UN Security Council has been obstructed and contaminated by the veto power of its permanent members, particularly of the Soviet Union (1950–70) and the United States (1970–90). As Austrian jurist Hans Köchler (1995) describes it, the veto power is a "normative contradiction" to the UN Charter's principle of sovereign equality of states. It needs to be changed. In the meantime, however, no one forces the UN Security Council members to use, or threaten to use, their veto. It is not the law itself but the subversion and rejection of law, particularly by powerful states, that is chiefly responsible for the ongoing failures.

In particular, two requirements for implementing international law will have to be met in order for us to move toward Option A:

1. *The law must be applied equitably.* If there is a law against murder but it is applied selectively, and not applied when someone rich and powerful commits murder, then there can be no rule of law. If there is a law against aggression but that law is not applied when a powerful state commits aggression, then there can be no rule of law.

2. *The law must be applied consistently in accord with its most fundamental purposes and principles.* If the law against murder is invoked when three people have been murdered, as pretext for the slaughter of three hundred people, there can be no rule of law. If the law against aggression is invoked as pretext for a massive escalation of violence and further acts of aggression, it repudiates the international legal system's most fundamental purposes and principles. There can be no rule of law until treachery of this kind is ended.

Both these requirements were violated immediately after the end of the Cold War, thus aborting progress toward Option A. An object lesson from this part of our history is provided in chapter 5, "The Case of Iraq." We now live in an increasingly dangerous time because the rule of law has been rejected by the most powerful states. Something better is possible.

PRINCIPLE 7
Democracy and law are interdependent.

"The price of freedom is eternal vigilance." This statement, attributed to Thomas Jefferson, is of course open to more than one interpretation and usage. It might be used to persuade a population to support their troops, for example, or to place absolute trust in their government as the "guardian of their liberty." Jefferson certainly had something very different in mind.

Thomas Jefferson was one of many who have thought carefully about the meaning of democracy. Another is Hans Köchler, a contemporary Austrian jurist who has written extensively on democracy, international law, and the relationship between the two. Both Jefferson and Köchler arrive at the same conclusion: that direct citizen participation in governance is the cornerstone of viable democracy.

> The dignity of every individual as an *active* (not merely passive) subject ... allows for a more precise formulation of the idea of human rights as a basis for a genuine democratic system. It will be demonstrated that democracy in the sense of *direct* (that is to say, unmediated) participation of the individual in the decision-making process in a community is the *only form of political organization concurring with human rights.* (Köchler 1995, 7; emphasis original)

Eternal vigilance — that means *your* eternal vigilance — is the price of creating and maintaining a world that is in your best interests. In practice, of course, "your best interests" means the best interests not only of you personally, but also of your children and other members of your family. It also means the best interests of others in your community. Pushed to the wall, human beings are quite capable of making things unpleasant for each other. So it is in your best interests not to contribute to a world that pushes a lot of people to the wall and instead to envision and work to implement conditions (a global community) that encourage active contributions for the common good from every person.

This line of reasoning leads inevitably to a framework of human rights as a basic necessity, and to the necessity for governments to comply with that framework. And that means that your eternal vigilance must include watching your own government for any deviations from the most important purposes, principles, and prescriptions of law.

In opposition to this line of reasoning is the theme, familiar to all of us, that your government and its military forces will protect your interests and provide for your security against threats arising from other states, and that your primary responsibility is therefore loyalty to your country, not vigilance with regard to your country's violation of international law. The state in which you hold citizenship, according to this map, is your protector; and it is your government, not the requirements of international law, that deserve your primary allegiance.

A comparison of these opposing concepts, along with evidence from the real world, leads to the insight that your government best serves your interests and best provides for your security by complying with international law. Furthermore, when we allow our government to violate international law and threaten the well-being of others in other parts of the global community, it is a critical failure of vigilance on our part.

If we understand *democracy* as it is defined in a standard dictionary and with the emphasis added in the foregoing paragraphs, then it is necessarily intertwined with international law, and both are dependent upon a fundamental acceptance of the primacy of human rights over state power. This understanding helps clarify why some standard ways of conducting foreign policy are illegitimate. Power politics means contempt for human life. It leads to the outrageous statements of a government official (Madeleine Albright) explaining why the lives of half a million children were a reasonable price to pay for this or that objective of the government. It leads, in fact, to fascism, and the road to that destination is not particularly long or winding.

Fascism, as we have all been instructed, is the negation of

democracy. But isn't law emphasized in a fascist state? Obsession with crime and punishment has been cited as one of the characteristics of a fascist state, and police in such a state are given almost limitless power to enforce laws. Isn't that a more robust commitment to law than we have in our "democratic" society?

What passes for law in fascist societies is that atavistic notion of law in which the supreme power in the state is above the law. Fascism is the negation not only of democracy, but also of law. Law means a framework for controlling power in the interest of human well-being. The law is to serve human beings and not the other way around. If it does not mean this, then law means something very dangerous indeed.

The characteristics of fascism include powerful and continuing nationalism, disdain for the recognition of human rights, identification of enemies and scapegoats as a unifying cause, controlled mass media, and obsession with national security, among others (see Britt 2003). The use of the spectacle in fascist states serves the purpose of impressing on the individual how impotent they are in the face of large aggregates of power, a very useful doctrine when your purpose is to destroy any vestige of democracy. In a fascist state, the individual is interpreted as a consumer and an object for manipulation, not as a vigilant, competent, responsible citizen. When we look at the list of characteristics of fascism, based on studies of fascist states such as Italy under Mussolini, Spain under Franco, and Germany under Hitler, we find features familiar to us in our own society.

A system that claims to protect the interests of any group of people, and on that basis claims the right to conduct foreign policy in ways that violate international law and threaten the well-being of other groups of people, is making a fraudulent claim. Such a system is in fact a threat to those whose interest it claims to protect.

An effective democracy is the only reliable enforcer for international law. International law is the guarantor and guideline of effective democracy. Both are essential for protection and promotion of our best interests, and both are our responsibility.

PRINCIPLE 8
Democracy and law are evolving.

Neither democracy nor international law is static. And neither is currently in a robust state of health. They must grow and change into something different from what they are now. In what direction do we want them to change, toward Option A or Option B? And what are we going to do about it?

Hans Köchler is one of those who have recognized the grotesque perversion of international law that took place in response to Iraq's invasion of Kuwait in 1990. It was a point at which the uses and concepts of international law underwent a change toward Option B. He refers to that travesty as he alerts us to the potential treachery behind words like "democracy" and "a rule of law." Hearing the words can so easily catch us off guard as the reality to which the words refer moves, step by step, down the road to hell.

> In its management of the Gulf Crisis, the USA factually had its power monopoly recognized by the other members of the Security Council, and it used this *fait accompli* in the spirit of the traditional doctrine of international law based on power politics for a reinterpretation of the UN Charter ... in a manner which effectively undermined the Charter itself....
>
> It is self-evident that "democracy" and the "rule of law" become instruments of cynical *realpolitik* when used under such circumstances. They degenerate into mere ideological phrases. (Köchler 1995, 46–47)

At the same time, Köchler understands very well the need for change in a different direction.

Therefore, if one actually propagates democracy as the new paradigm for international order — in distinction to the power-political maxims of classical international law — then such an idealistic program has to be followed by action. In particular, those provisions in the UN Charter that secure the privileged position of the post-war powers must be eliminated because they express nothing more than a power-political immunization which *legally* allows the respectively strongest power to turn the other states into hostages of its veto right and to initiate aggression itself without fear of instigating legal sanctions. (44)

Democracy and international law are on the move. Where do we want to take them, and where do we want them to take us? They can become more effective in promoting human security and a healthy global community, or they can mask and exacerbate a growing threat to human security and the global community. It's a choice that we must make and that future generations must live with.

PRINCIPLE 9
Nationalism has both creative and destructive effects on the state itself.

An *inclusive nationalism* can mitigate conflicts among ethnic communities and promote cooperative effort for the public good. This potential accounts for much of the historical success of nationalism. But nationalism has a strong tendency to become malignant: to make political power (state power) an end unto itself, and in serving that priority, to become exclusive, setting "us" against "them." This is *militant nationalism*, and it is the dominant form of nationalism today. It is pervasive in the culture of militarily powerful states, and it influences the culture of their allies. This is apparent even in so simple an observation as the difference between the attention that our mass media pays to deaths of "our troops" (who happen to be agents of our violations of international law in Iraq and Afghanistan) and the lack of attention that same mass media pays to civilian deaths in the countries with which we are at war.

Nationalism would not have survived and flourished if it had not been associated with impressive benefits for millions of people. Nationalism sometimes arises as a response to aggression or murderous oppression. The rise of Zionism in response to murderous oppression of Jews and the rise of various nationalisms in response to imperialism are familiar examples from the twentieth century.

Nationalism often promotes community. Because that community tends to be exclusive ("us" against "them"), it is a long-term threat to those in the community, but that does not prevent the nationalist social bond from being heartfelt and widely shared. It can be a very positive human experience accompanied by overwhelming emotions. The sense of national community may be strongest in a time of warfare if there is a real external threat to the nation. Veterans may remember their war years as the most positive time of their lives because of the sense of mission, community, and effectiveness.

Nationalist enthusiasms can also be intense in a powerful and secure state in times of peace, perhaps especially so, for their new home, among immigrants and refugees from the ravages of violent nationalism in other parts of the world. Nationalism promotes human rights for some even as it threatens human rights for others.

Anyone who has lived in a powerful state is familiar, not only from propaganda but from personal experience, with the benefits of nationalism. Consider the late twentieth-century differences between life in the United States and life in Colombia, where death threats, civil war, and kidnapping have for many years ravaged the fabric of society. Colombia is an "ownership society" in which wealthy individuals and groups refused to relinquish sufficient power to form an effective central government. It is a state threatened by one of the worst forms of anarchism. Militant nationalism is the lesser of two evils if we put it in the dock with a state that is disintegrating or tearing itself apart from within. The irony is that militant nationalism itself leads the state toward self-destruction. The trajectories of Germany under Adolf Hitler and of Iraq under Saddam Hussein provide dramatic examples. And what happened quickly for Iraq and Germany is happening more slowly for the world's superpower. As public resources are squandered on the negative capital invested in militarism, as the global community turns away from the United States as a model for the future, the United States looks more and more like an empire in decline.

PRINCIPLE 10
Every powerful state has both conveyed significant benefits and committed major atrocities.

Without exception, every powerful militant nationalist state in history has facilitated major achievements that benefited the citizens of that state. And without exception, every powerful militant nationalist state in history has been responsible for murderous atrocities.

Under conditions of militant nationalism, the growth of state power requires the deployment of public resources not only in international contests for power but also to maintain popular support. Having lived the first four decades of my life in the United States and the more recent two decades in Canada, I can attest to enormous benefits conveyed by each of those two states. I assume readers are familiar with many of these benefits from personal experience, so they need no elaboration here.

Readers will also be familiar with the fate of earlier inhabitants of North America after arrival of the Europeans at the end of the fifteenth century. Historically we Europeans have shown that we are capable not only of extinguishing entire populations but also of feeling quite proud of ourselves for doing it. Trafficking in slaves, murderous civil wars, aggression, torture, the use of weapons of mass destruction against civilian populations, and a long list of other atrocities characterize the history of Europe and its diaspora. European governments and their offshoots (including the governments of the United States, Canada, and Latin America) are far from unique in their barbarity, but most readers will be particularly familiar with the European and North American part of world history.

The atrocities a state commits are often associated with a relative increase in military power and with militant nationalism. But the state must simultaneously promote benefits for its citizens to ensure public support for its atrocities. And the militant nationalism itself can be deeply gratifying to the public in some situations, as exemplified in Germany before World War II.

By the early 1930s, many Germans had become impatient with their situation. There was the humiliation to which Germany had been subjected at Versailles in 1919 and the failure of a liberal government to solve the ensuing problems: hyperinflation in 1923, discrimination against German minorities in various parts of Europe in the 1920s, and the catastrophic effects of the world economic depression after 1929.

By 1933 unemployment in Germany had reached 40 percent. After Hitler's accession to power that same year, Germans witnessed a rise in national fervor, a dramatic fall in the unemployment rate, and Hitler's firm challenge to any further humiliation of Germany in the international arena. The trains ran on time, Germany won the 1936 Olympics, and the German army advanced its reputation as a fighting machine, much admired to this day for its military excellence. In films and photographs taken at the time of Germany's annexation of Austria (1938), there is jubilation on the faces of young Austrians about reunion with the fatherland.

Who could argue with success like that? The world was taking notice, and there was widespread admiration for the achievements of German nationalism.

Germany was a rising world power in the 1930s; Iraq was a rising regional power in the 1970s. The government of Iraq was murderously repressive, but there were significant advances in health, education, and other programs for public benefit. The government promoted a secular society and a vision of a powerful modern state. The role of women in public life and in professional fields such as medicine was expanding. Iraq was seen by many as an example for other Arab states to follow.

The atrocities committed by the government of Iraq under Saddam Hussein and by the government of Germany under Adolf Hitler will need no repetition for a reader of this book. We often congratulate ourselves on not being quite as bad as they were. And of course, that self-congratulation is part of the pathology.

Can we rationalize our own atrocities? You bet. Can we find a way of thinking that lets us sleep at night and continue feeling that we are quite okay? Obviously. Will intellectuals and experts and best-selling authors in our culture help us with that process? Of course. Will such commentators be well paid for their efforts? Sometimes handsomely.

These are not serious questions or serious challenges for our time. A serious question for our time is whether we can get ourselves out of the trap of self-destructive behavior that our culture has shared with defunct states and empires of the past. That serious challenge for the future provides a reference point for any serious and responsible discussion of world affairs.

PRINCIPLE 11
Nationalism is legitimate only when it serves human well-being within the constraints of international law.

It is essential to understand the difference between a culture that takes state power as priority (old paradigm, Option B) and a culture that takes human well-being as priority (new paradigm, Option A). The values in the old-paradigm culture have evolved, and continue to evolve. In the late nineteenth and early twentieth centuries, there was a strong association with notions of self-sacrifice (for the fatherland or some other idea) and heroism. As the twentieth century picked itself up from the ashes of war, there was less and less patience for that particular kind of heroism. Following a centuries-old pattern, the old paradigm was forced to pretend it was the new paradigm. Militant nationalism took on phrases such as "making the world safe for democracy" in order to pursue its agenda of dominance through military power and avoid public recognition.

The early twentieth-century version of glorious patriotism persists to some extent, and it must here be emphasized that its basic value of willingness to sacrifice for the good of others is a feature of healthy human psychology, and very much in accord with new-paradigm thinking. Its fatal flaw is that the "service to others" has been subverted to the service of illegitimate political power. Propaganda for war promotes a corrupted version of healthy human psychology. It is not so much the soldiers who are indoctrinated in this madness who are chiefly to blame but all of us who tolerate this malignancy in our culture.

This distinction — between devoting one's life to the service of others following the precepts of international law and devoting one's life to the service of state power following the precepts of militant nationalism — is one that makes a difference between life and death in human history. A positive nationalism is theoretically possible, but in a state that maintains a military-industrial-ideological-political complex, positive nationalism remains largely illusory, constantly undermined by the destructive foreign policy of the state.

The limits of legitimate nationalism are defined in part by international human rights law and the closely related law of non-aggression. International law recognizes both state sovereignty, with the associated right to self-defense against armed attack, and the responsibility of the state to respect and foster basic human rights.

[106]

The limits of legitimate nationalism are further defined by concepts in social psychology such as those that emerge from the work of Erich Fromm (see the section in chapter 1 titled "Pathogenesis: Nationalism and Warfare").

By its constant preparations for war, a state undermines whatever positive contributions it makes anywhere in the world, including within the state itself. Individuals who serve this self-destructive process likewise undermine whatever positive contributions their lives may make. That does not mean that the positive contributions of a militant nationalist state or a professional soldier should be ignored. It means that doing the math of the long-term positive or negative effects of that state or that individual's life must take into account both positive and negative elements of the equation. A militant nationalist culture severely undermines the positive contributions that countless lives of individuals brought up in that culture could otherwise have made.

PRINCIPLE 12
Violence begets violence. Militant nationalism sustains that dynamic in the global community.

Violence begets violence. This is well and widely understood, and easily forgotten. A cycle of violence and threats will tend to be sustained if one of the perpetrators refuses to acknowledge responsibility for the downward spiral. Warfare is *intentionally* sustained by a warfare system; militant nationalism is its ideology.

Fascism is a particular form of nationalism. Fascism was defeated in World War II, but the victors were also nationalists and, like the fascist states they had defeated, they pursued power through violence and threats of violence. They continue to do so, in flagrant violation of international law. Nationalism has passed the point of diminishing returns. It currently represents a real and present danger to our future.

Militant nationalism provokes endless cycles of violence. This phenomenon has been placed under the magnifying lens in many books, from various perspectives: *In Search of Enemies: A CIA Story* (1978) by John Stockwell, former chief of the CIA Angola Task Force; *Endless Enemies: The Making of an Unfriendly World* (1984) by Jonathan Kwitny, a *Wall Street Journal* reporter; *The Rise and Fall of the Great Powers* (1987) by Paul Kennedy; *Hegemony or Survival: America's Quest for Global Dominance* (2003) by Noam Chomsky; and a recent trilogy (2000–06) by Chalmers Johnson, to mention a few.

The fact that I am a human being is more basic than the fact that I am a citizen of the United States. Militant nationalism threatens the global community of which I am a part, and therefore it threatens me. It also threatens "our troops," as well as women and children in Baghdad and Beijing and Boston, and anyone else who is a human being. *The choice to support militant nationalism is a choice to continue that threat.*

PRINCIPLE 13
Militant nationalism begets militant nationalism.

It has been a while since I saw the film *Cabaret*, but if my memory is on target, a scene in that film, set in the early years of the Nazi movement in Germany, portrays both the seduction of resurgent nationalism and the distaste for that resurgence among a few of the older and wiser Germans at the time. A young man at a German *Wirtschaft* sings an inspiring song about the fatherland, "Tomorrow Belongs to Me," while an older German at one of the tables witnesses this with much less enthusiasm than the singer. The young man is wearing an armband with the Nazi swastika. The old man's expression seems to say, "Oh no, here we go again."

There was already a strong tradition of militant nationalism in Germany well before the 1930s. That nationalism was driven not only by a sense of superiority but also by a sense of victimization. In the 1920s, many Germans believed that they had been dominated and deprived of their rights; that they had been humiliated, particularly by France, at Versailles in 1919; and that their soldiers had been betrayed by citizens of Germany itself during World War I. Other nations had extensive empires; Germany had never had the empire it deserved. The German people deserved far better than this, said the National Socialists, who were determined to restore Germany's national honor and establish a German empire to last a thousand years.

"Tomorrow" belonged to the Nazis for less than twenty-five years, but their militant nationalism triggered other militant nationalisms. The virus spread. It destroyed Germany, boosted the militant nationalism of the major victors of World War II, and exacerbated militant nationalism in the Middle East and elsewhere.

In a sense, Germany and Japan were lucky because their militant nationalism was so overheated that it quickly showed its inherently self-destructive nature. Germany and Japan learned from the disaster, and their subsequent behavior as states shows a considerable advance in worldly wisdom. The victors, and various other states infested with militant nationalism by the events of 1930–1945, would take longer to learn the lesson. One of the iron laws of history appears to be that victory plants seeds of the victor's subsequent defeat. Nazi Germany and Imperial Japan had early victories that encouraged their march down the road to Option B.

Militant nationalism in one state or ethnic group tends to trigger militant nationalist responses in other states and ethnic groups. Remarkably, it does this even when the catastrophic effects of militant nationalism on states such as Germany and Japan of the 1930s are so glaringly apparent.

PRINCIPLE 14
The warfare system sustains and is sustained by a culture of cynicism.

Our culture is characterized by cynicism (self-centeredness). This has economic, social, cultural, and political consequences. We tend to emphasize competition (social Darwinism) over cooperation. We have chosen consumerism, careerism, ego-worship, and polarization of wealth over the alternatives.

In fact, human society depends on cooperation. Robert Axelrod's *The Evolution of Cooperation* (1984), a useful book on this necessity, summarizes information from computer models in which cooperative strategies were found to have an "evolutionary" advantage over cutthroat strategies. The author uses examples from history and politics to illustrate the same concepts.

Competition has its usefulness, but should be kept in per-spective. A healthy society would intentionally direct human competitive-ness toward healthy outcomes for all members of that society. In sports, commerce, and social encounters, competition can enrich community and evoke extraordinary achievement from individuals and groups, who characteristically compete in producing individual and social benefits of various kinds. However, competition can easily be misdirected or driven beyond the point of diminishing returns. Regulatory mechanisms must play a part in discouraging such misdirection and excess. The same principle applies to a healthy global community; hence the need for international law such as the Charter of Economic Rights and Duties of States, the UN Charter, and other instruments of human rights law and humanitarian law.

Richard Wilkinson has long studied the effect of economic and social inequality on advanced industrial states such as the United States, Canada, the United Kingdom, Sweden, and Japan. His observations are immediately relevant to the concept of a healthy society or a healthy global community. Option A and Option B are well expressed in the following passage from *The Impact of Inequality: How to Make Sick Societies Healthier:*

> There are two contrasting ways of dealing with the potential for conflict, and the extent of inequality is a fairly good indicator of where we are on the spectrum between them. At one extreme are the dominance hierarchies, based on power and coercion, in which the lion's share goes to the strongest and social relations are ordered according to differentials in power as a reflection of the potential for conflict [Option B]. At the other extreme is the egalitarian solution, based on fairness and a recognition of each other's needs [Option A].... The contrast is between relationships based on power and fear and those based on social obligations, equality, and cooperation. The extent of inequality in any society tells us a lot about where on this continuum the society lies. (Wilkinson 2005, 22)

The relationships connecting human well-being, wealth, and conflict have been a subject of interest for centuries. In the first letter of Paul to Timothy (New Testament), the writer contrasts the peace that comes from contentment with the ruin and destruction that come from avarice, concluding that "the love of money is the root of all evils." In Hindu tradition, the Bhagavad Gita depicts life as a battle, with a choice of adversaries. One option is to oppose your ego, to subdue the short-sighted selfish desires within you, and live your life in service to others. By engaging in that battle against your ego, you can discover your true self, which is at one with the Creator. To do battle with your ego and transcend your very human limitations is to actualize your uniquely human potential. It is to move beyond the Darwinian constraints affecting animals, to become increasingly at one with God. Self-fulfillment and abiding joy are the rewards of victory in that warfare. The other option is to submit to your ego, which will put you endlessly in conflict with fellow human beings as you pursue personal prestige, pleasures, profit, and ephemeral power. If you choose that battle, it will lead repeatedly and at last to disappointment and abiding sorrow.

These are profound insights into human psychology, and similar themes are extensively developed by twentieth-century social psychologists such as Erich Fromm and Abraham Maslow. This body of literature is encouraging because it points directly to a major cause of contemporary malaise and describes a way by which each of us can counteract it.

Contemporary Western culture is in opposition to such insights into human nature. Its pervasive cynicism is an ideology, of course, however vague or scholarly the formulation of it may be. One of its central doctrines is that acquisitiveness is sublime.

The choice of serving the ego leads to endless strife with others: interpersonally and internationally. To sustain that strife, we have the military-industrial-ideological-political complex. Advertising lures the consumer into an incessant restlessness, to be stilled only by incessant consumption. Wealth is polarized, ensuring that our house will be divided against itself.

The profits in the arms industry, sustained with public resources, help keep the cultural and political institutions inside the old paradigm, working toward Option B. Maintaining these profits becomes an end in itself for some parts of this military-industrial complex. Profits for the arms industry become more important than the life of a six-year-old child in Iraq, and more important than functional democracy, which would threaten the profits system.

Since the public are paying for all this, it is essential to recruit their support for it. In a powerful state, that is particularly easy to do. Since every powerful state is conveying significant benefits to the public and has much in its history to be proud of, the maps provided by the state have only to emphasize those benefits and reasons for pride. The atrocities committed by the state are ignored, obscured, or rationalized. For targeted adversaries, the emphasis is reversed. This leads to ways of thinking such as:

- Our weapons of mass destruction are okay; our adversaries' weapons of mass destruction are not okay.
- When we kill tens of thousands of people, it is an unfortunate necessity in pursuit of a noble goal; when our adversary kills tens of thousands of people, it is an atrocity.
- When we invade another country and overthrow its government, it is an act of liberation; when our adversary does the same, it is an act of aggression.

And so on and so forth.

The impoverishment of large parts of society and of the global community — and the sense of need for consumer goods, acceptance, and security — ensures an unending flow of recruits to military organizations. In Hubert Sauper's brilliant documentary film *Darwin's Nightmare* (2004) about events in Tanzania, two of the individuals interviewed make clear that they are willing to be agents of death to others because their economic straits make it necessary. One of them is a middle-aged Tanzanian man working as a night watchman, who explains why Tanzania needs a war. If there were a war, he says, the government would need soldiers, and they would pay the soldiers well, and that would give Tanzanian men brighter prospects for the future.

That's in Africa. Where we live, the major newspapers and news magazines provide the intellectual framework, broadcast media and parades promote the popular versions of militant nationalism, politicians in Congress ensure the continuation of public funding, and the financially disadvantaged provide the hands-on dirty work that serves the system. The ideology ensures that soldiers have an identity (an immortality system); the public funding ensures they get a paycheck. And so the sickness continues.

Beyond a certain point (diminishing returns), investments in "defense" become negative capital. Public resources are diverted from education, health care, and other programs that could have promoted human creative potential. This diversion occurs not only within the superpower state but also within states that feel threatened by the growing aggressiveness of the superpower, and by other states naïve enough to follow the example set by the superpower. By militarizing and destabilizing the international community, this use of public resources also undermines the security of citizens in the militant nationalist state itself.

Karl Marx and a good many modern economists have argued that people tend to think the way they do because of the material conditions of their existence. In other words, the reality they have to deal with influences their paradigms; the territory influences the map. Of course, this must be true. A friend of mine whose earlier life was spent in Eastern Europe once told me that in his opinion, none of the inter-ethnic violence in that part of the world would have taken place if everyone had had a job and a secure future.

It is also true that the map influences the territory: the way people think influences the reality they have to deal with. Public relations experts, the advertising industry, philosophers, historians, and parents who are trying to persuade their child to eat his spinach — in short, most of us — understand this pretty well. If you are trying to persuade people to buy your product, you give them a sales pitch. Both ideology and polarized wealth sustain the warfare system.

Recall that the world's major spiritual traditions have often created Option A challenges to the Option B status quo, but were then co-opted back into Option B. Historically, cultures that adopted Christianity rationalized their warfare and their polarized wealth and power in various ways. In a medieval society, the poor would always be with us, but each part of society had obligations to the other parts, and all were included in God's plan for the world. And of course the essential transition from Option A to Option B Christianity involved the concept that war could be used to promote God's purpose in the world. How convenient!

There was little support for a rise from rags to riches in such a world. Each individual had his or her place, and being a good person meant knowing your place and staying there. A little later, after the Industrial Revolution, it became possible to eliminate poverty, and many people thought that's exactly what would happen. Thorstein Veblen didn't think so and presented his reasons in his 1899 book, *The Theory of the Leisure Class*. With increasing wealth, he said, any barbarian would be attracted to the possibility of seizing as much as possible for himself. And since barbarians were still very much with us, said Veblen, poverty was likely to persist. Writing in the late nineteenth century, Veblen gave us memorable phrases such as "conspicuous consumption." Many of his readers thought he was just a humorist.

It turned out that his prediction was exactly right. Making a lot of money had already become quite acceptable after the Reformation in Europe and was all the rage by the 1920s in North America. The association of greed and virtue happened in societies of people who considered themselves Christians. In *The Protestant Ethic and the Spirit of Capitalism*, originally written in 1904–05, Max Weber provides an account of how a religion that had emphasized the virtues of poverty began to accommodate the entrepreneur. It was connected with the wonderful idea that as the entrepreneur became richer and richer, he would give more and more to society, and that his increasing wealth was a sign that he was on good terms with the Lord.

The history of thinking about economics and rich and poor is vast. Adam Smith and many other contributors to economic paradigms were concerned not only with wealth production but also with human well-being. This tradition has become increasingly marginalized in contemporary mainstream economic thought. A pragmatic guide that puts some of that history into perspective is *For the Common Good: Redirecting the Economy toward Community, the Environment, and a Sustainable Future* (1994) by Herman E. Daly and John B. Cobb, Jr. The book represents a collaboration of an economist (Daly) with a theologian (Cobb) and provides the kind of binocular vision that other works on economics so often lack.

The rationalizations for warfare and for helping the rich get richer have often made reference to human rights. Thus, in Charles Krauthammer's (2005) map of (way of thinking about) the invasion of Iraq, we find emphasis on the "democracy" that U.S. armed forces brought to Iraq (see chapter 5.) And in Milton Friedman's (1999) map of "capitalism" in the global community, we find an emphasis on its positive relationship to "freedom." The destructive effects of an invasion supported by Krauthammer or of the international economic order favored by Friedman are ignored, denied, obscured, or rationalized. A skilled mapmaker must be aware of his purpose and design his maps accordingly.

Here again, it is important to refer to the navigation system provided by Martin Luther King Jr. We can orient ourselves with reference to our priorities. The priority of the public relations experts and old-paradigm intellectuals who work for the warfare system is power. My priority is different from theirs, and so the map you are reading here is different from their maps.

The fact that the poor are particularly vulnerable to military recruitment raises a related question. How can we create alternatives — new-paradigm careers that will assure capable young people of food, clothing, shelter, and a promising future for their families? How can we redirect the economy to give them Option A as a realistic choice for their lives and their work? That's a problem we are going to have to solve, and the sooner the better.

Understanding the reciprocal support connecting militarism with our economic, cultural, and political institutions is an essential part of the curriculum for global citizenship (Option A). It is essential to political, economic, social, and cultural self-awareness. In the paragraphs that follow, I make reference to three writers on globalization—Thomas Friedman, Naomi Klein, and Joseph Stiglitz. For further reading relevant to the practice of global citizenship, I recommend David C. Korten's book *When Corporations Rule the World* (2001) and related work found at www.pcdf.org.

British military power was an essential enforcer for British imperialism in the nineteenth and early twentieth century. Today, U.S. armed forces play an analogous role as enforcers of globalization, free markets, and neo-liberalism. Thomas Friedman, who is somewhat enthusiastic about these economic paradigms, expresses it this way:

> The most powerful agent pressuring other countries to open their markets for free trade and free investment is Uncle Sam, and America's global armed forces keep these markets and sea lanes open for this era of globalization, just as the British navy did for the era of globalization in the nineteenth century. (1999, 381)

Friedman refers to a "winner-take-all world," in which America currently has "the winner-take-a-lot system." He is aware of globalization's "downsides," but does not emphasize them; he prefers to look on the bright side. By contrast, Naomi Klein does emphasize them and sees them as being inherent in the system of globalization in its contemporary form. She refers to the system driving globalization as "corporatist."

> A more accurate term for a system that erases the boundaries between Big Government and Big Business is not liberal, conservative, or capitalist but corporatist. Its main characteristics are huge transfers of public wealth to private hands, often accompanied by exploding debt,

an ever-widening chasm between the dazzling rich and the disposable poor, and an aggressive nationalism that justifies bottomless spending on security. For those inside the bubble of extreme wealth created by such an arrangement, there can be no more profitable way to organize a society....

This book is a challenge to the central and most cherished claim in the official story — that the triumph of deregulated capitalism has been born of freedom, that unfettered free markets go hand in hand with democracy. Instead, I will show that this fundamentalist form of capitalism has consistently been midwifed by the most brutal forms of coercion, inflicted on the collective body politic as well as on countless individual bodies. (2007, 18)

Providing detailed analyses of specific cases, Klein shows that it is exactly in the context of disasters that the rich often have opportunities to become richer and gain increasing control of goods and services. For example, when the democratically elected government of Chile, headed by Allende, was overthrown in 1973 and replaced by the dictatorship of Pinochet, the dictator imposed policies that had been conceived by Milton Friedman and his disciples at the Chicago School of economics. Milton Friedman was one of the enthusiasts of economics as a science, with "laws" that were as inescapable as the law of gravity. In Chile, apparently, the Chicago School of economists was trying to find experimental conditions optimal for testing their economic theories. It was only in the context of the political shock of the violent events in Chile in 1973 and subsequent years that the policies favored by the Chicago School could be imposed. These policies had devastating effects on the lives of many Chileans.

In the overthrow of Allende, U.S. covert operations had been instrumental; in the case of Iraq, U.S. policies played a much more public and dominating role. Naomi Klein provides her analysis of events, particularly those following the invasion of Iraq by U.S. armed forces in 2003. Here the point made by Thomas Friedman, that "Uncle Sam" is the most powerful agent pressuring other countries to open their markets for trade and investment, is illustrated with a specific and detailed case study.

Using Klein's analysis along with those of other authors, it is possible to see with much greater clarity some absolutely essential features of the real world. In particular, it becomes clear that concepts inherent in international human rights law, such as a duty of states to use their resources for the benefit of all their citizens, become marginalized or swept off the table in the corporatist paradigm for globalization.

Based on her experience and attention to conditions and events, Naomi Klein insists not on the elimination of market systems but on the necessity of applying some well-recognized ways of improving outcomes. Klein makes specific reference to a mixed, regulated economy that has had some well-documented successes in the twentieth century, with John Maynard Keynes as one of its architects.

An economist who has been directly involved in decision-making in the U.S. government and at the World Bank, Joseph Stiglitz shared the 2001 Nobel Prize in Economics. Like Friedman and Klein, he is aware of the detrimental effects of globalization, but in his book *Gobalization and Its Discontents*, he contributes his own perspective to the literature on globalization.

> I have written this book because while I was at the World Bank, I saw firsthand the devastating effect that globalization can have on developing countries, and especially the poor within those countries. I believe that globalization — the removal of barriers to free trade and the closer integration of national economies — can be a force for good and that it has the *potential* to enrich

everyone in the world, particularly the poor. But I also believe that if this is to be the case, the way globalization has been managed, including the international trade agreements that have played such a large role in removing those barriers and the policies that have been imposed on developing countries in the process of globalization, need to be radically rethought. (2002, ix-x)

Stiglitz emphasizes misguided policies of the International Monetary Fund in his analysis. His perspective differs somewhat from that of Klein, but he reaches conclusions that are in many ways complementary to hers.

The IMF's policies, in part based on the outworn presumption, that markets, by themselves, lead to efficient outcomes, failed to allow for desirable government interventions in the market, measures which can guide economic growth and make *everyone* better off. What was at issue, then, in many of the disputes that I describe in the following pages, is a matter of *ideas*, and conceptions of the role of government that derive from those ideas. (2002, xii)

The same policies that polarize wealth and create a dysfunctional global community can bring down even those who are doing relatively well. The history of the 1929 stock market crash and the subsequent worldwide depression is accessible to every well-informed person. Financial setbacks that affect rich folks like me have received considerable attention in the major media recently, and in the work of contemporary economists. The wiser economists are certainly conscious of the need for attention to the public space and the common good if we are to have a healthy economy.

One of my acquaintances is a young man from Oklahoma, Joshua Key, whose limited economic prospects were part of the reason he enlisted in the U.S. Army. Contrary to what he had been led to expect, he was posted to Iraq, where his experience included participating in raids on homes of Iraqis. Returning to the United States, he faced a crisis when he was supposed to report for another tour of duty in Iraq. He chose not to report, and he and his family fled to Canada, joining a growing number of war resisters. He also chose not to remain silent about his experience and co-authored a book about it, from which the following testimony is an excerpt:

> I had always seen my fellow Americans as upholders of justice in the world, but now I had come face to face with the indecency of our actions in Iraq.... We had become a force for evil, and I could not escape the fact that I was part of the machine. (Key 2007, 108, 110)

My own tour of duty with the US Army Medical Corps (two years, of which I spent a little over one year in South Korea during the Vietnam war and the rest in the United States) was much more comfortable that Joshua Key's, but I learned similar things. I also learned how much personal courage it takes to resist the warfare system. Joshua Key showed a fortitude that I did not have.

Two other young men I know are from middle-class backgrounds in New York and were among the dinner table guests one night in Schenectady when I asked: "Why are we so impotent as citizens?" Jeff answered that we think of ourselves as consumers, not as citizens, while Andrew responded that we think there is nothing we can do that will make a difference, so we prefer not to think about it.

A great deal of public policy is based on unrealistic and naïve assumptions that relegate citizens to the role of spectators. "You can't change the world" is one of the mottoes for this ideology of impotence (or "cult of impotence," to use Canadian journalist Linda McQuaig's term). Linked to this fallacy is the concept that you need to be a certified "expert" on world affairs to participate substantively in the decisions and actions that shape history. The idea that citizens have no substantive role to play in the conduct of public and world affairs is insolent and arrogant, of course, and it is also false on the evidence. Yet the idea somehow manages to maintain its credibility in our culture.

It would be a mistake to underestimate the magnitude of the problems we will face in the century ahead. It would be a bigger mistake to assume they cannot be solved. And perhaps the greatest mistake is to assume that as citizens we are not competent or responsible for the work of identifying these problems and finding solutions.

Many people seem to think they elect a political representative to be a scapegoat for their own failure of responsibility as citizens. The limits of possibility for the organization of power are — by their nature — such that, if mature and wise and loving human beings who respect human potential and human rights do not engage in the public space, then it will be dominated by people who are something less. The culture that will create or solve the major problems we will face, and create or extinguish the brightest possibilities for our future, is the one to which we contribute by our ways of thinking — including our assumptions about our own power, humanity, and responsibility.

PRINCIPLE 15
Militant nationalism is associated with contempt for law, democracy, and human rights. It is associated with the pathology of power.

In *The Pathology of Power*, Norman Cousins notes that power tends to "distort and damage the traditions and institutions it was designed to protect" (1987, 23). In a democracy, all legitimate political power is based in law and constrained by law. The United States has made important contributions to the concept of the rule of law, and the evolution of the law in the United States was instrumental in some of its landmark advances of the twentieth century, such as enfranchisement of women and advances in civil rights.

Undermining that very positive tradition have been the pathological tendencies associated with power in the United States. It is easy to recall the contempt for law and democracy in many other states, such as the erstwhile German Democratic Republic or USSR, but that knowledge is not nearly so important in practice as knowledge of how this pathology is manifest within our own government and its allies. Critical attention to the history of U.S. foreign policy, and a reading of many of the sources cited in this book, can provide the relevant background for this fifteenth principle. An even quicker way is to pay attention to the pronouncements of various intellectuals who support the pathology, some of whom have held prominent positions in the U.S. government themselves. That quip by Henry Kissinger captures the concept memorably and concisely: "The illegal we do immediately; the unconstitutional takes a little longer."

In the international arena, Kissinger was well aware of the disregard for international law among powerful states:

> Empires have no interest in operating within an international system; they aspire to be the international system.... That is how the United States has conducted its affairs in the Americas, and China throughout most of its history in Asia. (1994, 21)

More recently John Bolton (U.S. ambassador to the United Nations with the George W. Bush administration) had this to say about international law:

> It is a big mistake for us to grant any validity to international law even when it may seem in our short-term interest to do so — because, over the long term the goal of those who think that international law really means

anything are those who want to constrict the United States. (As told to *Insight* magazine February 28, 1999.)

International law (interpreted to mean what it says) and a functional democracy (meaning active citizen engagement in governance) are threats to the "national interest," as nicely stated here:

> Since the Cold War's end, a number of international organizations, human rights activists, and states have worked to transform the traditional law of nations ... into something akin to an international regulatory code. This "new" international law purports to govern the relationship of citizens to their governments, affecting such domestic issues as environmental protection and the rights of children. Among other things, it would: nearly eliminate the international use of military force.... Recast as such, international law constitutes a real and immediate threat to U.S. national interests. (Rivkin and Casey 2000)

Old-paradigm legal experts sometimes argue that international law must simply accommodate the paradigm of power politics (with its murderous effects on human beings). One such expert, writing on the failure of the UN Charter and the UN Security Council to deter the United States from its 2003 invasion of Iraq, had this to say:

> A second, related lesson from the UN's failure is thus that rules must flow from the way states actually behave, not how they ought to behave. (Glennon 2003)

Militant nationalism is associated with contempt for law, democracy, and human life. The foregoing quotations are a small sample of intellectual support for this pestilence.

PRINCIPLE 16

*Militant nationalism has destructive effects
on individuals, families, and communities.*

At its core, militant nationalism is a profoundly pessimistic ideology. It assumes that the global community will always be dysfunctional and that individuals must subordinate themselves to state power, accepting cycles of violence in the contests for power among states. It should not be surprising to find such attitudes associated with personal unhappiness. The pessimism of the ideology has profoundly destructive psychological effects on individuals within the militant nationalist state. Post-traumatic stress disorder and violence in military families are familiar problems. The family violence includes violence of husbands against wives and children, and violence of individuals against themselves. A recent study in Australia revealed that the *children* of Australian veterans of the Vietnam War were committing suicide three times as often as other Australians their age. Suicide is but one indicator of profound personal unhappiness. (For background on the Australian study, see http://www.aihw.gov.au/publications/index.cfm/title/5861).

One of militant nationalism's destructive effects on individuals is the psychopathology of domination and subordination. This relationship is explicit policy in the military and in political hierarchies. Much of the important progress in the history of the past two centuries has been related to the rejection of various forms of domination: monarchical power, slavery, the subjugation of women, and so on. That progress is incomplete, and militant nationalism is part of the next major barrier.

It is easy for me to recognize many signs of the psychological and physical damage that militant nationalism and warfare impose on individuals, families, and communities. It is much more difficult for me to estimate the extent to which militant nationalism encourages criminal behavior among returning veterans or the general public. The violence in which he participated as a U.S.

soldier in the Middle East may have played a role in Timothy McVeigh's act of violence in Oklahoma. The extent of this kind of corrosive effect on our society remains largely unknown, but it is not unheralded. Decades ago, Supreme Court Justice Louis D. Brandeis pointed out that when the government becomes a criminal, it sets an example for its citizens.

> Decency, security and liberty alike demand that government officials shall be subjected to the same rules of conduct that are commands to the citizen. In a government of laws, existence of the government will be imperiled if it fails to observe the law scrupulously. Our Government is the potent, the omnipresent teacher. For good or for ill, it teaches the whole people by its example. Crime is contagious. If the Government becomes a law-breaker, it breeds contempt for law; it invites every man to become a law unto himself; it invites anarchy. (*Olmstead v. United States* 277 U.S. 438 [1928])

Brandeis was referring to national laws; the same principle applies to the law of nations. If senators and presidents and Harvard intellectuals have contempt for the law, why should anyone expect higher standards in the streets?

Militant nationalism is a deeply pessimistic ideology based on the false premise that we have no choice but to continue destroying each other. If we confine ourselves within the prison of this premise, we will never be able to explore the possibilities of a healthy global community.

PRINCIPLE 17
A militant nationalist government is a threat to its own citizens.

Militant nationalism takes as the first priority the power of the state; human well-being is relegated to a lower priority. At its peak in the first half of the twentieth century, the ideology of militant nationalism was a major part of the pathogenesis of two world wars.

In *The Rise and Fall of the Great Powers* (1987), Paul Kennedy examines the economic dimensions of this connection between power rivalries of states and their subsequent decline. Any government that decided to enter the contest for "the grandest tiger in the jungle" had to raise money to pay for its participation in the contest. Taxes were one source of such funding; borrowing was another. Either route, or any combination thereof, gradually or swiftly led toward bankruptcy of the state. The "winners" could be expected to drift toward bankruptcy a little more slowly than the "losers."

If we examine the financing involved for the world's last remaining superpower, we find both financing devices in place. Public funding provides several hundred billion dollars a year in support of the warfare system in the United States. As anyone paying attention to the U.S. economy will understand, the United States is in a very unstable financial position, with an enormous national debt, and is possibly at the threshold of a major economic setback.

Predictably, after the publication of Paul Kennedy's book, there were sustained efforts from the old-paradigm intellectual community to provide reasons why the United States was an exception to the rule. Such efforts reappeared at intervals after economic disasters in other parts of the world. Economic disasters in East Asia and Argentina were followed by articles in the North American press about why it would not happen here. Not long before the watershed events of September 11, 2001, we find Thomas Friedman commenting on Paul Kennedy's thesis in the following way:

> Kennedy traced (quite brilliantly) the decline of the Spanish, French and British empires, but he concluded by suggesting that the American empire would be the next to fall because of its own imperial overreaching.... I believe Kennedy did not appreciate enough that the relative decline of the United States in the 1980s, when he was writing, was part of America's preparing itself for and adjusting to the new globalization system — a process that much of the rest of the world is going through only now. Kennedy did not anticipate that under the pressure of globalization America would slash its defense budget, shrink its government and shift more and more powers to the free market in ways that would prolong its status as a Great Power, not diminish it. (1999, xx)

In the corridors of power, delusion springs eternal. The enormous investment in the negative capital of warfare is one aspect of the threat that militant nationalist governments pose to their citizens. Another is the intuitively obvious fact that the creation of a monstrous military apparatus in any state — by its very existence — will quickly be perceived as a threat to other states, forcing them to develop some response in kind. Threats provoke counter-threats.

Any government that threatens another government thereby constitutes a threat to the global community. Since citizens of the militant nationalist state are part of the global community, every militant nationalist government is a threat to the citizens of its own state. The militarily most powerful state in the global community, the United States, is no exception to this rule. In the political culture of the United States, there is contempt for the UN Charter, for other basic principles of international law, and for the

United Nations itself. The consequences of that lawlessness will be visited upon all of us for a long time to come.

PRINCIPLE 18
Militant nationalism is particularly toxic to the global community when it dominates the culture and politics of a powerful state. Powerful states are the major violators of international law and the major threats to global community and human survival.

Weak or fractured states such as Colombia, the former Yugoslavia, Rwanda, and Sudan have committed murderous atrocities and violations of international law, but the criminality of such states does not have the global reach of a superpower and cannot corrupt and obstruct the UN Security Council and other institutions designed to advance the purposes of international law. Only powerful states are capable of that kind of obstruction and perversion of international law and its institutions.

The essence of any atrocity is the outrage against human well-being. Somehow when the perpetrator of such an outrage is a powerful state, the culture of that state makes it okay. A truly powerful state can impose policies, with international collusion, that lead to the deaths of half a million children. A suicide bomber cannot kill so many. In the minds of those who have succumbed to the anesthesia of the powerful state's culture, the obscenity perpetrated by the superpower that kills half a million is unfortunate but sort of acceptable, while the obscenity perpetrated by a suicide bomber that kills a few is an intolerable outrage. And that perception is part of the pathology that keeps both kinds of atrocity going.

Nationalism can become particularly virulent in a powerful state. That insight is essential. If we face the identity of warfare as a disease, militant nationalism can be seen as an ideological pathogen. The ideological pathogen cannot cause the disease by itself, but it contaminates the political process and persuades politicians to funnel the state's economy, its metabolic capacity, into fuel for the fire. The pathogen also infects the major cultural institutions and the public.

"The Case of Iraq" (chapter 5) illustrates these disease mechanisms for both Iraq and the United States. Saddam Hussein was a murderous violator of international law, and his violent nationalism arose within a context of murderous violations by states far more powerful than Iraq. From those states, the government of Iraq first received support, then savage reprisal, for its violations. Both phases of Western policy toward Iraq radically betrayed the fundamental purposes and principles of international law.

The treachery and violence of governments have historically been tolerated or supported by citizens and allies. A standard way of achieving that toleration and support is the argument that "our" treachery and violence are necessary to overcome the treachery and violence of our adversary. In 2003 the government of the United States carried this to a *reductio ad absurdum*. Its invasion of Iraq killed tens of thousands of people and was conducted on the basis of the argument that the government of Iraq might do something similar in the future. Violence and treachery were promoted on the pretext of preventing violence and treachery.

To the extent that these perfectly obvious insights are understood and begin to influence the culture and the policies within the most powerful states and their allies, the global community can begin to move toward Option A.

PRINCIPLE 19
International power politics provoke internal repression, dictatorships, and civil wars.

The U.S. government does not routinely place its Japanese citizens in concentration camps, but it did so during World War II. It does not ordinarily threaten to end the livelihood of intellectuals who would write a book like this one, but it did so during the McCarthy era, and earlier, through activities of the House Un-American Activities Committee in response to perceived threats from "international communism." It does not ordinarily slaughter its citizens, but it did slaughter tens of thousands of them during the Civil War (1861–1865) for reasons of nationalism. It does not ordinarily carry out ethnic cleansing, but in its early days the United States carried out acts of ethnic cleansing against parts of the indigenous North American population. It can be safely assumed that if there were serious efforts in progress to overthrow the government of the United States, the government would increase its internal repression.

Internal repression is part of a pathological process, typically in response to some threat, real or perceived, legitimate or illegitimate. The threat is almost invariably related to militant nationalism and violent contests for power among states. The principle holds true for states far more repressive than the United States. In 1954 the elected government of Guatemala under Jacobo Arbenz was overthrown with the help of the American CIA. The series of dictatorships that followed quickly made Guatemala one of the world's most notorious charnel houses. This murderously repressive government enjoyed the support of the U.S. government for years. The arguments for supporting the atrocities were based on threats from "international communism."

The history of Guatemala from 1954 onward had many consequences, including an early lesson for Fidel Castro and others involved in planning the Cuban revolution. The Cuban revolution was of course a response to repression from the pre-revolutionary government of Cuba. The revolutionaries learned this from Guatemala (and previous examples of U.S. intervention in Latin America): any government with a vision challenging U.S. hegemony runs the danger of being overthrown through internal subversion supported by CIA covert operations. Open governments such as that of Jacobo Arbenz are particularly vulnerable to internal subversion. Some measures to preserve state security are necessary to survival. Under existing circumstances, there will have to be a fairly pervasive internal security apparatus to ward off threats to the state. That was the lesson. The governments of many states throughout the world have understood one or another version of the lesson. The support for subversion might come from China or the United States or Russia or some other source, but subversion will provoke measures to counteract it.

Were these threats real? Did the United States really face any significant threat from its Japanese citizens during World War II, at a level sufficient to justify internment? Did the dictatorship of Guatemala really face a significant threat from citizens of Guatemala sufficient to justify imposing a reign of terror? Did the post-revolutionary Cuban government really face a significant threat from U.S. subversion? These questions, as well as whether (assuming they were real) the threats were *legitimate* (whether for example the overthrow of the Guatemalan dictatorship by citizens of Guatemala could be justified), can be examined for each individual case. For present purposes, the point is that internal repression and violence do not occur in isolation. They occur in the context of other problems that have global dimensions. *They occur as part of the pathology associated with militant nationalism in the global community.*

Departures from fundamental human rights standards will predispose a state or region to cycles of violence and repression. When people have been deprived of power and basic rights beyond some critical point, the resulting crisis may lead to infighting, even to the point of genocide, or the development of a defense mechanism — one or another form of militant nationalism. Like militant nationalism, civil war and internal repression are elements of a pathology that must be understood to be effectively treated or prevented.

To end the cycles of violence and repression, a series of changes are necessary, of which two are emphasized here: 1) reliable progress in a rule of law protecting human rights worldwide, and 2) an end to the threats of governments against other governments, including covert actions. To bring all dictatorships to an end, we must abandon Option B and make the paradigm shift. Failing this, it can reasonably be expected that dictatorships and internal repression will persist.

PRINCIPLE 20
Militant nationalism is an ideology whose time has passed.

Any ideology is a fraud if it claims to be humanitarian, yet dismisses the constraints of international humanitarian and human rights law. It is recognizable, for example, by the primary importance it places on support for "our troops" and the lesser importance it places on the lives of civilians endangered by "our troops." That is the ideology of militant nationalism. It is currently the dominant ideology in our culture, but its time has passed. Militant nationalism is a toxic remnant, a dangerous anachronism from a time in human history when we did not have nuclear weapons. In our time, it is an ongoing threat to the conditions of human existence and the chances of human survival.

The corruption, waste, and hypocrisy necessary to sustain militant nationalism have critically undermined its credibility. Enormous resources are currently being squandered to maintain this ideology, making our current options and our future very dark indeed. The sooner those resources are redirected toward Option A, the sooner we will see the light of dawn.

[133]

The evidence is in. Militant nationalism is an ongoing and perhaps terminal danger to our security. With time and the sustained level of risk inherent in the militant nationalist paradigm, disasters such as the destruction of Iraq and the incineration of the World Trade Center will recur, in various forms. This raving insanity will continue until militant nationalism is brought under control and governments are brought into compliance with the rule of law — or until, having squandered our resources together as fools, we have eliminated the possibility of continuing. Option B, the choice to continue violent contests for power in contempt of law, may lead, in this century or the next, to the end of the game. At the very least it will continue the profligate waste of human life and human potential that has been its ignominious legacy in our time. The hundreds of billions of dollars spent on militarism each year by the U.S. government and by other governments are steadily undermining the human security of Americans and others in the global community. In a democracy, citizens are ultimately responsible for solving such problems.

Each of us leaves a record of some part of what the human spirit can be. For each of us, our life will be our legacy. Each era, each generation, also leaves its legacy. This time, our time, is our chance, and it will not come again. We face our share of danger and opportunity. Complacency will increase the danger and waste the opportunity. Militant nationalism is an ideology that has robbed humanity of its potential. The sooner we put it behind us as a global community, the sooner and better we can explore the farther reaches of human potential.

CHAPTER FIVE

The Case of Iraq

In 2003 military forces from the United States and the United Kingdom invaded Iraq. By the time of that invasion, the economic sanctions, which had been imposed on Iraq more than a decade earlier, were already estimated to have cost the lives of more than half a million Iraqis, many of them children under the age of five. On May 12, 1996, Madeleine Albright, speaking as a U.S. government official on the television show *60 Minutes*, expressed the view that the cost of several hundred thousand deaths among Iraqi children had been "worth it."

The invasion of Iraq in 2003, and the events it precipitated, had by late 2004 caused tens of thousands of additional deaths among Iraqi civilians. In the first year of the invasion and occupation, most of those deaths were directly caused by the invading military forces, and since that time most have been caused directly or indirectly by the occupation. More than a million Iraqi lives have been extinguished or devastated beyond hope of repair since January 1, 1991. For none of those lives can the perpetrators of that catastrophe provide even a remotely adequate answer to the question: What has the world lost because of what you have done?

These are facts, but whether these things are good or bad, or of any importance whatever, is not an empirical question. In the old paradigm, these deaths are acceptable because they are leading toward a "noble goal." In that way of thinking, the governments of the United States and the United Kingdom are not a threat to international peace.

The map is not the territory. How we think about the case of Iraq will not encompass that part of reality, whether we use old-paradigm or new-paradigm ways of thinking. But it will certainly influence the reality of the world a century from now. How *you* choose to think about the case of Iraq will be part of that process. We choose our maps, those maps influence our action (and our inaction), and our action (or inaction) changes the course of history.

The axioms and principles presented in the foregoing chapters could be illustrated with any armed conflict, particularly one in which any of the most powerful states are directly involved in the violence. The case of Iraq is chosen for reasons indicated earlier: it directly involved the world's military superpower; the conceptual framework used to rationalize Western policies will be familiar to most readers; and as citizens of the United States or Canada or both, we have a more direct responsibility for what the government of the United States did to Iraq (with the collaboration of various governments including Canada's) than we have for, say, what the government of Sudan is doing in Darfur.

But a study of this or any conflict does not merely illustrate the concepts. When each case is studied within the framework of the new paradigm, it points to further basic principles or corollaries. It produces basic as well as particular new learning, which can then be applied to understanding other cases and to responding to events constructively (toward Option A). Study of a conflict or any epoch in history cannot illuminate reality in this way if the conflict, the conditions, and the events are perceived only within the conceptual framework of the old paradigm. The lessons of history are limited by the paradigm within which the case is studied.

The following synopsis is intended as an illustration of concepts presented in other parts of this book. As a guide to what has happened in Iraq, it cannot possibly substitute for the excellent and ongoing work of others: Robert Fisk, Phyllis Bennis, Dilip Hiro, Naomi Klein, Paul William Roberts, and many others who have through the years contributed to the necessary paradigm shift. References to works by several of these authors are included in the section on Further Reading.

Under ten headings, the synopsis presents a new-paradigm way of thinking about the case of Iraq. The old-paradigm map will be more familiar to most readers, and will receive attention only for comparative purposes here.

Saddam Hussein and the U.S. government before and after August 1990

Old-paradigm maps use at least two basic approaches to recruit support for Option B. The first is the "political realist" approach, which assumes that the violent contests for power are inevitable and therefore we have no choice but to play the game to win. It focuses on power relationships, game theory concepts, and the like. It prides itself in being "objective," meaning that it will not be much bothered by Saddam Hussein's nationalism and will often support his atrocities if they happen to advance the cleverly conceived goals of our own nationalism.

The second old-paradigm method of persuasion could be referred to as the "crusader" approach, which assumes that there is a battle between good and evil in the world and that "our" violence is essential to ensure the victory of good over evil.

A common solution to the problem of justifying one's aggression is to depict the enemy as evil. If your enemies are pure evil, there is little need for additional explanations of why you want to fight against them. Hence, the more thoroughly one can assimilate the enemy into the myth of pure evil, the less one needs to provide valid reasons for one's aggression. (Baumeister 1997, 85)

The slightly more liberal versions of the crusader approach are a little less self-righteous and a little more inhibited than fundamentalist versions, but otherwise generally similar. The deaths of tens or hundreds of thousands of Iraqis or Japanese or Europeans or Americans are the price we must all be willing to pay in the battle of good against evil.

Prior to August 1990, the political realist approach dominated the representations of Saddam Hussein in the Western media. Hussein's atrocities were generally accepted as part of the inevitable struggles for power in the world, and relatively little attention was devoted to them in the news. With few exceptions, media representations reflected U.S. government policies toward Iraq, which were essentially devoid of the hostility that emerged after August 1990.

After the 1979 revolution in Iran, in which the Shah was overthrown and a theocratic regime under Ayatollah Khomeini assumed power, Saddam Hussein's importance as a potential U.S. ally increased in the calculations of political realists. Khomeini's militant nationalist/theocratic regime was hostile to the secular dictatorship in Iraq, as well as to the Islamic family dictatorships in Kuwait and Saudi Arabia. The United States and other governments supported Saddam Hussein during the 1980s. It was in that decade that Hussein's threat to international peace and his savage violations of human rights were at their peak as Iraq carried out a long war against Iran, subsequently meting out savage retaliation against Iraqi Kurds for their collusion with Iran during the war. The threat and the violations would not have been possible without support from the United States, Kuwait, Saudi Arabia, and others.

Chemical weapons were used against Iran and against the Iraqi Kurds. This was well known to the U.S. government and was largely irrelevant in the maps of political realism — maps that ignore, obscure, or marginalize humanitarian considerations. Therefore, it scarcely made a ripple in the mainstream print or broadcast media.

With Iraq's invasion of Kuwait (a U.S. client state) in August 1990, the U.S. policy priorities shifted again. It is now clear that the U.S. policy objective from that date forward was to replace Saddam Hussein's government with a more compliant regime. For several reasons, this could not be accomplished immediately. Regime change was obviously illegal, and the conduct of operations ejecting Iraq from Kuwait had been conducted under UN auspices, with a good deal of public relations fanfare about a "new era of promise for the UN Charter." Furthermore, the coalition of states that had provided some support for the U.S. forces had been recruited within that framework of a UN initiative, with the limited objective of reversing Iraq's invasion of Kuwait. This context placed constraints on what the United States could do in 1991. There were also other regional strategic considerations at stake in the calculations of the U.S. administration. President George H. W. Bush not only called a halt to the forward movement of U.S. forces, leaving Saddam Hussein in power in Iraq; he also refused to allow U.S. support for a subsequent uprising against Saddam Hussein in southern Iraq. The United States was well aware that Iran was a greater regional power than Iraq. If the Ba'ath government had been toppled in Iraq, the regional influence of Iran might well have expanded and become far more of a challenge to U.S. "national interest" than a chastened and hobbled Saddam Hussein. Based on purely cynical considerations of power politics and public relations, the time was not propitious in 1991 for an immediate removal of Saddam from power. The government of the United States would have to bide its time.

But the maps representing Saddam Hussein shifted instantly in the Western media. From August 1990 onward, they were dominated by the crusader approach, which was perceived as more effective in propaganda for war. The old-paradigm maps about Saddam Hussein are familiar to everyone who followed the news in the 1990s: Saddam Hussein was a brutal dictator, a madman, another Hitler, a threat to international peace, and a violator of international law.

The new-paradigm map accommodates the factual information from the old into a more comprehensive representation of reality. Saddam Hussein was a brutal dictator and a militant nationalist, and the two aspects of his political profile were closely related.

The brutal internal security apparatus of Saddam Hussein was designed exactly to prevent what had happened in Chile in 1973, in Guatemala in 1954, and in Iran in 1953. In each of those cases, a more open government had been overthrown with the help of the U.S. CIA and replaced by a murderous dictatorship, which then enjoyed U.S. government support for years. Those in Iraq who had supported Saddam Hussein's dictatorship no doubt saw it as necessary to protect Iraq from internal conspiracies supported by foreign enemies. Internal repression tends to increase as external and internal threats increase. *Militant nationalism tends to push governments toward internal repression.*

Saddam Hussein used a carrot-and-stick approach to pursue the goal of an independent and unified Iraq. Iraq was to become strong enough to protect its "national interests" in the region, to counter threats from the hostile states that surround Iraq, and to discourage the armed Kurdish insurgency and other internal threats to Iraq's security.

Iraq's oil wealth provided resources for a fairly impressive carrot, including social programs such as free education and health care, and a secular political agenda, advancing the role of women in public life, that had been perceived by many as a model for Arab states. For the Kurds, the carrot included an accord of March 1970, which by regional standards was remarkably progressive: Kurdish was recognized as one of Iraq's national languages, a Kurdish university would be established, and representation of the Kurds in the central government was assured. Edmund Ghareeb's book *The Kurdish Question in Iraq* (1981) is a useful source on this subject. That was the carrot. The stick included savage retaliation for Kurdish treason during the Iran-Iraq war and a murderous internal security apparatus designed to prevent overthrow of the Iraqi government. Saddam Hussein's nationalism, and the support for it among other nationalists in Iraq, made the government of Iraq both a murderous violator of human rights internally and a threat to international peace externally.

Saddam Hussein had a remarkable combination of cleverness, nationalist enthusiasm, addiction to power, and grotesque ignorance of the value of human life. An account of the tyranny of fear even for "friends" of Saddam is given by Zainab Salbi, whose family "enjoyed" a personal relationship with the great leader.

> I hate all wars.... Still, I think the day I learned Saddam Hussein had been removed from power was the happiest day of my life. (Salbi and Becklund 2005, 272)

Saddam Hussein inspired not only fear but also intense hatred, which is easy to detect in the works of various writers about his regime. A vendetta against Saddam is evident in various works published in the West after 1990. Pursuit of that vendetta has already cost hundreds of billions of dollars and hundreds of thousands of lives. The costs are still coming in, with no end in sight.

Militant nationalism creates the conditions under which such poisonous personalities rise to power. Saddam Hussein was a murderer and torturer, but the CIA and Iraqi nationalists each thought at one time or another that he was *their* murderer and torturer, and at one time or another each was right.

U.S. government support for Saddam Hussein, like its hostility to Saddam Hussein, was based on militant nationalism rather than any deep concern for the people of Iraq, Iran, or the United States, either before or after August 1990. Henry Kissinger understood the concept. What he said about covert action applies also to militant nationalism: it should not be confused with missionary work. Or, in other words, never let humanitarian rhetoric deceive you about power politics.

The militant nationalists on both sides of the Iraq conflict thought that somehow they were doing something good. Saddam was moving Iraq, and with it all Arabs, toward a glorious new era in their history. And surely that would have been good if the powers of "evil" — led by the government of the United States — had not extinguished the vision. The presidents of the United States and all their minions were leaders, first in support and then in repudiation, of a murderous dictatorship. But even when the United States supports murderous dictators, can anyone doubt that the United States has done great good in the world?

All of them were murderous violators of the law of nations, which is designed to protect human beings from these hideous contests for power. Their militant nationalism has extinguished hundreds of thousands of lives and darkened the prospects for human survival. Not one of them has the faintest idea of what they have destroyed. From the ethically neutral perspective of political realism, the US-Iraq conflict is normal; in the crusader version, it is an illustration of how a savage dictator was defeated, the triumph of good over evil. These are two versions of old-paradigm maps. In the map presented here, the US-Iraq conflict is an illustration of the pathology that human beings inflict on one another, an affliction that as human beings we should try to bring under control.

The U.S. invasion of Panama, Iraq's invasion of Kuwait, and the 1991 Gulf War

The reader can supply an old-paradigm map as well as I can: The invasion of Kuwait was an unprovoked act of naked aggression. Iraq, on the verge of invading Saudi Arabia, was prevented in the nick of time by Operation Desert Shield. The international response to Iraq's aggression was a rare example of implementing the UN Charter to address a breach of international peace. Iraq refused to withdraw from Kuwait. The ejection of Iraq from Kuwait under the UN banner demonstrated the use of force within the framework of international law.

The U.S. aggression against Panama eight months earlier would be largely irrelevant in old-paradigm maps of Iraq's aggression against Kuwait. However, it is relevant to the issue of establishing a rule of international law, and therefore it is important in the conceptual framework of the new paradigm. The U.S. government was effectively unchallenged when it violated the law in Panama. When Iraq violated the same law, it was destroyed. If implementation of law is inequitable, there can be no rule of law.

Was Iraq's invasion of Kuwait unprovoked?

In 1990, Kuwait was overproducing oil by the standards of OPEC (the Organization of Petroleum Exporting Countries) and causing a fall in world oil prices. This was severely damaging the Iraqi economy, undermining Iraq's efforts to recover from its misadventures with Iran. Iraq's economy was more narrowly based on oil than was Kuwait's or Saudi Arabia's. Kuwait and Saudi Arabia had a broad portfolio of investments, many of which saw increasing profits as world oil prices fell. Iraq didn't have the portfolio, so it was hemorrhaging economic power. Kuwait had also been slant drilling at the Iraq-Kuwait border, siphoning off Iraqi oil. Iraq saw its own sacrifices in the Iran-Iraq war as a defense of Arab governments, including Kuwait's. From the Iraqi government perspective, Kuwait's actions were intentional provocations that almost certainly had U.S. backing. None of that in the least contravenes the fact that Iraq's invasion of Kuwait was an act of aggression and a fundamental violation of international law, but the invasion was hardly unprovoked.

Was Iraq on the verge of invading Saudi Arabia?

The evidence for this is essentially zero, and the evidence against it is compelling. But it was temporarily useful as pretext for getting U.S. troops into Saudi Arabia. A sense of the towering hostility among some Saudis to the presence of foreign troops in their country is conveyed by the attacks ten years later on the World Trade Center and the Pentagon by a group of men from Saudi Arabia. It would have taken a good part of those ten years to conceive, plan, prepare, and execute the attacks of September 11, 2001. Militant nationalism killed several thousand civilians in the United States on that day. Iraq's militant nationalism triggered U.S. militant nationalism, which triggered a renegade form of militant nationalism based in Saudi Arabia, illustrating the concept that violence begets violence. In 1990, the subterfuge that Iraq was about to invade Saudi Arabia served as disinformation used to overcome the Saudi resistance to a U.S. military presence. And that disinformation helped maintain the cycles of violence, which included attacks on U.S. territory a decade later.

The events unfolding after Iraq's invasion of Kuwait can best be understood as a conflict between two militant nationalisms, one of a government (Iraq) at a middle level of power by regional standards and the other of a government (the U.S.) with global reach and the ability to subvert international legal institutions to serve its militant nationalism.

It is true and important that chapter VII of the UN Charter was initially invoked as a legitimate response to Iraq's act of aggression in August 1990. The implementation was deeply flawed but even so was pushing events toward a peaceful resolution of the crisis. That process was blocked by the U.S. government under then-President George H. W. Bush. These points will be elaborated in the paragraphs below.

A few months before Iraq's invasion of Kuwait and violation of the very cornerstone of the UN Charter, the U.S. government had violated the same law. In December 1989, George H. W. Bush ordered the U.S. invasion of Panama and the kidnapping of its head of state, Manuel Noriega. A UN Security Council resolution condemning that violation was precluded by the U.S. veto. *The law must be applied equitably.* If there is a law against aggression but that law is not applied when a powerful state commits aggression, there can be no rule of law.

But it was not the inequitable application of the law that has chiefly discredited the UN Security Council in the case of Iraq. It was the fact that the UN Security Council allowed the Charter to be used as pretext for a massive escalation of violence after the invasion of Kuwait, and subsequently to conduct an economic siege of Iraq for the covert purpose of regime change. *The law must be applied consistently in accord with its most fundamental purposes and principles.* When the law against aggression is invoked as pretext for a massive escalation of violence, instead of pursuing an opportunity for peaceful reversal of the aggression, it repudiates the international legal system's most fundamental purposes and principles. There can be no rule of law until treachery of this kind is ended.

Was a peaceful resolution of the crisis available?

Iraq had refused the U.S. demand for an unconditional withdrawal from Kuwait. It was actively seeking a negotiated peaceful withdrawal from Kuwait. Iraq's efforts were predictable under the circumstances and were exactly what mechanisms in the UN Charter were designed to elicit: a resolution of the crisis in a way that reduces the violence and mitigates the conflict. A series of Iraqi offers, conducted behind the scenes, culminated in this one of late December 1990, reported in a Long Island newspaper by Knut Royce:

> Iraq has offered to withdraw from Kuwait if the United States pledges not to attack as soldiers are pulled out, if

foreign troops leave the region, and if there is agreement on the Palestinian problem and on the banning of all weapons of mass destruction, U.S. officials disclosed yesterday.... The White House immediately dismissed the proposal as inadequate since it contains preconditions for a pullout.... A State Department expert described the proposal as a "serious prenegotiation position." (Royce 1991)

Iraq was calling for negotiations to arrange a peaceful resolution of the confrontation, hardly surprising under the circumstances. To test the seriousness of that call, it was necessary to enter into the negotiations. The response of President George H. W. Bush was "There will be no negotiations." The UN Security Council had effectively abdicated its decision-making authority to the U.S. president. By January 1991 the Security Council had for several months been responding as a militant nationalist instrument of U.S. foreign policy.

Each component of the Iraqi proposal for a peaceful withdrawal deserves emphasis. A pledge not to attack military forces that have withdrawn from fortified positions will be understood as an essential element of any legitimate arrangement for peaceful withdrawal. Such an attack would have violated international law, *and such an attack was conducted subsequently against an Iraqi convoy retreating from Kuwait*, in an infamous violation of humanitarian law by U.S. forces known as the "Highway of Death."

Had foreign troops left the region as called for by Iraq, it would have included the withdrawal of U.S. troops from Saudi Arabia. Had that been done in 1991, it is highly likely that the World Trade Center would not have been attacked ten years later by Saudi terrorists bent on forcing a U.S. withdrawal from their country.

An agreement on the Palestinian problem could have been negotiated, as the State Department expert surely understood when he described the Iraqi proposal as a "serious prenegotiation position." Such an agreement was negotiated subsequently and could almost certainly have been negotiated in January 1991 to resolve the Kuwait crisis peacefully. That option was rejected by the Bush administration, in favor of more bloodshed.

The banning of all weapons of mass destruction (WMD) sounds like a bit of a stretch, conceivably a trick put into the proposal by the Iraqis. But that's not likely. What is likely is that Iraq's focus on WMD was driven partly by the Israeli nuclear threat, and it was absolutely essential to put a reference to WMD into their prenegotiating proposal for peaceful withdrawal. Israeli nuclear weapons were threatening the security of other states in the region, and Israel had attacked Iraq in 1981 to abort the Iraqi nuclear development program. It is difficult to imagine that Iraq would not call attention to the WMD issue in its proposal for withdrawal from Kuwait. Legitimate arms control measures take into account the legitimate security needs of all parties affected by the arrangement. A negotiator aiming for a peaceful resolution of the crisis could have gone into the negotiations with a viable counterproposal on this fourth point: for example, to postpone discussions of the regional WMD issues until a set date following the withdrawal of all Iraqi forces from Kuwait. Assuming that the Iraqi government was seeking a face-saving way of resolving the confrontation, such a counterproposal would likely have been successful.

It is therefore highly likely that Iraq would have withdrawn peacefully from Kuwait under an easily negotiated arrangement. Hundreds of thousands of people, many of them children, would have lived. The environmental damage, the discrediting of international law and its institutions, the burgeoning hatred toward the United States for its atrocities and lawlessness — all of this could probably have been avoided. Instead, the possibility of negotiation was rejected, and the scourge of war was imposed on Iraq under the banner of the United Nations.

The conduct of the 1991 assault on Iraq repeatedly violated

humanitarian law in several ways, including the use of force disproportionate to any justifiable military advantage and the destruction of civilian infrastructure such as the capacity to provide potable water. For an analysis of these violations by the United States in its conduct of the 1991 assault on Iraq, see Simons (1998, 194-205).

Violence begets violence; militant nationalism sustains the cycle. Militant nationalism is associated with contempt for law and for human life.

Communication, scholars, the media, and propaganda for war

From August 1990 onward, propaganda for war against Iraq was pervasive in the Western media. The covers of *Newsweek* between August 1990 and April 1991 provided particularly graphic examples of propaganda for war, using standard devices of the war propaganda poster: demonization of the targeted enemy, glorification of war, and framing questions in a way that promoted violent outcomes. But *Newsweek* was only a small part of the propaganda effort. News reports were set in the framework of this propaganda, which continued throughout the 1990s. Published works of Western intellectuals include, years later, Christopher Hitchens' *A Long Short War: The Postponed Liberation of Iraqi* (2002), which supported the impending invasion of Iraq. The U.S. government was driving the propaganda effort. The Canadian government and Western cultural institutions played supporting roles. It was exactly against such incitements to violence that Article 20 of the International Covenant on Civil and Political Rights, adopted by the UN General Assembly in 1966, was directed. Paragraph 1 of the Covenant reads as follows:

1. Any propaganda for war shall be prohibited by law.

Western propaganda for war was largely successful in recruiting public support for the destruction of Iraq, played out over more than a decade and culminating in the invasion of 2003 and the current occupation and ongoing violence. The death toll is estimated now at more than a million. And as always, the death toll is just the tip of the iceberg.

In Rwanda in early 1994, one in a series of waves of violence was cresting. This history of violence was related to the country's environmental degradation, population pressures on available land, and colonial and precolonial versions of militant nationalism. These were incredibly intense pressures, and a mere spark could set the country ablaze. The spark was provided by explicit, publicly broadcast incitement to violence of Hutu against Tutsi. It led to one of the century's major atrocities, the Rwandan genocide. The death toll alone was estimated at 800,000. It was exactly against such incitements to violence that Article 20 of the International Covenant on Civil and Political Rights had been directed. Paragraph 2 of the Covenant reads as follows:

2. Any advocacy of national, racial or religious hatred that constitutes incitement to discrimination, hostility or violence shall be prohibited by law.

The International Covenant on Civil and Political Rights places Article 20 in the context of rights to freedom of expression (Article 19), which the Covenant recognizes must be practiced responsibly.

Canada and the United States have ratified the International Covenant on Civil and Political Rights but have failed to live up to its requirements. Warfare and massacres depend utterly on the ideas that promote them. In Rwanda in 1994, it was radio broadcasts that drove events toward the genocide. In North America from August 1990 onward, it was both print and broadcast media that cultivated the public support for what was done to Iraq. Powerful states (and certain very dysfunctional weaker states) develop ideological systems and maps that promote militant nationalism. Propaganda for war is part of that process.

Facts and comparisons such as these are largely excluded from old-paradigm maps. In a contemporary version of those maps, we might emphasize our freedom of speech and freedom of the press. These points of emphasis are both true and important *as far as they go*. By our advances over the lack of freedom of the press to be found in states such as Saudi Arabia, Nazi Germany, or Saddam's Iraq, we have created opportunities for the next advance.

It is exactly because of the generally greater freedom and access to information that we have the opportunity to advance the necessary paradigm shift. But that freedom of the press and of speech, the advances we have achieved, have not been sufficiently effective against propaganda for war and incitement to violence. Freedom of speech and freedom of the press do not include the right to libel and deliberate propagation of lies.

The old-paradigm maps are confronting a growing skepticism and challenge thanks to the work of authors such as Noam Chomsky, Ed Herman, Norman Solomon, John MacArthur, and Sheldon Rampton; websites such as Truthout, Commondreams, and Counterpunch; and organizations such as Fairness and Accuracy in Reporting and the Center for Media and Democracy, among many others. Excellent books on issues relevant to Iraq have become available; some of these are listed in the section on Further Reading. Yet such books are exceptional; many cultural institutions in North America have been slow to understand the pathology.

Policies imposed by the U.S. and allied governments restricted the flow of information to and from Iraq. Communication between North Americans and citizens of Iraq was sharply limited by those policies. My brother-in-law, a physician from Iraq, was unable to send medicine to his sister in Baghdad during her last months of leukemia, or to reach her by telephone for weeks before she died. That is but one molecule in the iron curtain effect of nationalism on the ability of people to communicate.

Despite such restrictions, many kept the lines open on Iraq, not only journalists but others: organizations such as Voices in the Wilderness, or the group of physicians who surveyed the effects of the Persian Gulf war on infant and child mortality in Iraq (Asherio et al. 1992), and many others. There is considerable freedom of the press in Canada and the United States when compared to states such as Iraq or Saudi Arabia. Those of us who were paying close attention to the conflict benefited from that advantage and have put it to good use.

Economic sanctions and weapons of mass destruction

Any state that possesses nuclear weapons, attacks other states, and kills tens of thousands of people is by definition a threat to international peace. Under international law, mechanisms are prescribed to reduce the violence and threats, not to destroy the state that has perpetrated them. International law does not prescribe the destruction of states that have been threats to international peace, such as Iraq, the United States, or other members of the UN Security Council.

In practice, because of the veto power of its permanent members, the UN Security Council is very limited in its ability to respond when the threats to international peace come from a permanent member of the Council. That makes it all the more important to respond to other threats to international peace in strict accord with the principles and purposes of the UN Charter — that is, not to permit destruction of the offending state under auspices of the United Nations.

That's international law, and a new-paradigm way of responding to threats to the peace. Militant nationalism and old-paradigm thinking have a different approach: It's quite alright to destroy a country that threatens international peace if that country is a targeted adversary of "our" government. It's not alright to destroy us, or even challenge us, if our government is a threat to international peace. In the old paradigm, it is unthinkable to challenge our own government because it is threatening international peace.

The asymmetry of old-paradigm thinking should be informative for any rational observer: we should be able to get away with murder but our enemies should be destroyed for committing the same crime.

During the 1990s, economic sanctions were used as the primary means to ravage Iraqi society and thereby effect regime change. That strategy ultimately failed, and was replaced by a military invasion in 2003. An old-paradigm map on economic sanctions and WMD in Iraq saturated the North American media and scholarly publications during the 1990s, but not without challenge from the new paradigm. In essence, the old-paradigm map held that Iraq was a threat to international peace and that the economic sanctions on Iraq were therefore legal and necessary.

Iraq's programs to develop weapons of mass destruction were an endlessly repeated detail in the North American propaganda for war after 1991. Those programs were very real before 1991, when they were supported by states such as France, the United States, Kuwait, Saudi Arabia, and others. That support was given in part because of concerns from those states about Iranian power and influence in the region. The WMD programs in Iraq after 1991 were hypothetical; there was little evidence to support the idea that they continuing, and a great deal of evidence that they had effectively been stopped. The old-paradigm map made strenuous efforts to obscure the "hypothetical" part. Evidence that they had been stopped was marginalized; evidence that they might be continuing was magnified and manufactured.

The new-paradigm map readily incorporates the factual parts of the old-paradigm map but places them in a more comprehensive representation of reality. The UN Security Council is empowered under the UN Charter to identify threats to international peace, but the Council is required by the Charter to conduct its affairs in accord with the Charter's purposes and principles. Insofar as it fails in this, it violates the Charter, which is its source of legitimacy. Law must be interpreted reasonably and applied equitably for any hope of moving toward Option A. Iraq's threat to international peace was effectively nullified by late 1991 because the international support for that threat had been withdrawn. The maintenance of economic sanctions on Iraq and the subsequent invasion were contrary to the law of the UN Charter. Unless the law is interpreted and applied in accord with its most fundamental purposes and principles, there can be no rule of law.

In the 1990s, the old-paradigm map of Iraq's threat to international peace had a clear but unstated purpose: propaganda for regime change in Iraq. That purpose was in violation of the very cornerstone of international law, the law of non-aggression, which is designed to promote international peace. The old-paradigm map emphasized Iraq's WMD because it was assumed this would best serve the purpose of regime change, while maintaining a façade of promoting peace.

Tim Trevan was an inspector with the UN Special Commission (UNSCOM) team in Iraq. By the time I met him in Geneva in 1998, he was saying that the inspections had outlived their usefulness and it was time to overthrow the Iraqi government. We were both on a panel at a UN conference on biological weapons, and he asked to speak after me because by then we had had several conversations about Iraq and UNSCOM and he wanted to have the last word.

In his book *Saddam's Secrets: The Hunt for Iraq's Hidden Weapons* (1999), Trevan repeated his call for regime change. Close reading of the book confirms that UNSCOM had found no active program for development of WMD. So Trevan came to the following conclusion:

> The threat to international peace and security comes not from the dual-purpose materials and equipment in Iraq, or even from its military capabilities. It comes from the ambitions of the regime, embodied in the person of

Saddam Hussein. The threat to international peace and security will not be removed until the regime's ambitions have been removed or changed....

The obvious and only real solution is for the international community to take concerted action to remove the regime of Saddam Hussein. This would not be an illegal action, inconsistent with the UN Charter's injunction not to interfere in the internal affairs of member states. Saddam, by his actions and ambitions, is a threat to international security and hence forgoes the protection of that injunction. (1999, 389–90)

In other words, the fact that Iraq had discontinued its program for WMD was for Tim Trevan largely irrelevant. And presumably he did not consider the ambitions of the U.S. government — including regime change in Iraq, which his book endorses — a threat to international peace and security. His imaginative interpretation of the UN Charter is a vintage old-paradigm usage of international law.

This and other evidence indicate that UNSCOM included team members who favored overthrow of the Iraqi government. For any Iraqi official interacting with UNSCOM, that bias would potentially be a deadly threat. Such Iraqi officials would have been terminally naïve not to be on their guard against UNSCOM inspections. The "lack of cooperation" by Iraqi officials had exactly this quality of distrust about motives in the UNSCOM team, and, whatever Trevan's intentions, a careful reading of his book conveys exactly that impression.

In the 1980s, Iraq's threat to international peace was supported by other governments, resulting in close to a million deaths in Iran and in Iraq. That support vanished in August 1990. The Iran-Iraq war demonstrated the sharp limitations on Iraq's power even when its military capabilities were at their peak. The subsequent voluminous journalism and scholarship on Iraq's "threat to international peace" was itself largely propaganda for war.

The transparency of this propaganda is evident in an article published in the *Globe and Mail* on November 13, 1998. The title was "Hussein arsenal still impressive" and the subtitle: "Although a mere shadow of 1990s armament, significant threat exists." In the text, retired U.S. Army General Binford Peay is cited as the source of the following insight:

> Mr. Hussein has been gradually improving the quality of his forces. Although he has not managed to even approximate the armament and manpower he wielded when his troops invaded Kuwait in 1990, he *still poses a significant threat to U.S. pilots who might bomb Iraq.* (emphasis added)

In fact, U.S. attacks on Iraqi territory were stepped up the following month, December 1998. To belabor the point: Iraq's "threat to the peace" was its residual capacity to defend itself. Readers familiar with Article 51 of the UN Charter will know that the right of every state to defend itself is recognized under international law.

Legitimate arms control measures take into account the legitimate security needs of all parties to the arrangement. Forcing one state to disarm while leaving other states free to attack it is not a legitimate arms control measure. And when the government imposing the disarmament itself carries out repeated military assaults on the state forced to disarm, the measure becomes an obscenity.

There is no substantive evidence of a program to develop WMD in Iraq after 1991. And yet the death rate from waterborne diseases among Iraqi children increased dramatically in the decade of the 1990s, as if biological weapons were actually being used in the country. Odd, isn't it?

The irony is that in contrast to [weapons of mass destruction], this device — economic sanctions — is deployed frequently, by large states rather than small ones, and may have contributed to more deaths during the post-Cold War era than all weapons of mass destruction throughout history. Comparing the record of these various threats to human well-being is an instructive exercise — and one that casts U.S. policy toward Iraq, which levies sanctions to impede WMD programs, in a new and disturbing light. (Mueller and Mueller 1999)

The UN sanctions on Iraq are believed to have contributed to the deaths of several hundred thousand Iraqi civilians between 1990 and 1996, most of them children under the age of five. The toll was in part related to the additive effect of the 1991 assault on Iraq's civilian infrastructure, particularly its capacity to provide potable water, and the economic sanctions that for years after the 1991 assault continued to hobble Iraq's ability to restore its public health system.

Madeleine Albright's response to the question of whether the deaths of about half a million Iraqi children had been "worth it" has become infamous (*60 Minutes*, May 12, 1996). Two UN officials who had been in charge of the Oil for Food program, Denis Halliday and Hans von Sponeck, resigned over the effects of the sanctions on the civilian population of Iraq. Each of them became a vocal critic of the sanctions. In a critical review of various economic sanctions regimes and criteria for their legality under international law, Belgian jurist Marc Bossuyt came to this conclusion:

The sanctions regime against Iraq is unequivocally illegal under existing international humanitarian law and human rights law.... Once clear evidence was available that thousands of civilians were dying and that hundreds of thousands would die in the future as the Security

Council continued the sanctions, the deaths were no
longer an unintended side effect — the Security Council
was responsible for all known consequences of its actions.
(2000)

In 2000 I was one of a group of Canadians making a presentation
to the Canadian Parliament's Standing Committee on Foreign
Affairs and International Trade (SCFAIT). We presented evidence
of the destructive effects of economic sanctions on the civilian
population of Iraq and on the illegality and blindness of the
policies underlying the sanctions. As a result of our testimony,
SCFAIT unanimously adopted a report recommending that the
government of Canada work to bring the sanctions to an early
end, and restore diplomatic relations with the government of Iraq.
The Canadian government rejected the recommendations.

Militant nationalism, which has been driving all of us down the
Option B road, has contempt for international law. The goal of
the sanctions was regime change. In old-paradigm thinking, the
deaths of a few hundred thousand Iraqi children and the economic
destruction of Iraq was not too high a price to pay to achieve the
goal. Militant nationalism has contempt for human life.

The U.S.-UK invasion of Iraq, March 2003

An old-paradigm version of the March 2003 invasion is that
it was an act of liberation, thus comparable to the liberation of
France in 1944. But France had been occupied by a foreign power
(Germany), whereas the invasion of Iraq in 2003 imposed a foreign
occupation on the country. There are several other differences
between the liberation of France and the invasion and occupation
of Iraq, which any well-informed high school student will be able
to identify.

It is a fact that the invasion and occupation of Iraq ended a
brutal dictatorship; therefore, the concept that it was an act of

liberation has some legitimacy. If Zainab Salbi, whose family were friends of Saddam Hussein, can celebrate the end of his regime as the happiest day of her life, consider what hundreds of thousands of others who suffered under that tyranny saw in the termination of that dictatorship.

But the policies behind the invasion and occupation of Iraq in 2003 were driven by the same paradigm and the same conditions that gave rise to the dictatorship in the first place. The invasion and occupation on the one hand, and the regime they displaced on the other, were rationalized reciprocally in perpetuating the ideology of militant nationalism. The violence of the dictatorship was rationalized by its perpetrators as a defense against regime change; the violence used to displace the regime was rationalized by its perpetrators as a way of solving the problem of dictatorship. These reciprocally reinforcing rationalizations serve to perpetuate the violence.

The concept that the invasion and occupation of Iraq was an act of liberation is an old-paradigm map, serving as propaganda for war to support the invasion. The point of this book is to make the choice process more conscious and better informed. Choose your map, but be aware of your purpose before you decide. Also be aware of the predictable consequences of the choice, consequences for which you share in the responsibility.

When Iraq invaded Kuwait in 1990, it violated the most fundamental requirement of international law. The death toll that resulted directly from Iraq's invasion and occupation of Kuwait is estimated at three to five thousand. When the United States and the United Kingdom invaded Iraq in 2003, they too violated the most fundamental requirement of international law. Within a year, the death toll resulting directly from the invasion and occupation of Iraq was estimated to have been several tens of thousands.

Iraq's violation was formally condemned by the UN Security Council and chapter VII proceedings were initiated, which might well have resolved the crisis peacefully had they been conducted in accord with the purposes and principles of the UN Charter. Instead the law was used as pretext for a massive escalation of violence and the imposition of the scourge of war, including economic warfare, on Iraq.

The U.S.-UK violation was handled somewhat differently. The UN Security Council is an old-paradigm institution whose legitimacy derives from a new-paradigm Charter. The Council is therefore one place to watch for evidence of the paradigm shift. Old-paradigm thinking still dominates the Council. Hence the U.S. government had reason to believe even in 2002 that the Council might endorse the invasion.

By 2002, however, the U.S. government had lost much of its credibility. The savaging of Iraq from 1991 onward, under UN Security Council auspices, and the worldwide reaction against it, had made the Council's membership more resistant to U.S. pressures. Even during the Kosovo crisis in 1998-99, the Council was no longer so easy to recruit to U.S. militant nationalism.

UN Security Council Resolution 1441 of 2002 used ambiguous language about consequences if Iraq failed to comply with weapons inspections, and clearly did not authorize a U.S. invasion. That did not prevent old-paradigm legal experts from arguing that the invasion of Iraq was legal (see, for example, Taft and Buchwald 2003, and Yoo 2003).

What is little understood is that *even if the UN Security Council had endorsed it, the invasion and occupation of Iraq would still have been a violation of the UN Charter.* This may be somewhat difficult for old-paradigm international legal experts to grasp, but the UN Security Council's legitimacy derives from the UN Charter, and the Charter requires the Council to act in accord with the Charter's purposes and principles. Endorsing an act of aggression is contrary to those purposes and principles. The effort to gain the endorsement failed, and at least the UN Security Council should be commended for that. That may seem faint praise, and it is so intended.

Iraq's violation of the law (the invasion of Kuwait) was used as pretext for the destruction of Iraq; the U.S.-UK violation (the invasion of Iraq) was ignored or tacitly supported. The UN Security Council is radically in violation of the UN Charter on both counts. There can be no rule of law until the law is applied equitably and consistently in accord with its fundamental purposes and principles.

Apparently the policy planners involved had hoped that the devastation of Iraq in the 1991 war, and the continuation of war by other means with economic sanctions, would eventually lead to the overthrow of Saddam Hussein, and that the entire process could be carried out behind a façade of international law. When that failed, the much cruder instrument of overt military aggression was used to accomplish the goal. The aggression easily accomplished the goal of regime change, of course, but the outcome surprised its perpetrators, because their concepts of what would happen were old-paradigm concepts, and the old paradigm makes its prisoners very poor students of reality.

Democracy, the occupation, and the ongoing violence in Iraq

By late 2004, several more tens of thousands of Iraqi citizens had been killed as a result of the invasion and occupation. The invasion and occupation were superimposed on years of military attacks on radar and defense installations, which degraded Iraq's ability to defend itself, as they were intended to do, and killed quite a few human beings, which was irrelevant to the purpose of the attacks. Economic sanctions had killed hundreds of thousands of Iraqis and destroyed the economic life of the country. The sanctions had been superimposed on the war of 1991, and the damage they caused to the country's infrastructure had never been adequately repaired. The environmental damage and the ongoing consequences to human health in Iraq caused by the policies of the U.S. government and its allies will never be adequately reckoned. Every phase of this history included major violations of international law by the United States and its allies against Iraq, under the banner of the United Nations.

Chief among the given reasons (part of the old-paradigm map) for this criminality and carnage had been that Iraq was developing WMD and was a threat to international peace. When no trace of the hypothetical weapons could be found even after the invasion and occupation, the old-paradigm mapmakers shifted their emphasis: it had all been done for the good of the people of Iraq.

At the same time, political realist versions of old-paradigm maps began to reappear. These realists readily acknowledged that the invasion and occupation were illegal, but they also argued that the illegality was now irrelevant. States seek security (or power) by the threat and use of force; it is unrealistic to try to change this, and warfare is not a disease to be cured but a normal form of human behavior, and so on and so forth.

The fact that Iraq had no remaining WMD programs was largely irrelevant to the purpose of regime change. Even so, exposure of the fraud on which the economic sanctions and the invasion had been based at least called for some public relations damage control. In principle, this should be easy to do. An invasion, however repugnant and criminal, always produces some advantages for some part of the population in the invaded country. The maps produced to support the invasion need only emphasize that aspect of reality and ignore, obscure, or rationalize the rest. With the end of a dictatorship, there would be little trouble in producing the necessary old-paradigm maps.

Several versions of the damage control have appeared, each with the same ephemeral quality of other masks for militant nationalism. "Making the world safe for democracy" was a standard mask (map) in the mid-twentieth century when the CIA helped overthrow the elected governments of Iran, Guatemala, and Chile, and establish oppressive dictatorships in their stead. The overthrow of a regime such as Saddam Hussein's made it much easier to use democracy as a mask:

> Then comes America, not just proclaiming democratic liberation as its overriding foreign policy principle but sacrificing blood and treasure in the service of precisely that principle.
> It was not people power that set this in motion. It was American power. (Krauthammer 2005)

Krauthammer also expresses the hope that American power will contribute to democracy and "modernity" for the entire Middle East, citing elections in various states as evidence that this is happening, including two (Afghanistan and Iraq) that had been targets of U.S. military attacks. He cites elections in Palestine and Saudi Arabia, and democratic progress in Egypt and Lebanon, all by inference somehow due to American power and not to people power, in Krauthammer's map of reality.

Iraq's oil reserves may also have something to do with the invasion and occupation. Some would argue that the deaths related to the invasion (recently revised upward to more than six hundred thousand) were more about gaining access to Iraq's resources than about bringing democracy to Iraq. A detailed analysis of economic motivations for the invasion of Iraq is beyond the scope of this book but can be found in a publication by the Research Unit for Political Economy entitled *Behind the Invasion of Iraq* (Monthly Review Press, 2003).

On December 12, 1974 a Charter of Economic Rights and Duties of States was passed in the UN General Assembly. The preamble of the Charter calls for the attainment of wider prosperity among all countries and of higher standards of living for all peoples; the promotion by the entire international community of the economic and social progress of all countries, especially developing countries; and the protection, preservation, and enhancement of the environment. In chapter 1 of the Charter, certain fundamental principles of international economic relations are specified, including the sovereignty, territorial integrity, and political independence of states; non-aggression; peaceful coexistence; peaceful settlement of disputes; respect for human rights and fundamental freedoms; no attempt to seek hegemony and spheres of influence; promotion of international social justice; and international cooperation for development.

The Charter was passed by a vote of 120 in favor, six against, and ten abstentions. Of the six states voting against the resolution that contained the Charter, two (the United States and the United Kingdom) became the major invading and occupying powers in Iraq. In the old paradigm that dominates the ideology of power, ideas such as those expressed in the Charter of Economic Rights and Duties of States are considered "a letter to Santa Claus."

At the time Krauthammer's commentary appeared, people feared for their lives in modern, democratized Iraq. Saddam Hussein's tyranny was gone, and there can be no doubt that there are some very good things about that change. But that is only one aspect of reality. The Ba'ath government had imposed the same sort of "stability" maintained by fear that was imposed by the Chilean dictatorship after 1973 and by the Guatemalan dictatorship after 1954, but with the addition in Iraq of strong social programs, advances for women in the workforce, and other aspects of a project to end the tyranny of the West over the Arab world. Saddam Hussein had a nationalist vision for Iraq of unity, independence, and strength. Iraq had oil reserves that could have been used to achieve that nationalist vision. The vision has now been extinguished as Iraq stumbles toward an uncertain future. Internally at least, militant nationalism is the lesser of two evils when placed in the dock beside a state that is disintegrating or tearing itself apart from within.

Saddam's tyranny and nationalist vision have been replaced with the violent factionalism of a state teetering on the brink of ruin. The road to this disaster began decades ago, and we have been driven along it by militant nationalism. At every point, international law offered a roadmap for the alternative, toward Option A: support for regional pacts of non-aggression, refusal to support governments such as Iraq's or Kuwait's when their policies violated international law, substantive work to achieve a peaceful withdrawal of Iraq from Kuwait, and specifying an endpoint to economic sanctions in accord with international law and then lifting the sanctions in accord with reasonable interpretation of international law.

As political realists will understand, both Iraq and the United States would have remained under the constraints of international power relationships; Iran and other states in the region represent quite formidable limitations on Iraq's militant nationalist options, and those constraints would have remained if international law had been followed and Saddam Hussein had remained in power. Major differences would have been that hundreds of thousands of Iraqis would not only have lived but would have found much more productive lives, and the United States and its allies would not have lost the credibility and the resources they have squandered on their pursuit of Option B.

Again and again such options were rejected by governments. Citizens calling for Option A were stiff-armed, and old-paradigm intellectuals such as Charles Krauthammer, Michael Glennon, and Christopher Hitchens gave us their old-paradigm maps of the road we traveled and continue to travel toward Option B.

The sources of violence in Iraq today remain directly or indirectly related to the illegal invasion and occupation. They include direct violence inflicted by the occupying military forces and violence directed against the military forces of the occupation; violence and threats against Iraqis, perceived as collaborators, who work for or with the occupying forces; sectarian violence that has grown out of that same perception of collaboration; and random violence that the Iraqi police force is unable to control. The police force's authority is undermined by the occupying military forces, for whom the prevention of rape and armed robbery, and alleviation of general fear in the civilian population are not operational priorities. The force's solidarity is also being destroyed by the same factors promoting sectarian violence.

From this analysis, a rational observer would conclude (and would years ago have concluded) that prompt withdrawal of the occupying military forces is an absolutely essential step toward diminishing the violence in Iraq. It is exactly the invasion and protracted occupation that have escalated the violence and have made the restoration of human security in Iraq increasingly remote and difficult. This analysis and the conclusion to which it leads are supported by all the available evidence.

In 2004 I wrote a working paper on Iraq and presented it to a citizens' organization with which I was associated: CANDIL (Canada, Democracy and International Law). The paper was posted on the CANDIL website and is still available at www. candil.org. The individuals in that organization, with others across Canada, had long called for the lifting of sanctions against Iraq and had insisted on the absolute necessity of international law as a standard for any constructive approach to the government of Iraq and the situation in that part of the world. The standards of international law enabled us as concerned citizens to see very early and with great clarity the self-defeating direction of policy being generated by the U.S. government and its allies. The new paradigm enabled a powerful and prescient analysis of the course of events. Within the old paradigm, such an analysis is not possible, and the conclusions are incomprehensible. That is why government officials are so incompetent in the arena of world affairs.

Once the disaster of a militant nationalist adventure becomes too obvious to ignore, it is standard practice for the erstwhile supporters to plead incompetence: Our intentions were good, but we did not realize... *In Retrospect*, Robert McNamara's 1995 assessment of the Vietnam War, lists a series of "lessons learned."

They include several that an intelligent high school student not confined by old-paradigm thinking could have explained to the U.S. government administrations responsible for that particular era of carnage and waste of public resources. That is why democracy is so important. Responsible, active, informed citizens can think outside the box.

Throughout the decade of the 1990s, such citizens were calling for a change of direction in policy on Iraq. But militant nationalism has contempt for democracy. The calls were rejected by the U.S. government, and by the Canadian government. Only in the late stages of the destruction of Iraq, just before the 2003 invasion, was the Canadian government partially brought to its senses and refused full-fledged participation in that particular violation of international law. The destruction of Iraq illuminates the failure of democracy in North America.

Terrorism and the destruction of Iraq

For those who, like Zbigniew Brzezinski, believe that U.S. power is "uniquely central to world peace," without which the world would plunge "almost immediately into a politically chaotic crisis" (2004, 17), it should be instructive to recall the sustained rise of violence in Iraq after the arrival of U.S. forces in that country. In October 2006 alone, the death toll among Iraqi civilians was reportedly 3,706, much of it related to sectarian violence.

Conditions promoted in the global community by the militant nationalism of powerful states are the conditions that give rise to tyranny and terrorism. The CIA has promoted terrorism as part of its covert operations, so it does have some understanding of conditions that activate political violence within a state. It is not surprising that the CIA realized that the invasion and occupation of Iraq were likely to increase the risk of terrorism.

Violence begets violence. From its previous status as a militant nationalist state with publicly funded health care and education systems, and as a secular Arab state advancing the role of women in public life, Iraq has descended into violence and disintegration. The dictatorship and state terrorism under Saddam Hussein were a murderous response to the murderous geopolitical conditions in which they arose.

The standard definition of terrorism draws no distinction between state and non-state actors. The former Iraqi regime did not allow competing forms of terrorism on its turf. The violent displacement of that violent regime and the violent presence of the occupation forces have exacerbated various forms of terrorism. All this has emphasized how powerful the United States is, and teaching adversaries that lesson is in the "national interest" of the United States. In the old paradigm, the national interest is a more important consideration than the lives of human beings.

Promoting this pestilence in the global community raises the chances of its outbreak in North America. Iraq is a canary in the mineshaft of the coming century. If the priority of national interest over human life prevails, there are very dark times ahead.

Responsibility for the destruction of Iraq

An old-paradigm map held Saddam Hussein and his regime alone responsible for the destruction of Iraq. The purpose of that way of thinking is clear enough, though it borders on psychotic ideation. Responsibility for the destruction of Iraq is widely shared but includes at a minimum the government of Iraq, the government of the United States and its allies, and the UN Security Council.

Militant nationalism works to the short- or long-term destruction of the state that promotes it. Hitler's militant nationalism provoked militant nationalism in response. Saddam Hussein's militant nationalism made Iraq vulnerable to the militant nationalism of states much more powerful than Iraq. Those states too are in the process of self-destruction. In the United States, there is a hemorrhage of public resources into the military sector of the economy, concomitant with pervasive social disintegration related to the pathology of power and contempt for human life.

This is blindly self-destructive behavior that should instantly and forcefully call our attention to the choice put forward by Albert Camus: it is up to us not to be on the side of the pestilence. To believe in the inevitability of warfare and the impossibility of a rule of law is to be on the side of the pestilence.

When the government of Iraq attacks Iran or Kuwait, or slaughters its Kurdish population, it threatens the global community of which I am a part. The government of Iraq threatened me, and people like me, when it did these things. When the United States corrupts the UN Security Council, carries out the economic strangulation of Iraq for purposes of regime change, and then invades and occupies Iraq with murderous consequences for hundreds of thousands of people, it threatens the global community of which I am a part. The government of the United States threatens me, and people like me when it does this. The national interest is contrary to the public interest.

We are in the process of deciding whether to hold all governments accountable for their atrocities or to continue making exceptions for our own governments and their allies. The government of Iraq under Saddam Hussein was responsible for hundreds of thousands of deaths in the Middle East and fundamental violations of international law. The government of the United States and its allies are also responsible for hundreds of thousands of deaths in the Middle East and fundamental violations of international law. If we do not hold our own and allied governments — and all governments — accountable for their atrocities, then we ensure continuation of such atrocities.

A way forward

The patterns of waste and self-destruction that produced the catastrophe in Iraq are clear. They indicate our failure as a global community. We can ignore this failure and continue business as usual, or we can change direction by bringing our policies and practices into compliance with international law. Either way, we are responsible for the choice. This should give serious historians, and the rest of us, a useful standard for analysis of current events.

The case of Iraq illustrates basic principles for global citizenship, the subject of this book. Properly understood, those principles can facilitate much healthier approaches to the politics of the future. As in medicine, competent practice must be based on knowledge of the disease and evidence-based approaches to therapy and prevention.

We can also use the analogy of an airline disaster. Without a prompt and aggressive inquiry into the disaster, leading to insight into what caused it, the disaster is likely to be repeated. Such an inquiry should lead to recommendations for how to avoid recurrence.

Public analysis of the disaster in Iraq has, for the most part, been old-paradigm analysis, which is useless for identifying the source of the problem. Most of the recommendations that follow are taken directly from the working paper on Iraq posted in November 2004 (www.candil.org). These recommendations can contribute toward human security for all of us, whether we live in Iraq or elsewhere.

Recommendation #1: *There must be public and explicit recognition of responsibility for the devastation of Iraq.* That responsibility includes, first and foremost, the government of Iraq under Saddam Hussein. Militant nationalist governments are a threat to their own citizens. While we have heard endless repetition of Saddam Hussein's responsibility since August 1990,

there has been no public recognition of the basic principle that power politics and militant nationalism are a threat to human security. This is applicable not only to the militant nationalism of Saddam Hussein but also to the militant nationalism of other actors responsible for the course of events.

Responsibility for the devastation of Iraq now rests chiefly with the governments of the United States and its allies, particularly Kuwait, Saudi Arabia, and the United Kingdom. This responsibility must be publicly acknowledged and universally recognized. Other actors responsible for the devastation of Iraq include the UN Security Council and non-state actors, including factions within Iraq. Kurdish militant nationalists in Iraq are but one example of the non-state actors involved.

The list does not end there. The mass media and intellectuals who contributed to promoting the policies that devastated Iraq share in the responsibility, as do all of us who were silent about the policies of our governments, or insufficiently active in reversing them, while we paid taxes that supported those policies. To recognize that responsibility is a necessary first step toward a healthier world for our grandchildren. Whether you take that step is obviously your choice, but your responsibility is inescapable.

There is a difference between guilt and responsibility. Feeling guilty about past failures is all too likely to be a substitute for changing the thinking and behavior that produced those failures. The point here is that responsibility must now be accepted and acknowledged if the choice is Option A.

Recommendation #2: *International law must be recognized as necessary framework for the recovery of Iraq.* International law is a *sine qua non* for the recovery and reconstruction of Iraq, and for global security. The violations and subversion of international law by the previous government of Iraq and by the international community are responsible for the devastation of Iraq and for endangering peace and security in the global community. Reliable progress in reducing the dangers globally and in the reconstruction and recovery of Iraq can be achieved only to the extent that the spirit, purposes, and provisions of international law are implemented and followed in the process.

The invasion and occupation of Iraq are major violations of international law and major threats to our future security. The United States and all others involved in the occupation of Iraq must comply fully with the requirements of international law governing that occupation, and rapidly bring the occupation to an end.

Recommendation #3: *The foreign military forces occupying Iraq must be withdrawn expeditiously and foreign military bases closed.* We emphasized the necessity of a timetable for expeditious withdrawal of foreign military forces from Iraq in the working paper posted in November 2004. It is commendable that President Obama has recognized this necessity, even though the date set as endpoint (December 31, 2011) is years later than it should have been. Setting a timetable is not the same as actually withdrawing the troops and closing the foreign military bases. Watch carefully for what ensues.

Recommendation #4: *Sovereignty and self-determination are inalienable rights of the people of Iraq; recognition of that right must become definitive for the policies of all governments.* Foreign governments, particularly the government of the United States, must abandon all efforts to delay, manipulate, or dilute the practice of those rights by the people of Iraq.

With the exposure of false pretexts for the invasion and occupation of Iraq, some observers have attempted to justify the invasion and occupation by suggesting that the incursions may promote democracy and human rights in Iraq. But promoting democracy and human rights in Iraq cannot justify policies that violated the most fundamental provisions of international law, extinguished hundreds of thousands of lives, and wasted incalculable human potential among Iraqis, losses that can never be recovered or adequately measured. The disaster in Iraq is a powerful illustration of the reasoning behind Louis Henkin's point (see chapter 4) that advances in human rights must take place within the legal constraints of the UN Charter. Sweeping aside the constraints imposed by the UN Charter makes a rule of law impossible and thus renders advances in human rights transient and illusory.

Recommendation #5: *The resources of Iraq must be used in accord with international human rights law, for the benefit of the people of Iraq.* The resources of Iraq belong to the people of Iraq. Those resources must be used in accord with the Charter for Economic Rights and Duties of States and the International Covenant on Economic, Social, and Cultural Rights. The invasion and occupation of Iraq are illegal, and any disposition of Iraqi resources arising in the context of the invasion and occupation should be kept subject to independent legal review. It is the responsibility of all governments and institutions to uphold the principles set forth in the Charter of Economic Rights and Duties of States. It is the responsibility of citizens to be aware of these requirements and to promote compliance with them.

Recommendation #6: *All competent governments and international organizations must play a sustained and effective supporting role in the reconstruction of Iraq and facilitate interactions involving civil society in Iraq and in the international community.*
Reparations for the devastation of Iraq — including the effects of economic sanctions, political isolation, and illegal acts of war against Iraq — are the particular responsibility of those governments and institutions in the international community that perpetrated and supported the sanctions and the unlawful use of force. These reparative resources must be placed under control of Iraqi institutions and an Iraqi civil society working for a strong,

independent, and inclusive Iraq, with its internal and external affairs guided by basic precepts of international law and free of interference from foreign powers. For more than ten years after its invasion of Kuwait, Iraq was illegally deprived of access to its own resources and repeatedly subjected to unjustifiable military assaults. Responsibility for restoration to Iraq of lost resources rests with the perpetrators of that injustice.

Recommendation #7: *There must be a rapid devolution of power to Iraqi institutions.*

Those institutions should represent all parts of Iraqi society, without prejudice against previous affiliations with the former government of Iraq, the occupying powers, or others. Proxy institutions of governance and manipulative control of Iraqi institutions and resources by the very governments responsible for the ravaging of Iraq are illegitimate. Instead, resources must be placed in the hands of Iraqi institutions, including Iraqi civil society and its non-governmental organizations (NGOs). It is essential to understand that such organizations, in collaboration with international NGOs and civil society, have long been at work in the process of healing the damage to Iraq inflicted by violence and lawlessness. It is Iraqi civil society and NGOs that represent the core of integrity and experience necessary for an effective and legitimate process of recovery of the country. Foreign governments have neither the experience nor the credibility to direct this process; their role must be to support the process driven by civil society in Iraq and in the international community.

Recommendation #8: *The people of Iraq are responsible for establishing and implementing the process of reconciliation and inclusive governance.*

All parts of Iraqi society face the urgent necessity to establish an explicit process of reconciliation and governance, and to implement the process without delay. Martin Luther King Jr.'s observation, "We must learn to live together as brothers, or perish together as fools," applies at the national and international levels. Both the international aggression of the Iraqi government under Saddam Hussein and the violent factionalism within Iraq have played major roles in the devastation of Iraqi society. Internal factionalism in Iraq was responsible for direct self-destruction and waste of Iraq's human and natural resources, and it also aided and abetted the violence of foreign powers directed against Iraq. The people of Iraq must end their factionalism and their support for international aggression, either by Iraq against other countries or by other countries against Iraq. Otherwise their process of self-destruction will continue, regardless of any action or inaction on the part of the international community. A house divided against itself cannot stand.

Factionalism in Iraq has been exacerbated by the presence of a foreign occupation. Factional distrust and conflict will worsen and its resolution will be made more difficult to the extent that occupation is prolonged. An occupied and divided country is at an extreme disadvantage in generating the basis for self-respect, independence, and social cohesion. To develop a program of independence and national unity, it is essential that all parts of Iraqi society work together in civic institutions and throughout the structures of governance. Education, the police and armed forces, judiciary bodies, and all levels of government must have effective participation from all parts of Iraqi society and must be independent of foreign influences that tend to divide the country or marginalize parts of Iraq's population. Exclusion of individuals and groups based on previous affiliation with the Ba'ath party or on other political or ethnic grounds will perpetuate the division of the country and vitiate efforts at reconstruction and recovery. It is of utmost importance that women's rights and empowerment, in which Iraq had played a leading role in the Middle East, recover their pace of progress and governmental support.

Recommendation #9: *The participation of UN or other peacekeeping forces must be contingent upon request from legitimate Iraqi authorities.*

After devolution of full governing authority to Iraq, and at the discretion of the legitimate Iraqi authorities, UN or other international peacekeeping forces may have a legitimate and useful role to play in maintaining peace and security in Iraq. No such legitimacy can pertain to UN or other military forces deployed in Iraq under the aegis of the current illegal occupation.

Recommendation #10: *Governments of states in the region, including the government of Iraq, must conclude and implement regional agreements on non-aggression, disarmament, and cooperation.*

Acts of aggression in the Middle East have had colossally destructive consequences, including Iraq's acts of aggression against Iran and Kuwait, the U.S.-UK aggression against Iraq, and other acts of aggression perpetrated or supported by governments in the region.

International law is concerned not only with the international use of force but also with international threats. For example, the hypothetical weapons of mass destruction in Iraq were used as a reason for UN actions against Iraq after 1990. Iraq had sought to acquire weapons of mass destruction prior to 1990, but these policies were pursued in part because of perceived threats from an armed insurgency in northern Iraq and from hostile states in the region. The concept that violence begets violence can be extended to recognize that international threats and hostility tend to be self-perpetuating and mutually destructive to all parties in the process, and are a threat to the global community.

For this and other reasons, civil society throughout the world has a legitimate concern with peace in the Middle East. Any government that threatens other governments thereby becomes a threat to the global community. There are numerous obstacles to peace and stability in the Middle East. Governments in the region bear the primary responsibility for solving the problems and moving past the obstacles. Other governments with regional influence are responsible for supporting regional processes toward binding agreements on non-aggression, disarmament, and cooperation.

Recommendation # 1 1 : *Civil society throughout the world, particularly in Western democracies, is responsible for bringing policies and practices of their governments into compliance with international law and for participating in the recovery of Iraq and restoration of dynamic and constructive interactions between Iraqi civil society and the international community.*

Citizens in all democratic societies, working through organizations of civil society, are responsible for bringing their government's policies into compliance with international law and for promoting reconciliation, and cultural and social interactions, with civil society in Iraq.

A government that acts as a tyrant in its external affairs thereby jeopardizes its legitimacy. If that government is a democracy, meaning that the government's foreign policy expresses the will of the people of that state, then the citizens of that country are responsible for the external tyranny and for the dubious legitimacy of their government. This relationship between a tyrannical foreign policy and the conditions of democracy is well expressed by Austrian jurist Hans Köchler:

> On the one hand, democracy in foreign policy grants every citizen the right to influence the international relations of [his/her] state (internal aspect). On the other hand, it means that a specific state bases its relations to other states on the principles of democracy (external aspect). Both aspects are mutually entwined. Any democracy that acts as a dictatorship externally (even though its dictatorial

foreign policy may internally be sanctified by its citizens) is a contradiction in terms. Such citizens must not claim to be credible in their so-called democratic activities. (Köchler 1995, 20)

Democracy is both a right and a responsibility for citizens. John Ralston Saul makes the following point in reference to the execution of someone convicted of a serious crime — his principle applies even more forcefully in foreign policy, in which the act of a government affects thousands of people who have been convicted of no crime whatever:

Once you reach the democratic idea of legitimacy rooted in the citizenry, an execution implies that the populace not only consents, but also assumes responsibility for the decision. You, as a citizen, are no less directly responsible than a president or a judge or the jury on which you do not personally sit.

Democratic consent means that you would be prepared personally to act as executioner. Execution is not an abstract theory. It is an existential act. To be for the death penalty is to consider the convicted one by one and answer affirmatively the question: Am I personally prepared to kill that man? Consciously or unconsciously that final level of responsibility explains why Western democracies, with one exception, have ended the practice. The citizenry found themselves face to face with the combination of an ethical reality and their personal responsibility and decided that legal murder was ethically unacceptable, whatever the conditions. (2001, 89)

By these standards, citizens of the United States, the United Kingdom, Canada, and other U.S. allies are responsible for their government's role in the destruction of Iraq. When Madeleine

Albright expressed her opinion on the television show *60 Minutes* (May 12, 1996) that the deaths of about half a million children in Iraq, related to economic sanctions on that country, had been "worth it," she indicated at once the tyranny of U.S. foreign policy, the questionable legitimacy of the government of the United States, and the failure of responsible citizenship in North America.

There had by that time been countless citizens of the United States, the United Kingdom, Canada, and other countries who had made a sustained effort to bring their government's policy into compliance with law and to halt the effects of economic sanctions on the people of Iraq. The efforts of these individuals and organizations represent the responsible practice of democracy. These efforts ultimately failed because they were not adequately supported by other citizens and were effectively ignored by the government. Democracy and international law are interdependent; democracy that fails to support international law is on the road to self-destruction.

With the disaster in Iraq as a sign of grave and universal danger to human security in the decades ahead, it is now imperative that citizens and civil society in Western democracies act responsibly and in cooperation with the people of Iraq to confront that danger: to bring the policies and practices of Western governments into compliance with international law, to initiate and develop dynamic and constructive interactions with civil society in Iraq, and to ensure international respect for the rights of the people of Iraq.

Recommendation #12: *It is the responsibility of civil society and of governments to facilitate reintegration of war resistors into civilian life, to abandon all retribution for resistance to the war, and to ameliorate the physical and psychological damage to all soldiers, former soldiers, and civilians affected by the U.S.-UK war on Iraq.*

For the government of Canada, this means welcoming and

providing haven for U.S. war resistors — U.S. military personnel who have come to Canada because of their refusal to participate, or participate further, in the illegal war in Iraq — until the U.S. government has lived up to its own responsibility on this issue. The Canadian government's position on war resistors will be one important indicator of its position on international law, and of its contribution to the future of human security.

Conclusion

The catastrophe in Iraq is a rich source for lessons of history. If we fail to learn the lessons of history, we will likely repeat them. To be effective in prevention, however, the lessons must be learned within the paradigm — the conceptual framework — that serves the purpose of prevention. That will require the paradigm shift referred to in this book.

Using the new paradigm as a frame of reference, I have here provided only a small part of the lessons we can learn from the case of Iraq. Contrary to what we have been told, responsibility for the catastrophe was never restricted to the government of Iraq under Saddam Hussein.

Militant nationalist governments have provided evidence again and again of their threat to the global community and to the chances of human survival. If the threat is recognized only as coming from a particular government and not from militant nationalism itself, then we have failed to learn the lesson and we will have to repeat it until we get it right, or until we perish as fools.

Governments, particularly those of militarily powerful states, are rooted in the old and self-destructive paradigm of militant nationalism. Those who choose to occupy political office have only a limited capacity to uproot the traditions, shift the paradigm, and change the course of history. Nonetheless, they do have a chance to move policies and practices toward compliance with international law and to promote structures that strengthen democratic process

— essentially structures that empower civil society. To the extent that political leaders make this effort, they should be supported by civil society. To the extent they fail, civil society should persuade them to make the effort. Civil society has become the Option A leader in world affairs. By civil society I mean those individuals and organizations that are identifying the challenges to a healthy global community and finding life-affirming ways to meet those challenges within the framework of international law. Because they are far less hobbled by the old paradigm, civil society has been able to identify problems and constructive solutions with a speed and adaptive intelligence that governments cannot match. At present, civil society represents far too small a portion of the citizenry in Western democracies.

The responsibility rests not just with government and cannot be shouldered just by civil society. The responsibility belongs to all of us. Cultural institutions — schools and universities, scholars, the media — share in the responsibility. Economic institutions also have a responsibility to bring their practices into accord with the requirements of international human rights law. Most importantly, and by definition, citizens in a democracy are responsible for the policies and practices of their government. These are terms of responsible discourse on world affairs for the foreseeable future.

CHAPTER SIX

Principles of Global Citizenship

A man who feels no pain or remorse when he kills a child places his humanity in doubt. A nation that listens in silence and inaction as its government causes the deaths of a million fellow human beings has placed its future on the auction block. "National interest also allows a member [of the nation] to disregard moral principles in defence of the nation. — it is permissible to lie, to steal and to murder" (Harris 1990, 16).

At its core, nationalism (and the political realism that supports it) is a profoundly pessimistic ideology: it holds that we have no choice but to continue killing each other. What is human life worth? That is in the eye of the beholder. And in the eye of an ardent nationalist, it cannot be worth much.

Nationalism always wears a humanitarian mask: democracy, socialism, the fatherland, Christianity, Islam, God and country, whatever. But deep down, the ideology of nationalism is connected with a profound doubt about whether life is worth living. And if human life is not worth living, then the human species is not worth saving. Joy in living, respect for human life, and the chances of human survival are interdependent. The personal is political.

It is essential to recognize not only the pathological nature of militant nationalism but also the pathological failure of the environment that gives rise to it. Militant nationalism is not the product of a healthy global community. Militant nationalism sprouts in the pathological void left by the failure of human beings to recognize and activate their humanity. In our time, this is a failure of responsible global citizenship.

If a North American politician were to promote a policy of slavery or of disenfranchising women, his political career would soon be terminated. But a politician who promotes nuclear weapons development, the use of nuclear weapons against adversaries, the militarization of space, and murderous violations of international law can become president of the United States or prime minister of Canada. He may have to use a rhetoric that obscures what he is promoting, but the rhetoric is not the reality. Such politicians are threatening our survival as a species, yet under the current set of political assumptions, that's okay.

One of the urgent tasks facing our generation is to remove mass slaughter from the menu of political choices. If we are depressed and skeptical of the value of human life or if we decide that we have no responsibility to make the necessary change, then we will never rise to the challenge.

Most of the problem, then, is pervasive in our culture: a way of thinking in which mass slaughter is acceptable. The fundamental changes we need to make — steadily, relentlessly, and soon — are extremely unlikely to originate within or gain much momentum from the dominant political institutions. If the changes are to take place at all, they must be driven from outside the institutions, by a change in the way people think. If it remains acceptable in the minds of a critical mass of the public to continue down the road toward Option B, then we will continue down that road.

The future cannot be predicted in detail, but we conduct our lives on the basis of reasonable assumptions. We should be approaching our collective future in the same way. It is a reasonable assumption that if we accept and effectively implement our responsibility to repudiate lawlessness as an acceptable political option, our future will be better than if we fail to accept that responsibility.

The same line of reasoning applies to each of us as individuals. Each of us is the final arbiter of how we think about the world and how we conduct our lives. We can decide that we have a responsibility to repudiate political lawlessness, or not. In either case, we unquestionably bear responsibility for the predictable consequences of our choice.

Stalin and Hitler were forceful personalities, but ignorant and incompetent in the terms set forth in this book. We have such personalities in our own culture — "people of the lie," as Scott Peck calls them — self righteous, strong-willed, and destructive of human well-being. They may be Sunday school teachers or your neighbour or the local constable or a successful politician or a political appointee. In our culture, their pathological desire to dominate finds its complement in a pathological willingness to be dominated — the failure of responsible citizenship.

The current president of the United States, Barack Obama, seems relatively wise and mature, but that advantage will be for naught unless there is a quantum advance in well-informed, competent, engaged citizenship in the United States. Anyone occupying the office of president will be subjected to pressures from old-paradigm institutions (the military-industrial-ideological-political complex), and those will prevail unless we as citizens provide the countervailing force.

The navigational system provided by Martin Luther King Jr., Erich Fromm, and others — that is, the one presented in this book — is the most reliable we have. Had we used it consistently in the twentieth century, we would not be stumbling down this dark passage in the twenty-first. The principles provided in chapter 4 and those which follow here are intended as guides in this navigational system — guides to personal growth, discovery of your potential, and development of your legacy. Your life is your gift to the world. Don't waste it.

The principles in chapter 4 emphasized some of the pathologic conditions in the global community, the necessity of being aware of that pathology within ourselves, and some of the high costs of failing to do this. Carrying these concepts further, I have found the following principles useful in thinking about my own interactions with government and civil society, about the nature and uses of power, and about the challenges of practicing global citizenship.

PRINCIPLE 21
Elected and appointed officials are limited by the paradigm of the political institutions they serve.

Those who serve established institutions are limited by the paradigms in which those institutions are rooted. Those who hold political office, whether elected or appointed, are limited by the paradigms on which the government is based. The limitations are particularly severe in (militarily) powerful states because governments of powerful states, and the related economic and cultural institutions, are locked into the paradigm of militant nationalism.

Elected and appointed officials in militant nationalist states, and in states allied with them, often have to behave as if they were out of touch with reality. In the case of weapons of mass destruction in Iraq, for example, the absence of evidence was taken to be, for government officials of the United States and their allies, not only *not* evidence of absence, but evidence that the weapons programs (which hypothetically existed) had been concealed. If you were in the government, you were obliged to maintain this delusion.

Psychosis is a mental disorder in which symptoms such as delusions indicate an impaired contact with reality. The concept of an institutional psychosis is a useful one: an impaired contact with reality imposed by the policy or doctrinal requirements of an institution — in this case, a national government. Some part of reality must be ignored, or a figment of the imagina tion must be treated as if it were real. This kind of psychosis is pervasive in our political culture.

One of the challenges of responsible citizenship is to gain personal sanity, and then to restore sanity to the community. Presidents and prime ministers, even if they have achieved a level of psychosocial sanity themselves, remain under old-paradigm pressures. Only if citizens relentlessly push political institutions toward a healthy global community will we be able to abandon the self-destructive patterns of the past.

PRINCIPLE 22
Civil society has emerged as the Option A leader in world affairs.

Civil society is the non-governmental, non-profit sector of society that is dedicated to the public interest and the common good. Civil society organizations are variously concerned with environmental or social justice issues, or other challenges. Organizations and individuals in civil society have moved with an adaptive intelligence and speed that governments cannot match to identify problems and potential solutions for the challenges of life-and-death importance to our future. They are much less restricted by old-paradigm thinking. Much like a market economy, they gather information from countless sources and communicate it to others, enabling wise decisions about the use of resources.

In the twentieth century, while governments were designing and implementing policies that gave us World War I and World War II, nuclear weapons, and the Vietnam War, civil society gave us countless organizations that called for sanity and advanced the work of cleaning up the mess that governments had made. Over the past quarter century, government policies have given us the destruction of populations through economic sanctions and acts of aggression; implementing those policies has cost hundreds of billions of dollars. Civil society has relentlessly called for governments to abandon their assault on human rights and has had to bathe the wounds inflicted by the atrocities of covert operations, paramilitary operations, and overt military operations, as well as other direct and indirect damage inflicted by governments. It is civil society in Iraq that has had to cope with the rubble left by the arrogance and violence of governments. It is civil society in Latin America that has rejected the failed policies of neoliberalism and the governments and institutions that have promoted it.

Governments have given us global apartheid; civil society has given us microcredit organizations. Our "elected" governments hold the nuclear sword of Damocles above our heads; our civil society organizations tell them to take it down. Civil society organizations in North America are in touch with civil society organizations in Latin America, people to people, a direct form of communication that deals with the environmental and social justice issues that governments and their international bureaucracies, such as the World Trade Organization and the International Monetary Fund, have exacerbated. Civil society has taken its financial power out to women in villages, to the poorest of the poor, in order to lend small sums that enable them to build the means of life with dignity.

Skeptics point out that civil society is not an elected body of people or organizations. Under present conditions in our society, however, elected governments do not represent the public interest as reliably as civil society, for reasons given in this book. Elected officials make decisions behind closed doors about hundreds of billions of dollars in public funds, decisions to finance things that are a threat to the public interest. Civil society does not spend public resources or conduct its affairs in that way.

Paul Hawken is among the many observers who have noticed the rising power of civil society. Surveying the increasing numbers of organizations in civil society, and its vitality and genius, he writes:

> I believe this movement will prevail. I don't mean it will defeat, conquer, or create harm to someone else. Quite the opposite. I don't tender the claim in an oracular sense. I mean that the thinking that informs the movement's goals will reign. It will soon suffuse most institutions, but before then, it will change a sufficient number of people so as to begin the reversal of centuries of frenzied self-destructive behavior. Some say it is too late, but people never change when they are comfortable. Helen Keller threw aside the gnawing fears of chronic bad news when she declared, "I rejoice to live in such a splendidly disturbing time!" In such a time, history is suspended and thus unfinished. It will be the stroke of midnight for the rest of our lives. (2007, 189)

PRINCIPLE 23

The Option A responsibilities of any national government include compliance with and promotion of international humanitarian and human rights law and the law of non-aggression, as well as promotion of mechanisms, structures, and competencies for effective democracy.

Claiming to be democratic, governments often become a fortress within which those in power wall themselves off from citizens. Fortresses reduce visibility. Bad visibility makes for bad decisions. Those in government are connected with other governments that are walled off from *their* citizens. And each government has its "intelligence" services, which gather information and interpret it through the lens of the old paradigm, us versus them. The information gathered in this way is used to compose the Big Picture that is very secret and special and leads those who have

[187]

"security clearance" to think that — far from being out of touch and largely blind — they are very well informed and can see with great clarity.

Like so many militant nationalist governments today, the National Socialist government of Germany in the 1930s claimed to be the great and necessary guardian of the best interests of its people. Because of their deference to that authority, Germans paid a rapidly escalating price, their country being reduced to ashes by 1945. The process can evolve much more slowly, as the reader will have had chances to observe.

A government that serves the best interests of its citizens can be recognized by its compliance with and promotion of international law, particularly humanitarian and human rights law, and the law of non-aggression; by its support for mechanisms, structures, and competencies for effective democracy; and by its responsiveness to civil society.

PRINCIPLE 24
Power is essential to fostering a healthy global community under a rule of law.

Power is essential to promote and maintain the health of any community, including the global community. Power has political, economic, and cultural dimensions. Underestimating the importance of power, including economic power, is a serious fallacy among some well-intentioned activists. To a very large extent, people will do what they are paid to do. If they are paid to promote revitalization of communities, they will promote revitalization of communities. If they are paid to work in the arms industry, they will work in the arms industry. If they are paid to kill people, they will kill people. If their job depends on their not being able to understand that their own government is violating international law, they will have trouble understanding it.

Consider a second-year university student who is faced with

the need to find a summer job, and after that to find a career that will provide adequate financial resources not only for personal needs but to support a family and the future security of the family. Economic uncertainty is a powerful motivator. The student considers her or his options.

Under present circumstances, there are careers available in various professions and corporations, including those associated with the military establishment. There are far fewer and far less lucrative choices available in careers that promote the changes needed for a healthier global community. If young people are to make career choices of the latter kind, then the economic resources must be found to create those career tracks.

Dedicated activists have emphasized to me that they do a lot with very little. Some of them, through their parsimony and effectiveness, have contributed much more toward healthy communities than I have. But that does not solve the problem faced by the university student, nor is it enough to counter the economic forces driving the malignant transformation of power.

Cultural and political power is also essential. Historically, the peace movement in North America has impressive achievements to its credit. It helped bring the Vietnam War to a halt. In the past two decades, it has sometimes organized to persuade a member of Congress to vote against the warfare system on a particular bill before Congress. Other monumental achievements include the School of the Americas Watch, founded by Maryknoll Father Roy Bourgeois. Even the quiet work of meeting and communicating can lay the groundwork for the next advance toward political sanity.

Yet the North American peace movement has had much less impact than it should have had. Those who are dedicating so much time and energy to the peace movement can enhance the impact of their efforts by incorporating the conceptual framework of international law into their cultural and political work. That one step can produce a major strategic and tactical advantage. Other observers who have come to a similar conclusion include Scott

Ritter, who added the UN Charter and the U.S. Constitution as appendices to his 2007 book *Waging Peace: The Art of War for the Anti-War Movement*. Public opinion is waking up to the need for a rule of international law, and the peace movement will lose a golden opportunity if it ignores that development.

To move toward health of the global community, an expansion of political, economic, and cultural power in the service of that vision is an inescapable necessity. The ideas that people hold about the world and their relation to it have a profound influence on their behavior. Economic necessities will heavily influence how they use their time and their creative energy. Their political choices, the political representatives they put in office, and the rigor with which they monitor those representatives will affect how public resources are spent: whether on developing the means of violence and threats, or the means of revitalizing and connecting communities worldwide. Our concepts of power must also undergo a paradigm shift, toward the power that comes with creative cooperation. As Frances Moore Lappé puts it, "To participate in power is to stop blaming and to become a problem solver.... The growth in one person's power can enhance the power of others" (2007, 35).

Recently, tremors have run through global financial markets. Some are worried about the economy, about their own future, about the future of their children. Our own governments have imposed conditions on other countries that devastated the economies of those countries and the lives of millions of people. Now there is a growing fear that economic devastation might befall *us*. The policies that Western governments have imposed on the developing world are the antithesis of intelligent cooperation. Intelligent cooperation will become increasingly important for human security in the future.

Dramatic economic and resource changes could produce panic and a catastrophic increase in dysfunctional behavior, or it could produce a major step forward in adaptive intelligence. The word *power* has often had very negative connotations because of the violence and stupidity with which it has been associated. Our thinking has too often been incredibly short-sighted and oblivious to the common good. Now it is up to us to change that. It's a choice.

PRINCIPLE 25
The pathology of powerlessness sustains the pathology of power.

The tendency of power to degenerate into pathological forms can be averted only by effective democracy and a rule of law. Effective democracy and a rule of law are possible only if citizens accept the responsibility and acquire the necessary knowledge and skills for global citizenship. The pathology of power is sustained by the pathology of powerlessness. If those who prefer Option A fail to support it effectively, or actively support Option B despite their preference, then Option B will prevail.

Stanley Milgram's experiments at Yale in the early 1960s became famous for their finding that, despite their reluctance to harm fellow human beings, ordinary people would override their compunctions when instructed to do so by an authority figure. In an article about the experiments for *Harper's Magazine*, Milgram wrote:

> This is, perhaps, the most fundamental lesson of our study: ordinary people, simply doing their jobs, and without any particular hostility on their part, can become agents in a terrible destructive process. Moreover, even when the destructive effects of their work become patently clear and they are asked to carry out actions incompatible with fundamental standards of morality, relatively few people have the resources needed to resist authority. (1973)

Hannah Arendt eloquently developed this concept of the "banality of evil," in her book *Eichmann in Jerusalem* (1963a). She pointed out that political leaders cannot carry out large-scale policies in violation of human rights unless they have the willing support of large parts of the general population. Adolf Eichmann was a man who believed that silence and obedience to authority made him a good person, so he expedited the transfer of Jews to concentration camps for the Nazi government, and he did it with businesslike efficiency. Milgram's study of Americans corroborates Hannah Arendt's thesis. If we accept that it is evil to do hideous things to other human beings, evil is very much with us today. Timidity, vacillation, and deference to the ideology of nationalism lead basically decent people to support Option B.

Good is also very much with us today if we accept that it is good to repudiate violence, oppression, and illegitimate authority. One of the individuals in Milgram's study who refused to comply with authority was a woman who, with composure and self-confidence, refused to continue when she heard the screams of the test subject. She had to confront power to do this, and she did it as if she were a professional in power confrontation. Any work of importance requires both strong masculine and strong feminine elements: empathy, a clear vision, a strong will, sensitivity to context and consequences, and courage and perseverance.

The pathology of powerlessness often takes the form of power avoidance. It is absolutely essential to distinguish non-violence from pacifism. The best-known proponent of non-violence, Gandhi, confronted illegitimate power and understood the need for power to make that confrontation successful. Christianity has sometimes been dismissed as a "slave morality," but my understanding of the life and teaching of Jesus of Nazareth is that they are about empowerment: the power and the attendant risk of being fully human, of having a reverence for human life, and of confronting those who hold human life in contempt.

This affirmation of the sanctity of life is deeply threatening to Option B leaders, for they depend utterly on that deference to power that Stanley Milgram identified in 65 percent of his subjects. Therefore, conflict is inevitable. The paradigm shift that must be made will lead inevitably to conflict. Those who persist in their new-paradigm thinking can expect hostility and violence to be directed against them. They can also expect to come into conflict with other members of their culture, even members of their own families. Jesus was crucified; Martin Luther King Jr. and Gandhi were assassinated. Option A is not a path for cowards, and the work of promoting Option A sometimes carries mortal risks. Anyone who knows the history of the civil rights movement in the United States will understand this instantly.

Taking power means taking responsibility. If those who prefer Option B avidly pursue power while those who prefer Option A avoid power, then Option B will prevail. The ease with which authority overrides conscience in ordinary people and the reluctance to take power (and the related responsibility), even among those who can clearly see the pathology of power, enables less scrupulous people to push all of us toward Option B. It is not a clash of civilizations that will be decisive in the future of human survival, but a clash of convictions about the value of human life.

PRINCIPLE 26
Problems are there to be solved. Identifying and solving problems is essential to personal growth.

Pragmatic realism involves the ability to recognize a specific obstacle or problem, to define it in terms that evoke possible solutions, and to test the solutions. It is based on the desire to solve the problem, a realistic appraisal of the problem (and whether it needs to be broken down into smaller problems, to be addressed individually), a pragmatic optimism about the effort, and resilience in response to failure.

Identifying and solving problems is essential to personal

growth. The literature on the psychology of personal growth emphasizes this theme again and again. It's an essential concept for any problem-oriented endeavor, including responsible citizenship.

In the field of global citizenship, the list of obstacles and problems is potentially endless: public ignorance about the basic principles and requirements of international law; overwork among those who would be most supportive of Option A; lack of financial resources to establish the paid positions needed to carry out the work; avoidance of serious discussion of public affairs among neighbors; walls of silence that divide ethnic communities; refusal of political leaders to engage in serious discussion of issues; lack of public awareness of any coherent approach to these issues; in particular, a lack of public awareness that Option A is even an option (the assumption that Option B is the only possibility); and more. These problems have solutions, and active, responsible, well-informed citizens are at work on some of them. Solving problems is the spice of life and the source of growth.

PRINCIPLE 27

The conditions of human existence and the chances of human survival depend largely on respect for self and others. Emotional intelligence is essential at both personal and global levels.

Respect for human rights is fundamental to contemporary international law, and the extent to which governments fulfill their responsibilities under that law will largely determine the future of human security. The behavior of governments reflects the respect — or lack of respect — that citizens have for themselves and for others. Hence the future of human security depends on self-esteem and respect for others in day-to-day personal interactions.

Nathaniel Branden has for many years emphasized the importance of self-esteem to every aspect of personal experience and effectiveness. His work can be applied as a powerful manual on active, effective, responsible citizenship. His comparison of the obedient student versus the responsible student (Branden 1994, 223–224) lists traits for each that might have distinguished the subjects in Stanley Milgram's study: the 65 percent that were *obedient* to authority from the 35 percent that were *responsible*, standing up to authority where their conscience demanded it. (See also Bluestein 1999.)

Life is difficult, and part of the challenge is to create the stability in the world around us that is necessary for meeting a hierarchy of needs. By meeting basic needs, we can move on toward self-actualization and self-transcendence in a progression outlined by another psychologist, Abraham Maslow. The experience can increase personal and collective self-esteem. And perhaps, as Richard Tarnas (1991) suggests, it will lead our civilization to transcend itself to something far, far better than what we have known.

In his survey of Western philosophy — the ideas that have shaped our view of the world — Tarnas finds that a large part of it has had a predominantly masculine orientation. He also finds that this imbalance may be coming to an end, an outcome he welcomes. Tarnas, like many other authors writing on the world today, is carefully optimistic. He suggests that some of the turmoil in our consciousness in these times may be related to this transition to something better than what we were capable of in the twentieth century:

> I consider that much of the conflict and confusion of our own era reflects the fact that this evolutionary drama may now be reaching its climactic stages.… Each perspective, masculine and feminine, is here both affirmed and tran-scended, recognized as part of a larger whole; for each polarity requires the other for its fulfillment. And their synthesis leads to something beyond itself: it brings an unexpected opening to a larger reality that cannot be grasped before it arrives, because this new reality is itself a creative act. (1991, 444–45)

[195]

What is your life worth? You are working out the answer to that question in the arduous process of living it. Far too many people live with the assumption that they are just consumers or careerists and that their life is not really worth much. That assumption can have a pervasive, negative feedback effect on their experience of life.

Each person carries the capacity to bring a unique gift to the world, or to withhold it. To see this unique potential within oneself and within others is a way of perceiving human beings. It can be used instead of social Darwinism and other mental maps, depending on your purpose. It's a choice. If we place on human life the same value that the U.S. government has placed on lives in Iraq, or the Israeli government on lives in Gaza, or the Iraqi government on lives in Iran (1980–88), we become toxic to the world around us.

In a nationalist culture we have a recurrent dream that political leaders and experts will get us out of the cycles of self-destruction. That is a false lead. Institutions, with their leaders and experts, are locked in the old paradigm. The responsible citizen understands that she, and not the political leaders, is primarily responsible for the well-being of the global community. As that awareness grows, along with the knowledge and experience needed to implement it, it will bring with it, for millions of people, a growth in self-esteem and in optimism about the future. Think about whether that's an outcome you prefer, and then act accordingly.

Daniel Goleman's book *Emotional Intelligence: Why It Can Matter More than IQ* includes a list of key ingredients for children's success in school, based on a report from the National Center for Clinical Infant Programs. "Almost all children who do poorly in school … lack one or more of these elements of emotional intelligence," he writes (1997, 193–194).

As with so many other excellent works on personal well-being, Goleman's book is a tremendously valuable source of insights for public life. The list of ingredients for children's success in school can be taken as skills essential for personal success throughout life, but also as essential elements of effective global citizenship: confidence, curiosity, intentionality (the wish and capacity to have an impact, and to act upon that with persistence, related to a sense of competence, of being effective), self-control, relatedness, capacity to communicate, and cooperativeness.

Individual citizens and civil society organizations can apply such insights in a way that militant nationalist institutions cannot. That is why, again and again, the vision and initiatives necessary for progress have come from civil society working outside the dominant political, cultural, and economic institutions. Democracy is necessary because it brings the emotional intelligence of citizens into the process of problem solving and changing the rigid assumptions of institutions. International law recognizes this necessity, and the conditions to make it decisive.

PRINCIPLE 28
Citizenship is a field for innovation, achievement, and creative public life.

Creativity has been studied from a number of different perspectives. The creative act is usually a revitalizing experience, producing enthusiasm, zest, and delight. Perhaps it has that effect on the creative person not only because of its association with discovery, self-actualization, and problem-solving, but also because the creative act is a gift that the creative person brings to others. There is an evolutionary advantage in the empathy and support that healthy human beings show one another, and perhaps that's why we find that something has evolved in human psychology that confers a strong positive feedback when we engage in giving to another person or to others.

The practice of medicine is one field in which the professional can devote himself or herself to the well-being of others. The practice of medicine can be taken as a model for the practice of citizenship. Challenging the pathology of power is essential to the health of the global community. The spice of life comes from around the world: we learn from other human beings and other cultures in art, mathematics, and literature; in everyday things such as good food and friendship; and in the myriad possibilities of the human spirit.

As in the field of medicine, our prospects for the future of human survival depend on innovation and discovery, and on sound principles and practice. Engagement in the practice of informed, responsible citizenship involves the solution of problems for the benefit of the community and the future of human security. Its rewards are comparable to those in the best research and practice in medicine.

A patient with a life-threatening disorder will be fortunate to have a physician who is optimistic, healthy, alert, well informed, competent, confident, focused on her work, and genuinely interested in the patient's well-being. Conversely, a physician's work will be compromised if she is depressed, apathetic, ignorant, isolated, doubtful that she can make a difference, and so distracted by personal problems of her own that she is indifferent to the patient's well-being or is unable to bring her empathy to the level of effective action. The personal well-being of the physician is relevant to optimal outcomes for the patient.

The personal well-being of individuals and the health of local communities are relevant to outcomes for the global community and the future of human security. The global community is in imminent danger and desperately in need of responsible, well-informed, active citizens. The same pragmatic realism that informs the very best research and practice in medicine can inform progress in the practice of citizenship.

PRINCIPLE 29
Awareness, support, and active engagement are three stages of responsible citizenship.

If this book is ever made into a movie, there will have to be a character who says something like this:

> Listen, that's nice but nobody has time or interest for all that stuff. I've got three kids, I work part time, my husband and I are so tired by the end of the day ... The point is, it ain't gonna happen if it depends on people like me. Even if I had time and interest, I wouldn't know where to begin. And my impression is it's all hopeless anyway. You can't change the world.

This character is, I confess, a straw woman (could have been a straw man) who mouths the maps of our time. She alludes to four familiar problems: lack of time and energy, lack of working knowledge, lack of interest, and lack of hope.

Each person is court of last resort on how his or her life will be passed or spent. But let's take a critical look at the problems. As so often happens with complex situations, an effective solution to one of the problems can contribute to the solution of the others.

Awareness of basic concepts is the beginning of working knowledge and does not take much time. It takes less than 90 seconds to understand that international law is designed to protect basic human rights; that the most powerful governments and their allies (and that includes *your* government) are violating international law and threatening basic human rights, including the future security of their own citizens; and that political leaders are unable to escape that historical maze. So your tax dollars are being used to promote Option B, to being lost in the maze.

That's the beginning of a formal awareness. What if twenty million people on the continent where you live were to develop that awareness? How would that change prospects for survival? I don't know. Neither do you. It sounds like an interesting experiment.

The concepts advanced in this book might take as much time to read and understand as it takes to watch the six o'clock news every night for five nights. And the six o'clock news isn't really all that new anyway. What is new is a citizen who is as conscious of his responsibility to the global community as a surgeon entering the operating room is of her responsibility to the patient on the table.

There are individuals and organizations that have made the paradigm shift and are working toward Option A. The next stage of responsible citizenship is support for one or more of those individuals or organizations.

But it is in the stage of active engagement, the hands-on practice and thinking that go with full-fledged responsible citizenship, that the problems (lack of time, energy, working knowledge, interest, hope; and other obstacles) are reconfigured as something else, something potentially more intriguing than sudoku.

PRINCIPLE 30
Optimism is essential; complacency is dangerous; pessimism is a waste of time.

The human spirit is resilient. It dances in darkness, catches the light from stars, and rises like a phoenix from the embers of defeat. If you find out tomorrow that you have cancer and have less than two years to live, you will cope with it. If a century or a millennium from this moment humans are facing extinction, they will cope with it. There are always reasons for optimism.

There are also plenty of reasons for complacency. We live in an affluent society that fosters certain kinds of complacency. The dangers of complacency are famous, of course. Most disasters come as a shock. No one could have predicted that the *Titanic* would hit an iceberg and sink, but an alert person could have expressed scepticism about the idea that the ship was unsinkable, or concern about the shortage of lifeboats or about the lack of attention to messages coming into the signal room that were warning of icebergs. Complacency takes various forms, one of them being a punctilious insistence on "proof" that a danger exists. How would you prove, at a point in time when it matters, that a shortage of lifeboats on the Titanic is potentially a danger to those making the voyage? Being alert to the destructive tendencies in human behavior and the toxic foreign policies of powerful states can lead to corrective measures with beneficial effects. Academic complacency and the inertia of old-paradigm thinking can paralyze the effort.

It would be difficult to overstate the importance of our paradigm (our map or mindset). The future will be largely what we make it, and your own thoughts play a part in the shaping of it, every day.

Jared Diamond's four phases for failed decision-making, leading to collapse of a society, have been noted previously in this book: failure to anticipate the problem before it arrives, failure to perceive the problem even after it has arrived, failure to make an effort to solve the problem even if it has been perceived, and failure to solve it despite an effort to do so. The problem has arrived. It has environmental, spiritual, political, and economic dimensions. Millions of voices are calling our attention to it. Hundreds of thousands of people are engaged as a global community to solve the problem. Whether we will solve it depends on whether we reach critical mass, the tipping point: whether enough of us wake up and assume our responsibility as citizens.

Diamond follows his outline of the four phases of failure with this:

> While all this discussion of reasons for failure and societal collapses may seem depressing, the flip side is a heartening subject: namely, successful decision-making. Perhaps, if we understood the reasons why groups often make bad decisions, we could use that knowledge as

a checklist to guide groups to make good decisions.
(2005, 421)

I prefer optimism for pragmatic reasons. Optimism encourages action; pessimism leads to passivity. Nonetheless, it is essential to keep some of the reasons for pessimism in mind, both to avoid a false optimism and to identify problems that need to be solved.

In 1900 there was a world peace movement. The Peace Palace at the Hague, the establishment of the International Court of Justice, and other achievements led to a premature and false kind of optimism. An exhibit at the World's Fair in St. Louis in 1904 suggested that war might soon become obsolete. It didn't. The exhibit offered ideas for teachers, businessmen, and others to use in promoting peace. Ten years later came World War I. Later still, the efforts at achieving a rule of law for the international community through the League of Nations became a famous failure. Pessimists love to invoke this failure as they try to promote Option B: There's no hope. Look at what happened to the League of Nations.

More recently the UN Security Council became an agent of militant nationalism, an accessory to the destruction of Iraq. This was a major blow to the credibility of the United Nations and to prospects for a rule of law. I have already indicated other reasons for pessimism. There is no end to them. The reasons for pessimism can be used to sustain the old paradigm and to push societies toward Option B, or they can be used for creative problem solving, to move societies toward Option A.

Pessimism is basically a waste of time. If you want to find a cure for cancer, you don't spend a lot of time thinking about reasons why it can't be found. The conditions that led to failure a hundred years ago have changed. The things that have been accomplished in other times and places — on meager resources, under conditions of oppression, and with hardly a wisp of the opportunity we have today — leave those of us in the West little excuse for defeatism.

Winds of change

Other authors have emphasized deteriorating environmental conditions, or demographics, or economic indices in trying to sense which way the wind is blowing. Obviously these things are important. In this book, however, I have emphasized our ways of thinking, our maps, because we have much more direct control over them than over other factors. Moreover, by changing how we think, we can better prepare ourselves for the economic, demographic, and environmental challenges ahead, and we can influence how severe those challenges will be. Our ways of thinking are winds of change. Not only can we set our sails to take advantage of them, but also to a significant extent we can actually control the wind.

Many writers who emphasize emerging dangers are optimists. For example, Jared Diamond (in *Collapse: How Societies Choose to Fail or Succeed*), Noam Chomsky (in *Hegemony or Survival*), and Ronald Wright (in *A Short History of Progress*) are clearly emphasizing the dangers because they believe that by being aware of dangers we can improve outcomes. I agree. I write this book from a similar perspective. It is also essential to emphasize opportunities and alternatives for the future, as do many of the authors I have cited in this book.

Predictions of the future often tell us more about the person making the prediction than about the future: whether they are a new-paradigm or an old-paradigm thinker, for example. Human beings also differ significantly in their attitudes toward dependence and independence. There are individuals with a pathological desire to control others, and they can be remarkably strong-willed. There are also people who seem to want to be controlled. Dostoyevsky's Grand Inquisitor was well aware of this; Erich Fromm wrote about their dilemma and why they choose to "escape from freedom." The pathology of power and the pathology of powerlessness, the pathological desire to control others and the pathological willingness to be controlled — these are among the dangers that we face in the decades ahead.

Others have chosen personal freedom and responsibility. No one knows how prevalent those free spirits are among us, but perhaps it's about 35 percent — in Stanley Milgrams's study, the prevalence of those who could repudiate unethical demands from an authority figure. Thirty-five percent isn't bad. If our society could harness the power of that 35 percent, we could achieve takeoff.

We can face the challenges and take personal responsibility for the health of the local and the global community. It's a choice. If we make that choice, the success is an indicator of our adaptive intelligence. If we fail to make that choice, the failure is our responsibility. We are the winds of change.

The power of one

Sociologists are familiar with a remarkable feature of groupthink, the tendency of individuals in a group to defer to a dominant opinion in the group (Shepard 1987, 151). In one version of the classic experiments that reveal this very human tendency, a small group of people are asked to pick which of a set of lines is the longest. Suppose the lines are labeled *a* through *e*, and suppose an independent observer would essentially always recognize line *a* as the longest. But the experiment is run as a groupthink experience. Before each member of the group is asked to make his or her own assessment and answer accordingly, the lines are examined and discussed as a group. Then each member of the group marks his or her choice on an individual answer sheet. Furthermore, the experiment is a set-up: all but one member of the group, without the knowledge of the real "test subject" member of the group, has been instructed to select line *b* as the correct answer. In this context, the naïve member of the group will often follow the group's example and pick the wrong line (*b*) rather than believing his or her own eyes and own analysis, which tells him or her that line *a* is the correct choice.

In his own way, Henry David Thoreau noticed and commented on this tendency to groupthink, as it affected the practice of citizenship, in his essay, "Civil Disobedience":

> The mass of men serve the state thus, not as men mainly, but as machines, with their bodies. They are the standing army, and the militia, jailers, constables, posse comitatus, &c. In most cases there is no free exercise whatever of the judgment or of the moral sense; but they put themselves on a level with wood and earth and stones; and wooden men can perhaps be manufactured that will serve the purpose as well. (1849, 226)

Thoreau proposes that the true patriot serves the state with his conscience. This refers to exactly the concept of a positive, healthy nationalism, discussed earlier, of which Gandhi was an example and Erich Fromm so astute an observer. In fact, the works of Thoreau had an influence on Gandhi.

Under Principle 22 above, I alluded to the emerging power of civil society worldwide. But what if your own local culture is out of touch with this reality and sees the world through a distorting lens, perhaps that of a corporate news channel? What if everyone around you is supporting Option B? What difference does it make if you are the only one insisting on Option A? What is the use of resisting the majority's support, for example, of the warfare system? Thoreau had a sharp answer to that question, reminiscent of the story of the emperor's new clothes. The one voice that calls attention to the right answer shakes up the system that supports the wrong answer:

> For it matters not how small the beginning may seem to be: what is once well done is done forever. (1849, 397–398)

Outrageously, Thoreau suggests that if you do or say or think consistently in the service of your conscience, you will create a situation that forces change. No one can erase what you have expressed. In our society today, you probably won't face the dangers that Gandhi, Nelson Mandela, or Martin Luther King Jr. faced, but you will put your feet on the same road.

> Action from principle, the perception and the performance of right, changes things and relations; it is essentially revolutionary, and does not consist wholly with anything which was. (Thoreau 1849, 395)

Each person's life is part of the process of defining what the human spirit can endure and what it can attain. The power of one is what you make it.

Civil disobedience

Critical readers of this book may notice that I have placed little emphasis on civil disobedience and the practice of non-violence. My emphasis on the necessity of law may even seem to ignore the importance and necessity of civil disobedience in making progress toward Option A. For the record, I am well aware of that importance and that necessity. If I had engaged much in civil disobedience myself, I would have had much more to say about it in this book. In the absence of that personal experience, I have to refer the reader to works by others: Thoreau, Martin Luther King Jr., Gandhi, Nelson Mandela, Gene Sharp, and Per Herngren, for example. A PBS documentary series, *Eyes on the Prize*, provides a history of the civil rights movement in the United States.

Per Herngren provides a definition of civil disobedience:

- Civil disobedience is a public action.
- It is based on nonviolence.

- The action is illegal or defies a command or decision.
- The direct intent of the action is to preserve or change a phenomenon in the society.
- The personal consequences of the action are an important part of the message. (1993, 8–9)

Thus the act of civil disobedience is characteristically illegal, but an even more essential characteristic is its non-violence. Herngren elaborates:

Civil disobedience is not putting oneself above the law. Even when a law is broken, it is not ignored. The participants in an action do not sneak away from the consequences of the action....

Civil disobedience is effective only if it functions as a moral challenge. That is why civil disobedience is ineffective for immoral purposes, or more exactly purposes that are generally perceived as being wrong. Of course, there are examples of bad civil disobedience. When resistance groups block the possibility of a dialogue they strengthen and confirm the opponent's power. This can be perceived as a negative dialogue: the possibilities for citizens to understand and give their opinion are reduced with each action, and support for the opponent is increased. However, if the opponent for purely tactical reasons breaks off a dialogue, then this can increase the possibility for the resistance group to create a dialogue directly with other citizens. This development is, as a matter of fact, the most common. When the opponent sees that silence reduces its influence and power, then the chances for a fruitful dialogue increase again. Silence on the part of the opponent can therefore be viewed as an important element in the dialogue. This should, however, not be confused with a negative dialogue that arises when the resistance group blocks the possibility for dialogue.

We see here how the circle closes. Civil disobedience weaves together ethics and method; you cannot entirely separate one from the other. (1993, 15, 17)

Governments are under no circumstances in a position to equate the illegality of an act of civil disobedience with their own violations of the law of non-aggression. Under modern concepts of law, the legitimacy of any government is based in law, and the measure of justice of law is its service to human well-being. An act of aggression serves the interests of power and undermines human well-being, which is the reason for the law of non-aggression. Civil disobedience, as practiced for example in the American civil rights movement and as defined by Per Herngren (1983), must serve human well-being; it must represent a "moral challenge" as Herngren puts it. As such, civil disobedience is directed against unjust laws, as writers such as Henry Thoreau, Gandhi, Martin Luther King Jr., and Herngren have emphasized. This difference is, literally, of life-and-death importance.

Civil disobedience is one method of advancing social justice, but the game can be played in other ways. One of the most gifted civil rights activists the United States has ever produced was Saul Alinsky. Out of his direct experience with poverty, he developed an approach to organizing for action that has had a lasting influence on civil society in North America. Feisty, iconoclastic, and witty, he honed his methods in the mean streets of Chicago. He was a gifted tactician when it came to seizing a specific beachhead, such as opening the hiring policies of a business to include non-White job applicants.

But Alinsky did not use civil disobedience as defined above. One of the features of his tactical approach was to keep the action legal, but highly effective. His tactics could catch the targeted business so off-balance that the response might be instant accession to the conditions set by the organizers. An excellent source on his approach is his book *Rules for Radicals: A Pragmatic Primer for Realistic Radicals* (1972).

Alinsky had long personal experience with ghettos. He saw the suburbs as "gilded ghettos" in which the middle class had isolated itself. Reflecting on his life and work not long before he died, he made this comment during a 1972 interview with *Playboy Magazine*:

> One thing I've come to realize is that any positive action for radical social change will have to be focused on the white middle class, for the simple reason that this is where the real power lies.

This book, *The ABCs of Human Survival*, is based largely on my own experience and way of thinking at the time of writing. Responsible citizenship as I practice it can lead to ostracism and other dissonant encounters, but those I have experienced have never been particularly uncomfortable to me. As for active hostility, I recall no physical threats against me in response to my activism. Arguments and intellectual adversity are not something I feel I need to avoid, although my preference is to convert them into something more constructive. True, I have on occasion confronted legal authorities about issues related to law and human rights, but these efforts have never led to my imprisonment or physical injury. For the most part, I have stayed within in my comfort zone. I am not particularly holy. More bothersome to me is that I have not yet been sufficiently effective in moving history toward Option A.

I have quoted liberally from Henry Thoreau's essay on civil disobedience, but that essay is putting *me* on the spot. I omitted, for example, the following passage:

> Those who, while they disapprove of the character and measures of a government, yield to it their allegiance and support, are undoubtedly its most conscientious supporters, and so frequently the most serious obstacles to reform. (1849, 394)

In "Civil Disobedience," Thoreau came to the same conclusion about unjust laws as Martin Luther King Jr. later expressed in his "Letter from the Birmingham Jail": unjust laws must be resisted. I agree with that conclusion, but I have failed to act accordingly. Throughout the 1990s, the government of the United States, with the collusion of other governments including Canada's, imposed policies on Iraq that violated international human rights law and were largely responsible for the deaths of tens of thousands of Iraqi children. Not once during those years did I refuse to pay taxes to the government of the United States or of Canada.

Of course, it is easy for me to rationalize my unqualified compliance with the tax laws. I have defined my own domain of responsible citizenship, which emphasizes the necessity of just laws and living democracy. I have connected that entire field with the concepts of self-actualization and innovation. Chapter 7 provides a further account of all this. My point is that I have not reached the standards set by Thoreau. Thoreau gives me a discomfort I cannot shake. I am no Gandhi or Martin Luther King Jr. or Per Herngren. I have not passed the kinds of tests that Rosa Parks or, more recently, Kathy Kelly and countless others have passed. I have never engaged in civil disobedience.

What I present in this book is in some sense a story of my success in emerging from a darkness in which I found myself a long time ago, shadows of which persist inside me. Perhaps I could not have accomplished what I have had it not been necessary to find my way out of that darkness. The solution to that problem transformed me. Like almost everyone else, however, I know another version of my own story, a version in which my life has been a failure. The part of that failure that took place in my personal life is inseparable from my shortcomings as a global citizen. We cannot be part of the solution until we recognize that we are part of the problem. For many reasons, I am aware of my own part in the pathology that we human beings are inflicting on each other. Thoreau and Rosa Parks set higher standards than I have. By their standards I judge my own work. My self-transformation is not yet complete. I have miles to go before I sleep.

CHAPTER SEVEN

Practicing Citizenship

Practicing citizenship today means practicing global citizenship, for we are beyond the age when less mature forms of citizenship were acceptable. We know too much: we cannot claim ignorance as an excuse for persisting in old patterns of behavior and avoiding the responsibility that our epoch places before us.

Practicing citizenship requires awareness, including self-awareness. Individually and as a global community we must wake up.

Practicing citizenship requires imagination and knowledge. It requires goal-directed and evidence-based new learning. Basic and continuing education is as important to the practice of citizenship as it is to the practice of medicine.

Practicing citizenship requires connections. Not only is responsible citizenship directed toward fostering healthy community; to be successful, it requires community. This chapter includes a description of two projects in which I have been involved, each designed to promote connections at local and global levels.

Practicing citizenship requires active, creative engagement: problem solving and innovative action advancing the health of the local and global communities. Another goal of that creative engagement is personal growth, empowerment, and well-being. In practice, these are natural consequences of this creative engagement. We empower ourselves and promote our own well-being as we work toward empowerment and well-being of others.

The global citizen as hero for our time

In novels, stories, films, our culture has been fascinated with the hero, and has visited and revisited the question of what it means to be a hero. As human beings we have been doing this for millennia. In his classic study of myth and hero, *The Hero with a Thousand Faces* (1949), Joseph Campbell seeks to understand the essence of the hero as he or she appears in each epoch. Campbell comes to conclusions that differ significantly from the "myth of the hero" as a means of denying death. Instead of denying mortality, the hero must pass through a fully human struggle with limitations and full awareness of approaching death. The end of all that searching brings the hero to a transcendent vision for rebirth of his or her society and culture. And having made the arduous journey, the hero's second task is to convey that vision to the world.

In the concluding section of his book, entitled "The Hero Today," Campbell comes uncannily close to describing the work of the global citizen:

> The community today is the planet, not the bounded nation; hence the patterns of projected aggression which formerly served to co-ordinate the in-group now can only break it into factions. The national idea, with the flag as totem, is today an aggrandizer of the nursery ego, not the annihilator of an infantile situation.... And the numerous saints of this anti-cult — namely the patriots

[213]

whose ubiquitous photographs, draped with flags, serve as official icons — are precisely the local threshold guardians ... whom it is the first problem of the hero to surpass. (1949, 388–89)

Through our own efforts toward self-actualization, each of us can bring a unique gift to the world. The process of discovering and developing the unique potential that is within each of us is essential to the practice of responsible global citizenship. The hero is not someone out there, remote and exalted, but a possibility within ourselves.

Awareness

We live in a profoundly dysfunctional global community — even insane, in the terms of observers such as Erich Fromm and Eckhart Tolle. The practice of citizenship is a process of healing that insanity. Practicing global citizenship requires an acute and abiding awareness of the insanity, in terms conducive to healing it.

The illness is spread not by self-conscious wickedness but by ordinary people, usually in the course of doing things that are socially acceptable and often in the course of doing things that are considered good (patriotic, Christian, godly, self-sacrificing, or even heroic). The road to hell is indeed paved with good intentions. Adolf Eichmann was, in Hannah Arendt's view (1963a), an example of the everyday quality of evil. He facilitated the forced transfer of innocent people to incarceration and death because it was what the established authorities had ordered, and because for Eichmann, obedience — following orders without question — was a characteristic of the good person, a servant of the fatherland.

In the Nazi era, many Germans watched in silence or indifference as fellow human beings in Germany were being deprived of their human rights by the German government. This happened between 1933 and 1940, with full public knowledge of the process, *before* the Holocaust. Many of those who were silent and complicit called themselves Christians. And of course, those who were silent and complicit could have given you very good reasons for their silence and complicity.

In our era, many North Americans watched in silence or indifference as fellow human beings in Iraq were being deprived of their human rights by economic sanctions. Those sanctions, imposed and maintained by the government of the United States and its allies working through the UN Security Council, violated international human rights law. The UN Security Council was violating the UN Charter. The effects of the sanctions proceeded with full public knowledge of the process, *before* the invasion of Iraq. Many of those who were silent and complicit called themselves Christians. And of course, those who were silent and complicit could have given you very good reasons for their silence and complicity.

> If only it were all so simple! If only there were evil people somewhere insidiously committing evil deeds, and it were necessary only to separate them from the rest of us and destroy them. But the line dividing good and evil cuts through the heart of every human being. And who is willing to destroy a piece of his own heart? (Solzhenitsyn 1974, 168)

If we have any interest in advancing the health of the global community, we will have to begin by cleaning up our own act. That includes bringing our government and the governments of our allies into compliance with international law.

As individuals, each of us carries to some extent the pathology of our society, just as a drop of pond water from a polluted pond carries the toxins of its source. Cleaning up our own act necessarily includes healing ourselves. The restoration of sanity, if it is to happen at all, must take place both within individuals and within communities, locally and globally. That is essential to the practice of global citizenship as the term is used in this book. In serving the health of the global community, the individual (the citizen) must also heal himself. The process of serving the health of the local and the global community also serves the purpose of healing the person who is active in this way.

It is sometimes assumed that the state of consumerism, careerism, and cynicism of our society is the best we can do. Nothing significantly better is realistically possible. Even a casual examination of such a premise renders it dubious. By asking the right questions, we can challenge old assumptions and begin to create new facts that render the premise obsolete.

Should a person who is capable of ordering or facilitating the deaths of half a million children be elected to the office of president or prime minister? If you notice that such things are taken for granted in our culture, or if you think the answer to that question is yes, then consider how the world would be different if a critical mass of citizens decided that the answer would be no and that such things would no longer be taken for granted.

Increasingly and worldwide, such things are no longer being taken for granted, and it is within civil society that this rethinking is most active and effective. Civil society has done magnificent and necessary work in the practice of citizenship. However, that work remains largely disconnected from everyday life and from awareness of the general public. While hundreds of billions of dollars are lavished on the established old-paradigm institutions, civil society struggles forward on its dangerously limited budget, doing its indispensable work but lacking the leverage and power needed for an adequate rate of change.

Awareness of the obstacles, the inevitable frustrations, and the dangers in the current situation: all these are necessary. It is also necessary to understand that challenges, even quite daunting challenges, are essential to personal growth and self-actualization, as well as to progress in civilizations. Civil society is generating powerful forces for positive change. Our consumer and careerist culture is astonishingly limited in its capacity to harness this force, or even to be aware of it, because that culture is rooted in the old paradigm of the individual's impotence in the public sphere. The old paradigm severely limits what can be learned from reality. It will be a while before our society makes the paradigm shift, but don't wait for them. The faster you shift your paradigm, the faster society will follow you.

Imagination and knowledge

Imagination and knowledge have always been world-transformers and will continue to be so. Einstein may have said that imagination was more important than knowledge, but they work beautifully together. Imagination and new learning not only transform the world; they also transform the imaginative person. Depression can be thought of as a psychological state devoid of the capacity for imagination, new learning, and self-transformation.

The evil in the world comes from ignorance, and new goal-directed learning is an essential part of the practice of global citizenship. With that process comes growing awareness of one's own power to change the world, along with growing self-esteem. To engage in responsible citizenship is to refute the doctrine of impotence.

Imagination is conceptual blockbusting. As examples, I'll suggest three specific blocks to progress that can be busted by reimagining: 1) using narrowly conceived (compartmentalized) issues as the conceptual basis for activism; 2) neglecting the energy of conflict as a potential power source for positive change; and 3) underestimating the value of breaching walls of silence. For each of the blocks, I will provide an example of how a collective act of imagination has blockbusted.

Efforts to promote the common good are often too narrowly issue-based. Progress may depend on moving past the resulting compartmentalization of energy and effort. Instead of thinking of issues such as warfare, environmental devastation, poverty, homelessness, and hunger as unrelated, it is time to consider how progress on each of these issues can benefit from recognizing them as multiple aspects of one problem, and redesigning approaches to solving them, and the larger problem, on that basis. The history of the Vermont Housing and Conservation Board (VHCB) illustrates the concept. In 1987, thanks to a convergence of those who were passionate about affordable housing and others who were passionate about conservation, the VHCB was created by the Vermont legislature, and three million dollars in state funds were appropriated for its work. The following year, the legislature appropriated an additional twenty million dollars, and the VHCB became a line item in the state's budget. The state's commitment to land conservation and affordable housing was steadfast through subsequent difficult economic times.

> The principal key to Vermont's success has been the coalition of organizations with seemingly contradictory objectives: housing versus open space.... The original idea for a state trust fund was to protect farmland. Later, the proposal was expanded to include protection of wildlife habitat, recreation areas, and historic buildings. Despite a clear need to protect these lands from the pressures of development, it was not until affordable housing was added to the list that the idea captured the attention of the governor and legislative leaders. With this political support and favorable economic times, VHCB was established in a single legislative session. (Libby and Darby 2000, 267)

If you did not previously know this history of the VHCB, then you now have some new knowledge. If you are trying to address homelessness or some other challenge, that new knowledge and your imagination might just carry you past the next obstacle toward your goal.

Conflict is associated with energy, and that energy can sometimes be converted into a power source for a positive outcome. A project to establish a Calgary Centre for Global Community is described later in this chapter. The earliest step toward that project illustrates the concept of energy conversion.

Several years ago, a conflict arose over an event in Calgary hosted by the Palestinian-Canadian Students' Society at the University of Calgary. The event had been criticized in an article in the *Calgary Herald* and had generated some randomly directed energy. In particular, a few members of the Jewish community in Calgary were distressed by the idea, presented by a rabbi, that Judaism and Zionism are incompatible: one cannot, said the rabbi, be a good Jew and be a Zionist.

As luck would have it, we were able to convert the energy of the conflict into a constructive dialogue, choosing a goal of potential interest to everyone involved in the conflict. We discussed how to establish a standing forum on life-threatening conflicts, to be open to concerned citizens and connected to the media in Calgary. I invited the author of the article who had criticized the event to co-host the dialogue with me. We brought into the effort two journalists; various members of the Jewish community, including a co-founder of Stand with Israel (a Zionist organization); the president of the Palestinian Canadian Students' Society; the president of the Muslim Students' Association at the University of Calgary; and others.

Soon we had a draft of a short document on a Calgary Media Forum on Life-threatening Conflicts. It specified operating principles such as openness to all concerned, as well as the necessity of compliance with the Forum's code of conduct, including respectful listening. What was most remarkable, however, was the participation of such diverse and even adversarial advocates.

That year we were holding a larger conference entitled "Media

Coverage of Life-threatening Conflicts," with keynote speakers and panelists from the media. In one of the many sessions at that conference, the participants in the dialogue presented the concept of the Forum to an audience of about five hundred people. The president of the Palestinian Canadian Students' Society and the co-founder of Stand with Israel stood together at the microphone to explain how the Forum could work, and how it could be a substantial asset in advancing public understanding of extremely difficult issues of life-and-death importance.

The goal of the dialogue was to work out how to establish the Forum, not to take on the work of doing it. Years later, however, the document generated from the energy of that conflict became the seed for a project to establish a Calgary Centre for Global Community.

Conflicts become destructive and sometimes deadly when communication fails. Walls of silence surround us. Some of them are significant impediments to progress, and some may be remarkably easy to breach. Identifying such high-yield points for establishing communication can be a powerful strategy.

Here are some examples of walls of silence: Social activists may refuse to talk to people who are in the hierarchy of large corporations, or vice versa. Peace activists may find nothing to express except anger at academics in the field of military and strategic studies. Police officers may see no point in having any sort of ongoing communication with people who organize or participate in protests. Homeless people may feel the need for an effective channel of communication to others in the city where they live, yet be unable to find or create such an opening. And people may be so busy that they scarcely know the names or anything else about their next-door neighbours. The walls of silence are endless.

There are countless ways of creating openings in those walls of silence. Recently I learned of the Oasis of Peace Village, established in 1976, where fifty-four Arab and Jewish families in Israel have lived together with the goal of promoting "equality, mutual respect, and cooperation within the community and beyond." I learned about it through a member of the Canadian Friends of Oasis of Peace. This was not long before a traveling art exhibit was to arrive in Calgary featuring the works of children from Oasis of Peace and from the Tulkarem Refugee Camp on the West Bank. The exhibit is the outcome of an event in June 2008. Children from the refugee camp had attended an art workshop in the Oasis of Peace Primary School, together with twenty-five Jewish and Arab children from the village itself. About eighty pictures on canvas and paper came out of the event, as well as a day and a half of interactions among the children.

The establishment of the Oasis of Peace Village is epoch-making, an ongoing process of breaching walls of silence in the Middle East. An event such as the art project organized by the village involves cooperation between organizers in the village and in the refugee camp, interactions among the children and art instructors, cooperation and communication between the village and hosts for the countries receiving the artworks as a traveling exhibit, and interactions among visitors to the exhibit in the host country where it travels. This illustrates the number and diversity of ways that such an initiative can breach walls of silence. Notice also how the concepts presented so far in this section can generate synergies. Dissolving the narrow conceptual domains of issue-oriented advocacy, transforming the energy of conflict to enable a fresh initiative of potential interest to all the adversaries, and creating breaches in walls of silence all derive from and lead toward imagining new possibilities and generating new knowledge. Such is the work of civil society and, perhaps, the journey of the Good Life.

I have already mentioned many references in this book that I consider useful as sources for practicing citizenship. Here I will emphasize two short books, available in paperback, that convey this sense of growth, imagination, exploration, and empowerment. Anthony Weston's *How to Re-imagine the World: A Pocket Guide for Practical Visionaries* (2007) is lively and evocative. In fewer than 150 pages, Weston conveys the optimism, energy, and creative enthusiasm of citizenship. Because of its quick, light style and its emphasis on reimagining, Weston's book is a particularly effective antidote to the pessimism and impotence that dominate so much of our political culture today. Equally exhilarating is Frances Moore Lappé's short book *Getting a Grip: Clarity, Creativity, and Courage in a World Gone Mad* (2007). Based on decades of observation and experience, this book would be a good choice for a book club or discussion group. Among its many contributions, it includes a contrast between a "spiral of empowerment" and a "spiral of powerlessness." The author evidently prefers the first option. Each of these two books includes a short list of other references. The two books and their references are valuable resources for practicing citizenship.

Practicing responsible global citizenship may not be for everybody. Modern life seems hectic; it's hard to keep up. Just having a beer and watching the news or sports on television may be just the right thing for some after an exhausting day at work. Each person is the court of last resort on how his or her life will be spent, and each must accept how it has been spent when its end draws near. The extent to which this experience of practicing citizenship can enhance your life in the living of it, or enhance your sense of a life well-lived, is obviously for you to decide. But understanding the option will surely enable a wiser decision.

A 35 percent solution and the game of global citizenship

The vast majority of the work essential to a healthy society occurs every single day, everywhere, almost invisibly. We take for granted the work of parenting, teaching, and providing essential goods and services.

But there are significant differences among us in our potential for self-actualization as global citizens. Sociologists are familiar with a tendency to conformity and deference to authority figures as social characteristics. People differ in their abilities in this realm. Stanley Milgram's study revealed that 65 percent of his subjects could not stand up to unethical demands from an authority figure. That's the bad news. The good news is that 35 percent of his subjects *could* stand up to those same unethical demands, thus following their conscience instead of illegitimate authority.

Milgram was concerned with the perils of unconditional obedience. Society is made up of individuals with extremely diverse sets of strengths and weaknesses. Just as some are gifted athletes and others are not, some have a genius for citizenship in the terms described here. Others are less gifted, and some are probably uneducable. The 35 percent of Milgram's subjects who could repudiate illegitimate authority could be considered "natural athletes," if we take athletics as a metaphor for citizenship.

To pursue the metaphor of athletics: A large percentage of the general population, with coaching and the will to succeed, can become fairly accomplished at a game in which they want to excel. But of course they have to understand the game, learn the basics, and above all have some enthusiasm for playing the game well. Not everyone can rival a Michael Jordan on the basketball court, and very few people can match the accomplishments of a Gandhi. Nonetheless, a large part of the population can probably learn to become very competent global citizens *if the programs for promoting the basic knowledge and skills are put in place.*

So the evidence from Milgram's study gives reason for optimism. If 35 percent of the general population were able to repudiate unethical demands from an authority figure, even with no prior training in the game of responsible citizenship, there is reason to believe that good training programs could significantly improve the level of skill at responsible global citizenship in the general population — and produce some epoch-making athletes in the process.

[223]

In the culture of a militant nationalist state, there will probably be ferocious resistance to initiating programs based on principles such as those presented in this book. That should make the task interesting. Of the countless domains for practicing global citizenship, one is the field of education: the task is to establish the curriculum for learning to live together as human beings, school district by school district.

Certain aspects of this game of global citizenship make it particularly appealing, once it is understood. One is that skill at the game can continue to increase throughout life. A 75-year-old can be more skillful at the game than she was at the age of 25. Another appealing aspect of this game is that it has incomparably greater potential than ordinary sports for outcomes of lasting importance. The many people who contributed to advances in civil rights, for example, achieved something far more useful and of more lasting importance than the person who won this or that athletic trophy fifty or a hundred years ago.

Like athletics, effective citizenship and democracy depend on the support of communities. The next four sections focus on connections as an essential requirement of effective citizenship and democracy.

The basic building block of democracy

You can't have a democracy if you can't talk with your neighbors about matters of mutual interest or concern. Thomas Jefferson, who had an abiding interest in democracy, came to a similar conclusion. He was prescient in understanding the dangers of concentrated power, whether in corporations ("holding companies" in his day) or in political leaders or exclusionary political institutions. Direct involvement of citizens was what had made the American Revolution possible and given the new republic vitality and hope for the future. Without that involvement, the republic would die. Eventually, he saw a need for the nation to be subdivided into "wards" — political units so small that everyone living there could participate directly in the political process. The representatives for each ward in the capital would have to be responsive to citizens organized in this way. A vibrant democracy conducted locally would then provide the active basic unit for the democratic life of the republic. With that kind of involvement, the republic might survive and prosper.

In *On Revolution* (1963b), Hannah Arendt emphasizes this aspect of Jefferson's later life and thought. As Arendt explains in some detail, revolutions have had to decide between two different outcomes of the revolutionary process, one in which the freedom of individuals included their free and effective participation in governance and in public life, and the other in which their freedom was almost entirely confined to their private lives. The revolutionary spirit necessarily includes citizens' active engagement in public life — that is, the first option. If freedom applies only to their personal lives, then the people have lost the revolutionary spirit.

The French Revolution went through a phase in which popular societies and the Paris Commune had a voice, but this voice was soon suppressed by the central government. More than a century later, the Russian Revolution went through a similar experience, with the voice of the workers' soviets (local councils) being marginalized by 1921. The consequences for both those revolutions were catastrophic.

Jefferson was one of the few, even then, who understood the dangers of a lack of participation in public life by citizens. As Hannah Arendt makes clear, the point was also lost on historians. "Democracy" has been reduced to the level of a spectator sport.

Democracy, of course, is supposed to be a form of governance in which power is in the hands of the people. In New England in the eighteenth century, this was often remarkably close to the reality. Democracy was participatory. Townships were politically active, and direct political action was part of the experience of many New Englanders. In the process of forming the Constitution, many had assumed that this direct public involvement would be formalized in the machinery of the new government, through the process of representation.

In the American Revolution, and in others, political leaders not only lost sight of the necessity for effective, direct involvement of citizens in public life; they actively suppressed that involvement. And thus the people have lost the very essence of what they were supposed to have won in the Revolution. That is why, early on, Jefferson saw recurrent violent revolution as the only way to guarantee the survival of the republic. (It was only much later that he came to see the ward system as a non-violent alternative.) Even very early in the experience of the American republic, elected "representatives" ignored the basic necessity of responsible and responsive engagement with those who had elected them. One such representative, Benjamin Rush, suggested that power belonged to the people only on the day of an election (Arendt 1963b, 236). This was tantamount to abandoning the new republic's most important asset.

Hannah Arendt saw this failure to formalize the structures for direct citizen involvement in governance as a fateful turning point. While recognizing the important achievements of the Constitution, she also recognized its Achilles heel.

> What eventually saved the United States from the dangers which Jefferson feared was the machinery of government; but this machinery could not save the people from lethargy and inattention to public business, since the Constitution itself provided a public space only for the representatives of the people, and not for the people themselves.
>
> ... It was precisely because of the enormous weight of the Constitution and of the experiences in founding a new body politic that the failure to incorporate the townships and the town-hall meetings amounted to a death sentence for them. Paradoxical as it may sound, it

was in fact under the impact of the Revolution that the revolutionary spirit in America began to wither away, and it was the Constitution itself, this greatest achievement of the American people, which eventually cheated them of their proudest possession. (1963b, 238–39)

After all his experience, including his observations of the French Revolution and his time in office as president, Jefferson saw the ward system as essential. Arendt was well aware of the importance of this direct citizen participation in public life, based on very small, local units. The exhilaration of successful engagement in the public life, so familiar to Jefferson and many of his contemporaries, has again become *terra incognita*. It waits for rediscovery.

The basic assumption of the ward system, whether Jefferson knew it or not, was that no one could be called happy without his share in public happiness, that no one could be called free without his experience in public freedom, and that no one could be called either happy or free without participating, and having a share, in public power. (Arendt 1963b, 255)

In the late 1990s I no longer lived in the United States, but many of the obstacles to democracy where I lived in Calgary, in western Canada, were related to what Hannah Arendt had described and what Jefferson had recognized. Parkhill was a comfortable neighborhood in Calgary, with houses of modest size and residents from diverse walks of life. One evening in the spring of 1999, a group of us who lived in Parkhill decided to run an experiment.

The Parkhill Pulse

There were seven of us at the beginning. Well aware of the atomization of society, we were interested in revitalizing community in Parkhill. That first evening, we discussed what a neighborhood might be like if we had a real democracy.

Jeremy, the youngest, was in college. Allara and Peter were only a few years older, she a dancer and he a graduate student in mathematics. The others were into their fifties, professionals, including three who were on the faculty at the University of Calgary. Like many of our neighbors, the seven of us had only very infrequent, often accidental interactions with each other and with the other residents of Parkhill. I was in the habit of going to work early, coming home late, and scarcely taking time to say hello to my neighbors.

We certainly couldn't establish a ward system like the one Jefferson had envisioned. We set ourselves a different and potentially achievable objective. We would find out whether we could create at least some of the basic conditions of a living democracy in Parkhill. Specifically, we decided to create a forum for discussions on topics of interest to our neighbors. The topics would not be confined to political or even "public interest" issues and would be chosen by the participants.

The forum we established became known as the Parkhill Pulse. It was open to all our neighbors (and others). Personally, I thought it might last a year or so. Had it survived for three years I would have considered it a remarkable success and a pleasant surprise. In fact, it flourished for seven years.

Over those years, we held discussions about changes in the health care system, Islam and Western society, political developments nationally and internationally, and protests being planned (and later activated) at a meeting in Calgary of the World Petroleum Congress, among countless other topics.

The World Petroleum Congress protests was a topic chosen by the social justice club at a local high school, students whom we had invited to pick a topic and join us for the related discussions. That topic extended to several sessions, and we invited not only the high school students, but also some of the activists who were preparing the protests, as well as representatives of the Royal Canadian Mounted

Police (RCMP) and the Calgary Police Services. The sessions were held, as always, in one of the homes in the neighborhood. The experience was very informative, not least for the realization that the representatives from the RCMP and Calgary Police Services were less enthusiastic and less comfortable with the invitation and the discussion than the students or the activists who were planning the protests. Had we extended the discussions as a series, I think the RCMP and the Calgary Police would have become more comfortable with the process, and we could then have accomplished much more than we did in that limited series of Parkhill Pulse meetings.

The sessions were often facilitated (but not dominated) by someone with extensive direct experience on the topic. After the attacks on the Pentagon and the World Trade Center in New York on September 11, 2001, official pronouncements about violence and threats, and counter-violence and counter-threats became the norm, along with officially promoted fear. The Parkhill Pulse responded to the situation by inviting the imam of a local Muslim community to facilitate the discussion on Islam. In doing this, the Parkhill Pulse opened an urgently needed channel of local communication. The very existence of a neighborhood forum of this kind becomes the key for opening many other lines of communication.

From its inception, the Parkhill Pulse was designed to be versatile, to move in whatever direction its participants chose to take it. The topic or activity for any month was selected in advance, often at the closure of the previous month's meeting. That in itself was always a pleasure, for it encouraged participatory imagination. On two occasions in the summer, the group decided on an easy hike in the Canadian Rockies. In December each year, we developed a tradition of reading Christmas or winter poetry, or other seasonal literature. Once we did a play reading (Oscar Wilde's *The Importance of Being Earnest*); on another occasion we went to a film and then came home to discuss the movie over a glass of wine.

The "political" discussions were only one dimension in the life of the Parkhill Pulse. Topics included the meaning of love in your life, the meaning of art in your life, what dance can do for people of all ages, and the art of cooking. Some remarkable people facilitated these discussions, including, for the art of cooking, a chef who had competed in Japan and France in international cooking competitions, and, for the dance session, a young woman who had her own modern dance company and who happened to be a neighbor, a member of the Parkhill Pulse.

The Parkhill Pulse made some first steps toward connecting with other communities in Calgary by often including individuals from other communities. On one occasion, the Pulse met with Prairie Sky Co-housing, a small community in Calgary in which the residents themselves had been the developers, designing the housing units to promote a small, vibrant community that included a weekly common meal, monthly musical events, and a variety of participatory initiatives.

The Parkhill Pulse achieved a great deal, though it was only a small sample of what such neighborhood initiatives can accomplish. The possibilities — of connecting with other communities, with political leaders, with organizations in civil society; and of exploring the unique memories, experiences, and creative capacities of people in community — are almost limitless. The Parkhill Pulse actualized, in embryonic form, a simple message expressed by Canada25 in their 2007 report *Canadians & the Common Good: Building a Civic Nation through Civic Engagement* (p. 3): "Good things happen when people engage with others." Of course it is a bit of a stretch from getting neighbors together to promoting a healthier global community. To bridge that distance, one would have to imagine how to connect the local with the global.

The city as microcosm of the global community

The challenges and opportunities of a modern city reflect the challenges and opportunities for humanity in the twenty-first century. Ethnic and cultural diversity within a large city originate in rich traditions from various parts of the global community. The close proximity of those cultures in a city has sometimes produced conflict, but far more often it has produced creative renewal and fresh cultural initiatives.

Nationalism was one of the twentieth-century efforts to realize a healthy global community. Because of nationalism's tendency to turn malignant, this effort has become a dead end. Yet nationalism reflects a deeply felt human need for stability and reassurance through attachment to familiar cultural and ethnic roots. That kind of security should be accessible, but it should not distract anyone from the need to realize our shared humanity and unity in the global community.

A synthesis of these two visions — a cultural identity and a global human identity — is possible. The boundaries between cultures are not sharp lines but zones of enormous generative potential.

> A truly "urban" city is one which is complex enough to offer its inhabitants two fundamental kinds of experience. One is a stable space of continuity, where we can rely on our beliefs and self-identifications. The other is where we put ourselves — our beliefs and worldviews — at risk. Through confrontation with different truths, we question our beliefs, values, and identities and are thus led to expand our moral imaginations of what is possible and important. (Tajbakhsh 2002, 9–10)

The city can become a generator and transformer. It can do this best not by traditional top-down approaches to change but by creating structures and resources to actualize the creative potential inherent in individuals and communities within the city. Neighborhood communities can become a generator and transformer to the city. A city that realizes its potential can become a generator and transformer to the world.

A fundamental threat to human security is the failure of

democracy. This threat can be most dangerous where it is least visible, in powerful states that call themselves democracies. National governments of such states are perennial obstacles to progress. Civil society has become the world leader in Option A initiatives, of course, but cities, including city councils, also have the potential for leadership roles. Cities have historically been one point where citizens have gained leverage to move national governments. Cities and state legislatures in the United States have sometimes been voices of reason in response to regressive national policies.

If residential neighborhoods can become generators and transformers, they can extend that effect through alliances with organizations in civil society and through city-wide alliances that transform the city itself. I see this as an indispensable component of the work for any chance of realizing the vision set forth in the *Hague Agenda for Peace and Justice for the 21ˢᵗ Century*.

> The Hague Appeal proposes a citizens' Agenda for Peace and Justice for the 21ˢᵗ Century. This will entail a fundamentally new approach, building on the recent model of New Diplomacy in which citizen advocates, progressive governments and international organizations have worked together for common goals....
>
> ... Civil society has flourished since the end of the Cold War and launched campaigns aimed at eradicating landmines, reducing the traffic in small arms, alleviating third world debt, ending violence against women, abolishing nuclear weapons, protecting the rights of children, stopping the use of child soldiers and building an independent International Criminal Court. These grassroots efforts are having a major impact. They are succeeding because they mobilize ordinary people, because they integrate different sectors (human rights, the environment, humanitarian assistance, disarmament, sustainable development, etc.) and because they invite the full participation of women,

youth, indigenous peoples, minorities, the disabled and other affected groups.

These campaigns have generated unity and cohesion and demonstrate what can be done when people are listened to instead of talked at. (2000, 2)

The *Hague Agenda* designates specific themes, initiatives, and target areas for transformation to achieve its vision. Available as a United Nations document and online (www.haguepeace. org), it is a kind of strategic roadmap, a very useful outcome of a collaborative process. The project is supported by its offices in The Hague, Geneva, and New York, which facilitate and provide information on absolutely essential work in many parts of the global community.

What percentage of the population in Calgary, Alberta, Canada has ever heard of the *Hague Agenda*? I would guess that it's below the level of statistical error. What difference would it make if people in Calgary not only knew about the *Hague Agenda* but took possession of it the way they took possession of the Winter Olympics in 1988? I don't know, and neither does anyone else, but I think it's an interesting question. How difficult would it be for a neighborhood forum such as the Parkhill Pulse to inform their part of Calgary about the *Hague Agenda*? It would be a piece of cake.

What if the citizens of a modern city were to use the framework of the *Hague Agenda* as a guide in rejuvenating the "revolutionary spirit" described by Hannah Arendt (1963b)? What if their residential neighborhoods included awareness of the *Hague Agenda* among the many topics in their own agenda for neighborhood dialogues? What if it were part of an ongoing project to build social capital in their neighborhoods and citywide? And how could that kind of growth and change be translated into an advantage for the global community? What sort of project in a modern city could facilitate a visionary effort of that kind?

There are probably a lot of different answers to that last question. Here's one, a project many of us have recently initiated in Calgary, Alberta, Canada.

A Calgary Centre for Global Community

Civil society has in effect become the health and well-being system for the global community. The very legitimacy of governments can be measured by their responsiveness to global civil society. Yet civil society has never had anything analogous to a medical center for advancing its work. In a modern health care system, the medical center is the place where health care professionals from many specialties interact; where medical research is conducted; where medical students become competent physicians; where patients receive expert care; where conferences and symposia on medical advances are held; and where, at the interface of disciplines, innovative approaches to prevention and therapy of disease are developed.

In Calgary we have proposed to establish the counterpart of a medical centre for civil society. The following paragraphs are taken directly from a working paper on the Calgary Centre for Global Community:

> At the beginning of the twenty-first century, the global community faces growing challenges to human survival and well-being. Old paradigms of nationalism, of profit for profit's sake, and of environmental irresponsibility, continue to dominate many of our established political, economic, and cultural institutions. These old patterns of thought and behavior tend to make institutional responses slow and maladaptive. They are not adequate for the challenges of the twenty-first century.
>
> Civil society has been able to respond to emerging challenges with far greater adaptive intelligence and speed

than old paradigm institutions. Non-governmental organizations and individual citizens are identifying and activating evidence-based responses to inter-related challenges including environmental degradation, poverty, violent conflicts, inadequate public health infrastructures, and other threats to human survival. A concept of global citizenship is emerging, which connects individual well-being to the health of local communities, the health of the global community and environmental stewardship. This represents a paradigm shift of life and death importance.

But progress has been too slow. A rate-limiting factor in this progress is the level of public awareness, public support, and public engagement in the indispensable work of civil society. Public support and participation will largely determine the conditions of human existence and the chances of human survival in this century. The Calgary Centre for Global Community is designed to be a catalyst to accelerate this process. It is intended as the first of a new kind of forum for living democracy. (www.ucalgary.ca/md/PARHAD/ccgc_background.htm)

If the project is successful, it will benefit countless people in the years ahead: visitors and participants in its events and programs, people of all ages and every walk of life. They would come to the Centre not only for an enjoyable and informative experience but also for a process of self-discovery: finding *within themselves*, through their experience at the Centre, the potential to bring something to the world of lasting importance. The experience at the Calgary Centre would prompt visitors to explore the connections linking their creative potential, the vitality of local communities, and the health of the global community.

With the goals of the Calgary Centre in mind, we have developed a concept of three centres in one:

1. A **visitors centre**, where exhibits, films, live performance, and other features would provide enjoyable and informative experiences for casual visitors and where the program content would be closely related to more participatory activities at the other two "centres."

2. A **conference centre**, where workshops, courses of instruction, symposia, dialogues, meetings, and conversations would foster the knowledge, ideas, and interactions essential for well-informed, creative, responsible global citizenship.

3. A **connections centre**, where visitors and participants would find the information, connections, and resources for a wide variety of opportunities to engage in the work of civil society, to realize their own humanity, and to advance the health of the global community.

The mission of the Calgary Centre for Global Community is to raise public awareness of the conditions essential to human well-being and the challenges to human survival in this century, and to foster ideas and initiatives — and promote knowledge, skills, and participatory research — toward a healthy global community and responsible, effective local and global citizenship.

The Centre is designed with the following goals in mind:

- to extend the scope, reach, and impact of the work of civil society and its organizations;
- to facilitate interactions among citizens, communities, political leaders, the media, faith-based groups, businesses, and other institutions, and foster research and other initiatives to promote healthy local and global communities;
- to promote respect for the intrinsic worth and creative potential of each person, and the necessity of international law to protect basic human rights;

- to promote knowledge and competencies essential for responsible global citizenship; and
- to promote ways of transforming and preventing violent conflicts.

The concept for the Calgary Centre has inspired contributions from many talented and accomplished individuals and the civil society organizations with which they are affiliated. The proposals we have received for program content indicate the range and genius of the work of civil society and the evocative power of the idea for the Centre itself. Among the contributions has been an architectural design for the Centre by a group of visionary young architects. Marc Boutin's design received an international Progressive Architecture Award, one of eight projects from around the world recognized in the 54th annual competition in February 2007. A visionary structure connecting the external environment with its internal spaces, the design is extensively illustrated in the January 2007 issue of the New York magazine *Architect*.

The Calgary Centre will help connect neighborhoods and communities in Calgary. Building social capital locally is one of its primary goals. The Parkhill Pulse flourished for seven years, then came to an end. Its founders (myself included) had moved away from Parkhill long before the Pulse stopped. When we launched that initiative in 1999, we assumed it would last only for a relatively short time. We also thought that if it were successful, the memory of that success might inspire similar projects elsewhere.

That rebirth is now in progress. A successor to the Parkhill Pulse has been launched in another Calgary neighborhood. In this renaissance of the Pulse, we plan to spark similar initiatives in other neighborhoods, then bring them together for an annual symposium at the Calgary Centre for Global Community, where representatives from those neighborhoods would describe what they have done over the past year and share ideas for extensions of the concept. Those extensions would include connecting not only with other local communities, but also with communities elsewhere in North America and worldwide.

What discoveries could this project yield? What differences might it make in the lives of individuals and families in the participating communities? What advantages will it bring to the other programs and the visitors at the Calgary Centre for Global Community? How might that forum started in the Parkhill community in 1999 affect the global community years hence? We don't know the answers to these questions. We will have to run the experiment to find out.

The Calgary Centre is designed to foster community locally and globally, and to promote the connections essential for living democracy. You cannot have a democracy if you cannot talk with your neighbor about matters of mutual interest and concern. The Internet, for all its advantages, is no substitute for direct community connections.

Will the project to establish a Calgary Centre for Global Community be successful? Will we find the resources to accomplish the mission and the goals set out for the Centre? Will it draw visitors and observers from all over the world? Will it become a model for other cities to follow? Will it accelerate the transforming effect of civil society on the century ahead? We don't know the answers to these questions. We will have to run the experiment to find out.

The genius of citizenship

It is easy to think that we are not responsible for solving problems facing the global community and that such great works are the responsibility of great leaders and the experts they have selected to advise them. What a load of responsibility that takes off our shoulders! How gladly the old-paradigm thinkers take that burden and that treasure away from us! How ignorant and pathetic we are as we follow them in our darkness, down the road to Option B!

If you are waiting for a charismatic leader or, having found one, expecting him or her to solve the great problems of the ages or of this century, *you are looking in the wrong direction.* Look around you, not only for the counterpart of Susan B. Anthony and Rosa Parks, but also for the others, nameless but luminous, who have advanced the consciousness of humanity. Then look within yourself and ask whether the sun of that consciousness is also rising within you.

Just as human genius can be expressed in music or literature or mathematics or the natural sciences, it can also be expressed in global citizenship. This is the critical domain for transformative genius in our time. Technical progress without the genius of human value and empathy is a shot into darkness. It may lead to the final Dead End. If I have highly developed intelligence in science and math but have no love for fellow human beings, I can easily become a clanging gong, a robot, shuffling toward some Orwellian future. Personally, I would rather have my life serve Option A, whatever choice others may make.

There are many highly skilled intellectuals who lack the genius of empathy and the awareness referred to in the present context. They could be considered intellectually skillful, but not very bright. Our society seems to place a little too much emphasis on spectacle, on various kinds of physical and intellectual achievement, and on something referred to as "charisma." One sad residue of the heyday of monarchies is our contemporary enthusiasm for charismatic political leaders. That enthusiasm, particularly when it refers to a remote and exalted heroic figure, is misguided and dangerous. One need only consider charismatic leaders like Adolf Hitler to get the point. Any hope of a brighter future rests with individuals discovering their own creative potential and taking responsibility for developing it, guided by new-paradigm thinking. Charismatic leadership, as it is often understood, is a snare and a delusion.

Without doubt there are highly effective leaders whom we can use as good role models. Gandhi is one example. We are told that he was initially unpromising in his chosen profession of law, and physically unprepossessing. His effectiveness as a leader was not due to outward appearance or his success at various forms of competition. He was effective because of his heightened awareness of the worth of human beings, combined with spiritual creativity and tremendous self-discipline. From such examples we can conclude that effectiveness in a leader comes from a transforming vision, rooted in self-transformation, and the discipline and experience necessary to implement that vision, very much along the lines of what Joseph Campbell described for "the hero today." Imagination, wisdom, perseverance, self-reliance, responsible self-esteem, respect for other human beings, and enthusiasm for the possibilities of the human spirit — these are elements of effectiveness in a leader.

Presidents and prime ministers become more effective in leadership toward Option A when they recognize their own limitations and responsibility, as well as the necessity of law and the promise of democracy. It comes when they bring our attention to our own freedom and responsibility, and work with communities in actualizing human potential. Governments can be judged not only by their compliance with and promotion of international law, but also by their responsiveness to civil society and the extent to which they redirect public resources toward public interest (not the national interest) and foster the genius of responsible global citizenship.

CHAPTER EIGHT

Prognosis

Like Scrooge in Charles Dickens' *A Christmas Carol*, we are being visited by ghosts of the past, the present, and the future. They are showing us the consequences of our self-inflicted pestilence and giving us a chance to bring that pestilence to an end.

In my own country of origin, the United States, the government that was supposed to represent my interests has, in the past five years alone, thrown hundreds of billions of dollars in public funds into spreading the pestilence: devastating other countries, destroying hundreds of thousands of lives, and escalating the violence and hatred in the global community. And that government, my government, has given every indication that it intends to direct similar threats against other governments in the years ahead. Far from being immune to this plague, the Obama administration is helping to spread it in Afghanistan and Pakistan. In the past and in the present, my government has threatened and continues to threaten the global community of which I am a part. And it is an ongoing threat to the future, constantly undermining the chances of human survival and conditions essential to optimal human health.

Militant nationalism leads swiftly to the arrogance of power and glorifies our ignorance and incompetence. It has been said that much of our culture — the myth of the hero, the addiction to acquiring material possessions, the violent contests for power — can be explained by our efforts to deny our mortality. Being surrounded by possessions gives us a false sense of security, and dominating others deludes us into a sense of immortality. One consequence of this choice is that in denying our mortality, we are losing our humanity.

In everyday conversations with many people in the United States, or in listening to people talking in restaurants or on television or in the streets, I often find a surreal lack of awareness of what has happened and what is happening. A waitress tells me about "sleepers" who are waiting for orders from Osama Bin Laden to rise up and attack "us" in the United States. A taxi driver tells me that "we" can't let governments like Iraq's get away with stuff, and the rest of the world has to help "us" stop "them."

The waitress and the taxi driver are capable of greater sanity than their words convey. As I listened to them, I heard other evidence that affirmed their humanity, even as they expressed their paranoid and violent ideas.

In our culture, such ideas are not only okay, they are cultivated. Professionals with whom I converse often express slightly more sophisticated versions of the same kind of thinking. Sleeper cells, the latest version of Hitler, and other rehashed ways of frightening the public and seducing them into support for state violence — all this is, in significant part, the work of an endless parade of intellectuals. And these intellectuals, who serve the military-industrial-ideological-political complex, appear to be utterly ignorant of the pathogenesis of the plague they help to spread.

Militant nationalism is the major ideological disease-promoting factor in the warfare system. Warfare is a cancer, but also a communicable disease. Propaganda for war and mass violence can be communicated through radio broadcasts, as in Rwanda in 1994, or through news magazines, scholarly publications, and television broadcasts, as in our own culture today.

To counteract the disease effectively, we must find the cultural, economic, and political means for therapy and prevention. This search will have to be innovative, evidence-based, and constantly renewed. To wait until the threshold of the next outbreak of war is to guarantee failure. Though the two world wars are behind us, the warfare system is very much alive among us:

> [T]he plague bacillus never dies or disappears for good ... it can lie dormant for years and years in furniture and linen-chests ... it bides its time in bedrooms, cellars, trunks, and bookshelves; and ... perhaps the day would come when, for the bane and the enlightening of men, it would rouse up its rats again and send them forth to die in a happy city. (Camus 1947, 308)

Militant nationalism is diminishing the chances of human survival, undermining the conditions of human security, squandering public resources, and extinguishing possibilities for growth of the human spirit worldwide. In my own country and in many other parts of the world, this plague is ravaging individual lives, families, and local communities.

The warfare system is a plague and a cancer that depends on militant nationalism to sustain it and spread it.

What is the prognosis?

By 2050 the economic and military ascendancy of China may have become obvious to every well-educated person. Assuming that the global community continues down the road toward Option B, China will probably not only develop the means to shoot down satellites (as it has already done and demonstrated) and the ability to deliver nuclear weapons where and when it chooses, but may also with a coalition that it organizes gain increasing control of the world's dwindling oil reserves.

Will this affect the lives of your children?

Assuming the continued rise of China and Option B for the global community, it is easy to conceive of scenarios for North Americans in 2050. With climate change, dwindling access to oil, and other emerging challenges, North Americans could face hard choices, including some that lead to increasing social polarization. Society could fragment as it goes into economic decline. North American society might look more and more like "weasels fighting in a hole," to use the words of W.B. Yeats. To state the case rather gently: if social capital as well as economic wealth are in decline, life in North America three generations from now may no longer be the envy of the rest of the world.

We know that the world a century from now will be very different from the world of today. We can no more predict the details of that world than a stock market analyst can tell you what will be on television ten years from now. Nonetheless, trends are often discernible, and predictable consequences often follow from recognizable conditions. The provident person does not wait until the house burns down to carry out maintenance and repairs, or to purchase household insurance. Our ability to influence the future remains significantly greater than our ability to predict what that future will be. Learn or perish. We must learn to live together as human beings. That remains an option.

A patient with an immune deficiency is likely to succumb to an infectious disease that a healthy individual can easily survive. Climate change and other challenges are likely to be manageable if we meet them as a healthy, cooperative global community. A global community ravaged by militant nationalism and warfare is more likely to succumb. There is no point in wasting time with pessimistic and vapid predictions about the dangers ahead; it is essential to be aware of the challenges and prepare ourselves as a global community to meet them.

We are stuck in an old and dangerously maladaptive paradigm. The danger that the warfare system may lead to extinction of the human species has been a matter of public awareness at least since the attacks on Hiroshima and Nagasaki in 1945. Despite this mass of evidence, nuclear weapons states have repudiated their responsibility under international law to relinquish their nuclear weapons. The military superpower among them has assumed a belligerent posture toward other governments, which is guaranteed to elicit defensive responses from the governments that feel threatened. Violence and threats beget violence and counter-threats.

That pattern of behavior is a threat to the global community, meaning *us*. It is an inevitable consequence of militant nationalism and the warfare system. At this point in history, it requires profound ignorance or willful blindness not to understand this.

The warfare system is a plague and a cancer; militant nationalism is its ideological pathogen. Pervasive in our culture is implicit and explicit propaganda for war; an unremitting, and usually subtle, incitement to violence and to accepting the inevitability of violence.

We are imposing this pathology on ourselves; therefore, it is in our power to stop it. We are after all human beings and not plague bacilli or cancer cells. Human beings are supposed to be smarter than plague bacilli and cancer cells.

> Some generation of mankind was eventually bound to face the task of abolishing war, because civilization was bound to endow us sooner or later with the power to destroy ourselves. We happen to be that generation, though we did not ask for the honor and do not feel ready for it. There is nobody wiser who will take the responsibility and solve this problem for us. We have to do it ourselves. (Dyer 1985, 265)

Pessimism about the worst of the possibilities is a waste of time. The human spirit is resilient, and we will endure what we must, as Carthage once endured Rome's conquest, as the Romans endured their demise in the fifth century C.E., and as Iraqis have endured the plague of militant nationalism over the past quarter century.

Whatever befalls, the essential dynamic will involve not so much a clash of civilizations as a clash of convictions about the value of human life and the conditions that sustain it. That is a conflict that works itself out within each of us as individuals, as well as in communities worldwide.

Within each person — within *you* — there are values and mental pathways that provide information about the chances of human survival. Gratitude and reverence for life tends toward one set of futures; ingratitude and violence against life leads toward another. If life is not worth living, if we place little value on our own potential and even less on the lives of other human beings, then it follows that the human species is not worth saving. And almost all of the things we care about, which assume that the human spirit and human creativity have value, would then, by definition, be of little long-term interest.

Far more interesting to me is another possibility: that if we can significantly change our patterns of thinking and behavior toward healthier alternatives, we may discover a vastly expanded realm of human possibilities. This awakening may also involve a painful awareness of what we have destroyed and lost in the past, and of our own responsibility for that failure. However painful it may be, if it comes, it can enable a far, far better use of the opportunities that remain.

As a global community we are in the process of growing up. In *The Great Turning: From Empire to Earth Community* (2006), David C. Korten outlines five stages in the developmental pathway from the least mature to the most mature orders of human consciousness. Korten bases his map on the work of various psychologists who have studied human social and psychological maturation from infancy to adulthood. This sequence begins with Magical Consciousness, the consciousness of a young child two to six years of age. In this first order of consciousness, the child's behavior is impulsive and driven by emotions. The child looks to others to make things magically right, and is unable to take responsibility or even recognize the effects of his or her own actions.

The second order of human consciousness, according to Korten's map, is Imperial Consciousness, which normally occurs at about six or seven years of age. One of the discoveries the child makes in this stage of development is that actions have consequences and that pleasing authority figures is often rewarded. There is at this stage no internalized code of ethical behavior, of course. And bad behavior is rationalized with the claim of good intentions, or the dodge that "Everyone else is doing it." It is not difficult to recognize in this pre-adolescent order of consciousness some of the ideational and behavioral hallmarks of our own "adult" political culture. We can also recognize similarities to the ideational framework for quite a few contemporary intellectuals. Yet it is Korten's third order of consciousness, the Socialized Consciousness, that best fits with our dominant political culture today.

The transition from Imperial Consciousness to Socialized Consciousness normally takes place about the age of eleven or twelve years. In the individual, it corresponds to a time in which the norms of a large reference group become internalized. Advances in emotional intelligence and social skills help the individual gain security within a group. The individual learns to do what is necessary to gain acceptance by the group and to support the group against other, competing groups. This stage is associated with acceptance of rules and laws and legitimate authority, and with a morality that endorses such a framework. The individual also finds identity through primary reference groups as defined by "gender, age, race, ethnicity, religion, nationality, class, political party, occupation, employer and perhaps a favored sports team."

It is the consciousness of the Good Citizens, who have a "Small World" view of reality defined by their immediate reference group, play by the existing rules, and expect a

decent life in return for themselves, their families, and
their communities....

Highly adaptive to the dominant cultural and institutional context, the Socialized Consciousness is the
foundation of conventional good citizenship. On the down-
side, it is also susceptible to manipulation by advertisers,
propagandists, and political demagogues, and it is prone
to demand rights for the members of its own identity
group that it is willing to deny others. (Korten 2006,
45–46)

The Socialized Consciousness can be recognized as the level
of maturation our political culture has achieved, that of an
adolescent. The individual or the culture that has attained Socialized
Consciousness may be capable of further growth, or not. Our culture
has been stuck in this stage of maturation for a long time. The
Socialized Consciousness is at the core of old-paradigm thinking
and guarantees the Option B choice that we are making as a global
community.

Encounters with people from other cultures, from identity groups
outside one's own, can lead individuals to transcend their Socialized
Consciousness to what Korten calls Cultural Consciousness, the
fourth order of maturation of human consciousness. This step
involves a recognition that cultural diversity, like biodiversity, is
a natural and healthy phenomenon. Cultural consciousness is a
"profound step in the development of a true moral consciousness
based on examined moral principles."

A Cultural Consciousness is rarely achieved before age
thirty, and the majority of those who live in modern
imperial societies never achieve it, partly because most
corporations, political parties, churches, labor unions,
and even educational institutions actively discourage it.
Each of these institutions has its defining belief system

to which it demands loyalty.... But because those who achieve a Cultural Consciousness have the capacity to question the dysfunctional cultural premises of Empire, they are the essential engines of the cultural renewal and maturation.... Persons who have achieved a Cultural Consciousness have an "Inclusive World" view that sees the possibility of creating inclusive, life-affirming societies that work for all. (Ibid., 46–47)

Korten's fifth order of consciousness, Spiritual Consciousness, is one in which creativity in service to others becomes a source of self-actualization and joy. Korten describes Spiritual Consciousness as "the highest expression of what it means to be human" (Ibid., 47). This is a level of awareness in which conflict and paradox become new opportunities for growth, and what seemed to be constraints become the means of self-transcendence. He sees this deepening awareness of life's possibilities as an integral part of the process in which the individual relates to diverse people and situations.

The Spiritual Consciousness joins the Cultural Consciousness in seeking to change unjust laws. It recognizes, however, that at times it must engage in acts of principled nonviolent civil disobedience both to avoid being complicit in the injustice and to call the injustice to public attention. It undertakes such acts with awareness of the potential legal consequences. (Ibid., 48)

It is in self-actualization at the spiritual level of maturation that the necessary connection between personal well-being and the health of the global community becomes obvious. It is also at this level that the diametric differences between Option A Christians and Option B Christians can no longer be obscured. It is Option A Christians, Muslims, and Jews who can achieve Spiritual Consciousness. This concept is entirely in accord with the concepts presented by Korten. Option B Christians, Muslims, and Jews are stuck at an earlier stage of maturation, however famous they may be as religious figures. This is why the designation "Christian" or "Muslim" or "Jew" is so meaningless in spiritual terms.

Among the contemporary writers and visionaries who have understood this is Eknath Easwaran. His many excellent contributions include a three-volume work, *The Bhagavad Gita for Daily Living* (1975–84). It is profoundly important that India's ancient scripture, on which Eknath Easwaran's book is based, uses the metaphor of a battle for the challenge facing each of us in life. The adversary, however, is not someone or something "out there," but the Ego within each of us, which separates us from what we could become. To overcome that adversary requires tremendous discipline and dedication to the service of others. It is exactly this that we admire in the good soldier. It is not the discipline and the dedication to serving others that is the fatal flaw in the military or the soldier. It is that they have chosen service to something that is self-destructive, militant nationalism, which is to the nation and to the global community what the Ego is to the individual. Until this recognition dawns in our consciousness, we will continue down the road to Option B.

The purpose of this book is not to prompt a debate but to clarify a choice. It is not for me to make that choice for you, but I must state the choice as clearly as I can. The consciousness that dominates current history must be transcended if there is to be any hope of moving toward brighter human options. If we want Option A, then we will have to bring governments into compliance with law. Human well-being, not state power, must become the priority. The new paradigm is the *sine qua non* for progress toward Option A.

Your choice

The personal is historic. There is an undiscovered country within you. Through the exploration and development of that country, you can bring to the world something no other can achieve. Each generation leaves a legacy for the next: a set of problems and a set of opportunities. Your life and work will contribute in some way to the legacy your generation leaves for those who follow.

The generation that abolished slavery, the generation that established the vote for women, and the generation that established a five-day work week each created opportunities for us. Those generations swept aside all the false arguments for why it could not be done. Our generation will decide whether to establish a rule of international law as the framework for human security and human survival.

Political leaders are forced to make their decisions from a menu of viable options. It is no longer a viable political option in North America to sell human beings as slaves, to exclude women from public life, or to impose a seven-day work week on any of us.

Today it remains a viable option for our governments to massively escalate international violence, threatening the global community of which we and the generations that follow us are a part. International law is designed to remove that option. In the culture of militant nationalism, there will always be intellectuals who insist on maintaining it. They dismiss international law as unrealistic. They are the false prophets of our time.

What about tomorrow? For each of us, it is an option to support international law. *Awareness* of the requirements of international law, and of some of the major derelictions from those requirements by home and allied governments, is within easy reach of most adults. *Support* for organizations and for individuals who insist on government compliance with international law is also within easy reach. *Active engagement* in responsible, informed citizenship, in initiatives that promote your government's compliance with law and respect for health of the global community and human life, is also well within the reach of many.

To act on that opportunity is the essence of real democracy. Real democracy requires active, informed, responsible citizenship, using the prescriptions and honoring the requirements of law. Genuine democracy subordinates state power to a profound respect for human life. And it recognizes that the framework of international law is necessary for making that value system stick. Richard Falk, Albert G. Milbank Professor of International Law and Practice, Princeton, goes a step further:

> I believe that as an American citizen I would be better served by a government that accepted the constraints of law as surely in international affairs as in domestic. Indeed, I would even contend that the next leap forward in legitimate governance will be giving citizens an enforceable, constitutional right to a "lawful foreign policy." (1999)

Will we be able to establish a rule of law and thereby advance the chances of our survival? That is an empirical question. It can only be answered by sustained and visionary efforts to achieve the goal: by relentless pragmatic realism.

Whatever else happens, if you play an active and constructive part in the effort, it will be *your* gift to the future of human survival. Nothing can ever erase what you have contributed. And if your generation is able to establish a rule of law for the global community, it might just be the most important gift any generation has ever given to the world.

The prognosis is yours to decide.

BIBLIOGRAPHY

The following list, alphabetical by author, includes authors and titles referred to in the text as well as other titles selected from the vast literature that contributes to new-paradigm thinking. A very small minority of the following list are old-paradigm works that I have referred to in the text, and these authors too have contributed to new-paradigm thinking, perhaps unconsciously and in their own way.

Abunimah, Ali. 2006. *One Country: A Bold Proposal to End the Israeli-Palestinian Impasse.* New York: Henry Holt & Co.

Alexander, Titus. 1996. *Unravelling Global Apartheid: An Overview of World Politics.* Cambridge, UK: Polity Press.

Alinsky, Saul. 1972. *Rules for Radicals: A Pragmatic Primer for Realistic Radicals.* New York: Random House.

Arendt, Hannah. 1963a. *Eichmann in Jerusalem: A Report on the Banality of Evil.* New York: Penguin Books.

———. 1963b. *On Revolution.* London: Penguin Books.

Arnove, Anthony, ed. 2000. *Iraq Under Siege: The Deadly Impact of Sanctions and War.* Cambridge, MA: South End Press.

[253]

Ascherio, A., R. Chase, T. Cote, G. Dehaes, E. Hoskins, J. Laaouej, M. Passey et al. 1992. Effect of the Gulf War on infant and child mortality in Iraq. *New England Journal of Medicine* 327 (13): 931–36.

Ashford, Mary-Wynne. 2006. *Enough Blood Shed: 101 Solutions to Violence, Terror and War*. With Guy Dauncey. Gabriola Island, BC: New Society Publishers.

Axelrod, Robert. 1984. *The Evolution of Cooperation*. New York: Basic Books.

Bakan, Joel. 2004. *The Corporation: The Pathological Pursuit of Profit and Power*. New York: Free Press.

Baumeister, Roy F. 1997. *Evil: Inside Human Violence and Cruelty*. New York: Henry Holt & Co.

Becker, Ernest. 1973. *The Denial of Death*. New York: Free Press.

Bluestein, Jane. 1999. *21st Century Discipline: Teaching Students Responsibility and Self-Management*. Frank Schaeffer Publications.

Bopp, Michael, and Judie Bopp. 2006. *Recreating the World: A Practical Guide to Building Sustainable Communities*. Calgary, AB: Four Worlds Press.

Bossuyt, Marc. 2000. The adverse consequences of economic sanctions on the enjoyment of human rights. Working Paper, UNESCO Commission on Human Rights: Sub-Commission on the Promotion and Protection of Human Rights.

Branden, Nathaniel. 1994. *The Six Pillars of Self-Esteem*. New York: Bantam Books.

Britt, Lawrence. 2003. Fascism anyone? *Free Inquiry* 23 (2). http://www.secularhumanism.org/index.php?section=library&page=britt_23_2.

Brzezinski, Zbigniew. 2004. *The Choice: Global Domination or Global Leadership*. New York: Basic Books.

Buber, Martin. 1960. *The Way of Man According to the Teachings of Hasidism*. Wallingford, PA: Pendle Hill Publications.

Campbell, Joseph. 1949. *The Hero with a Thousand Faces*. Princeton, NJ: Princeton University Press.

Camus, Albert. 1947. *The Plague*. English translation 1948 by Stuart Gilbert. New York: Vintage Books, Random House.

Canada25. 2007. *Canadians & the Common Good: Building a Civic Nation through Civic Engagement.* Toronto: Canada25.

Chomsky, Noam. 2003. *Hegemony or Survival: America's Quest for Global Dominance.* New York: Henry Holt & Co.

Cousins, Norman. 1981. *Human Options*. New York: W.W. Norton & Co.

———. 1987. *The Pathology of Power.* New York: W.W. Norton & Co.

Daly, Herman E., and John B. Cobb, Jr. 1994. *For the Common Good: Redirecting the Economy toward Community, the Environment, and a Sustainable Future.* Boston: Beacon Press.

Derber, Charles. 2003. *People Before Profits.* New York: St. Martin's Press.

Diamond, Jared. 2005. *Collapse: How Societies Choose to Fail or Succeed.* New York: Penguin Books.

Dyer, Gwynne. 1985. *War.* Toronto: Stoddart.

Easwaran, Eknath. 1975–84. *The Bhagavad Gita for Daily Living.* 3 vols. Tomales, CA: Nilgiri Press.

———. 1992. *Your Life Is Your Message.* Tomales, CA: Nilgiri Press.

Falk, Richard. 1999. Letter to the editor. *Foreign Affairs* 78 (May/June).

Fischer, Louis. 1954. *Gandhi: His Life and Message for the World.* New York: Mentor Books.

Fisk, Robert. 1990. *Pity the Nation: Lebanon at War.* London: Oxford University Press.

Friedman, Thomas L. 1999. *The Lexus and the Olive Tree.* New York: Random House.

Fromm, Erich. 1941. *Escape from Freedom.* New York: Henry Holt & Co.

———. 1947. *Man for Himself: An Inquiry into the Psychology of Ethics.* New York: Henry Holt.

———. 1955. *The Sane Society.* New York: Rinehart & Co.

Geisler, Charles, and Gail Daneker, eds. 2000. *Property and Values: Alternatives to Public and Private Ownership.* Washington, DC: Island Press.

Ghareeb, Edmund. 1981. *The Kurdish Question in Iraq.* Syracuse, NY: Syracuse University Press.

Glennon, Michael J. 2003. Why the security council failed. *Foreign Affairs* (May/June).

Goleman, Daniel. 1997. *Emotional Intelligence: Why It Can Matter More than IQ.* New York: Bantam Books.

Hague Appeal for Peace. *Hague agenda for peace and justice for the 21st century.* 2000. http://www.haguepeace.org/index.php?action=resources.

Harris, Nigel. 1990. *National Liberation.* London: Penguin Books.

Hawken, Paul. 2007. *Blessed Unrest: How the Largest Movement in the World Came into Being and Why No One Saw It Coming.* New York: Viking Penguin.

Held, David. 1995. *Democracy and the Global Order: From the Modern State to Cosmopolitan Governance.* Stanford, CA: Stanford University Press.

Henkin, Louis. 1991. Use of Force: Law and U.S. Policy. In *Right v. Might: International Law and the Use of Force,* by Louis Henkin, Stanley Hoffmann, Jeane J. Kirkpatrick, Allan Gerson, William D. Rogers, and David J. Scheffer. New York: Council on Foreign Relations Press.

Herngren, Per. 1993. *Path of Resistance: The Practice of Civil Disobedience.* Philadelphia, PA: New Society Publishers.

Hiro, Dilip. 1992. *Desert Shield to Desert Storm: The Second Gulf War.* Lincoln, NE: Harper Collins.

———. 2002. *Iraq: In the Eye of the Storm.* New York: Thunder's Mouth Press.

Hitchens, Christopher. 2003. *A Long Short War: The Postponed Liberation of Iraq.* New York: Penguin.

Huntington, Samuel P. 1999. Robust nationalism. *The National Interest* 58 (Winter 1999/2000, 31-40).

International Commission on Intervention and State Sovereignty. 2001. *The Responsibility to Protect: Report of the International Commission on Intervention and State Sovereignty*. Ottawa: International Development Research Centre.

Johnson, Chalmers. 2004. *Blowback: The Costs and Consequences of American Empire*. (rev. ed.) New York: Henry Holt & Co.

————. 2004. *The Sorrows of Empire: Militarism, Secrecy, and the End of the Republic*. (rev. ed.) New York: Henry Holt & Co.

————. 2006. *Nemesis: The Last Days of the American Republic*. New York: Henry Holt & Co.

Kennedy, Paul. 1987. *The Rise and Fall of the Great Powers: Economic change and Military Conflict from 1500 to 2000*. New York: Random House.

Key, Joshua. 2007. *The Deserter's Tale: The Story of an Ordinary Soldier Who Walked away from the War in Iraq*. As told to Lawrence Hill. Toronto: House of Anansi Press.

Kissinger, Henry. 1994. *Diplomacy*. New York: Simon & Schuster.

Klein, Naomi. 2007. *The Shock Doctrine: The Rise of Disaster Capitalism*. Toronto: Alfred A. Knopf.

Köchler, Hans. 1995. *Democracy and the International Rule of Law: Propositions for an Alternative World Order*. Vienna: Springer-Verlag.

Korten, David C. 2001. *When Corporations Rule the World*. Bloomfield: Kumarian Press.

————. 2006. *The Great Turning: From Empire to Earth Community*. Bloomfield: Kumarian Press.

Korzybski, Alfred. 1933. *Science and Sanity: An Introduction to Non-Aristotelian Systems and General Semantics*. 4th ed. Fort Worth, TX: International Non-Aristotelian Library Publishing Company, 1958.

Kraft, Joseph. 1973. "Secretary Henry." *New York Times Magazine*, October 28.

Krauthammer, Charles. 2005. Three cheers for the Bush doctrine. *Time*, March 7.

Kuhn, Thomas. 1962. *The Structure of Scientific Revolutions*. Chicago, IL: University of Chicago Press.

Kurlansky, Mark. 2006. *Nonviolence: Twenty-five Lessons from the History of a Dangerous Idea*. New York: Modern Library.

Kwitny, Jonathan. 1984. *Endless Enemies: The Making of an Unfriendly World*. New York: Viking Penguin.

Lappé, Frances Moore. 2006. *Democracy's Edge: Choosing to Save Our Country by Bringing Democracy to Life*. San Francisco: Jossey-Bass.

————. 2007. *Getting a Grip: Clarity, Creativity, and Courage in a World Gone Mad*. Cambridge, MA: Small Planet Media.

Libby, James M. Jr., and Darby Bradley. 2000. Vermont Housing and Conservation Board: A Conspiracy of Good Will Among Land Trusts and Housing Trusts. In *Property and Values: Alternatives to Public and Private Ownership*, eds. Charles Geisler and Gail Daneker, 259–82. Washington, DC: Island Press.

Loeb, Paul Rogat. 1999. *Soul of a Citizen: Living with Conviction in a Cynical Time*. New York: St. Martin's Griffin.

————, ed. 2004. *The Impossible Will Take a Little While: A Citizen's Guide to Hope in a Time of Fear*. New York: Basic Books.

MacArthur, John R. 1992. *Second Front: Censorship and Propaganda in the Gulf War*. Berkeley: University of California Press.

Maslow, A.H. 1971. *The Farther Reaches of Human Nature*. New York: Viking Press.

McNamara, Robert S. 1995. *In Retrospect: The Tragedy and Lessons of Vietnam*. With Brian VanDeMark. New York: Random House.

McNamara, Robert S., James G. Blight, and Robert K. Brigham. 1990. *Argument Without End: In Search of Answers to the Vietnam Tragedy*. With Thomas J. Biersteker and Col. Herbert Y. Schandler. New York: Public Affairs.

McQuaig, Linda. 1998. *The Cult of Impotence: Selling the Myth of Powerlessness in the Global Economy*. Toronto: Penguin Books.

Melnyk, George, ed. 2004. *Canada and the New American Empire*. Calgary: University of Calgary Press.

Milgram, Stanley. 1973. The perils of obedience. *Harper's Magazine* (December): 62–77.

Mueller, John, and Karl Mueller. 1999. Sanctions of mass destruction. *Foreign Affairs* (May/June): 43–53.

Nathan, Otto, and Heinz Nordern, eds. 1960. *Einstein on Peace.* New York: Simon & Schuster.

Peck, M. Scott. 1978. *The Road Less Travelled: A New Psychology of Love, Traditional Values and Spiritual Growth.* New York: Simon & Schuster.

———. 1983. *People of the Lie: The Hope for Healing Human Evil.* New York: Simon & Schuster.

Phipps, Bill. 2007. *Cause for Hope: Humanity at the Crossroads.* Kelowna, BC: Copper House Press.

Putnam, Robert. 2000. *Bowling Alone: The Collapse and Revival of American Community.* New York: Simon & Schuster.

The Random House Dictionary of the English language. 1987. 2nd ed., unabridged. New York: Random House.

Research Unit for Political Economy. 2003. *Behind the Invasion of Iraq.* New York: Monthly Review Press.

Ritter, Scott. 2007. *Waging Peace: The Art of War for the Anti-War Movement.* New York: Nation Books.

Rivkin, David B. Jr., and Lee A. Casey. 2000. The rocky shoals of international law. *The National Interest* 35 (Winter). http://findarticles.com/p/articles/mi_m2751/is_2000_Winter/ai_68547471/?tag=content;col1

Roberts, Les, Riyadh Lafta, Richard Garfield, Jamal Khudhairi, and Gilbert Burnham. 2004. Mortality before and after the 2003 invasion of Iraq: Cluster sample survey. *The Lancet,* October 29.

Roberts, Paul William. 2004. *A War Against Truth: An Intimate Account of the Invasion of Iraq.* Vancouver: Raincoast Books.

Royce, Knut. 1991. Iraq offers deal to quit Kuwait. New York *Newsday,* January 3.

Salbi, Zainab, and Laurie Becklund. 2005. *Between Two Worlds:*

Escape from Tyranny: Growing up in the Shadow of Saddam. New York: Gotham Books.

Saul, John Ralston. 2001. *On Equilibrium*. Toronto: Viking Canada.

———. 2005. *The Collapse of Globalism and the Reinvention of the World*. Toronto: Viking Canada.

Schaeffer, Robert. 1990. *Warpaths: The Politics of Partition*. New York: Hill & Wang.

Schattle, Hans. 2008. *The Practices of Global Citizenship*. Lanham: Rowman & Littlefield.

Schell, Jonathan. 2003. *The Unconquerable World: Power, Nonviolence, and the Will of the People*. New York: Henry Holt & Co.

Sharp, Gene. 1973. *The Politics of Nonviolent Action*. Boston: Porter Sargent Publishers.

Shaw, Randy. 1996. *The Activist's Handbook: A Primer*. Berkeley: University of California Press.

Shepard, Jon M. 1987. *Sociology*. St. Paul: West Publishing Co.

Simons, Geoff. 1998. *The Scourging of Iraq: Sanctions, Law, and Natural Justice*. New York: St. Martin's Press.

Solzhenitsyn, Aleksandr. 1974. *The Gulag Archipelago 1918–1956: An Experiment in Literary Investigation*. New York: Harper & Row.

Stiglitz, Joseph E. 2002 *Globalization and Its Discontents*. New York: W.W. Norton & Co.

———. 2008. The three trillion dollar war in Iraq. *Toronto Star*, March 12. http://www.thestar.com/comment/article/339461.

Stockwell, John. 1978. *In Search of Enemies: A CIA Story*. New York: W.W. Norton & Co.

Taft, William H. IV, and Todd F. Buchwald. Preemption, Iraq, and international law. 2003. *American Journal of International Law* 97 (July): 557–62.

Tajbakhsh, Kian. 2002. Dialoguing in cities and civilizations. *Peace and Policy: Journal of the Toda Institute for Global Peace and Policy Research* 7: 7–10.

Tarnas, Richard. 1991. *The Passion of the Western Mind: Understanding the Ideas that Have Shaped Our World View.* New York: Ballantine Books.

Thoreau, Henry David. 1849. Civil disobedience. In *Walden and Civil Disobedience.* Page references are for the 1983 edition. New York: Penguin Books.

Tolle, Eckhart. 2005. *A New Earth: Awakening to Your Life's Purpose.* New York: Penguin Books.

Treitschke, Heinrich von. 1898. *Politics.* Vol. 1. Trans. Blanche Dugdale and Torben de Bille. London, 1916.

Trevan, Tim. 1999. *Saddam's Secrets: The Hunt for Iraq's Hidden Weapons.* London: HarperCollins.

Veblen, Thorstein. 1899. *The Theory of the Leisure Class.* Boston: Houghton Mifflin, 1973.

Weber, Max. 1958. *The Protestant Ethic and the Spirit of Capitalism.* Trans. Talcott Parsons. New York: Charles Scribner's Sons.

Weston, Anthony. 2007. *How to Re-imagine the World: A Pocket Guide for Practical Visionaries.* Gabriola Island, BC: New Society Publishers.

Wilkinson, Richard G. 1996. *Unhealthy Societies: The Afflictions of Inequality.* London: Routledge.

———. 2005. *The Impact of Inequality: How to Make Sick Societies Healthier.* New York: New Press.

Wright, Ronald. 2004. *A Short History of Progress.* Toronto: House of Anansi Press.

Yoo, John. 2003. International law and the war in Iraq. *American Journal of International Law* 97 (July): 563–75.

Dr. Arthur Clark is a Professor of Neuropathology and Clinical Neurosciences at the University of Calgary, and an active staff neuropathologist at the Foothills Hospital in Calgary. He carries lifelong experience with militant nationalist culture, having come of age during the Vietnam War and serving two years as Captain in the United States Army Medical Corps. In 1995, in honour of his late wife, he established the Dr. Irma M. Parhad Programmes at the University of Calgary, which focus on ways to improve worldwide health and well-being within the framework of international law. He is also currently involved in a project to establish a Calgary Centre for Global Community, to be based on the values and vision that informed *The ABCs of Human Survival.*